Gaston Vuillier, Frederic Breton

**The Forgotten Isles**

Impressions of Travel in the Balearic Isles, Corsica and Sardinia

Gaston Vuillier, Frederic Breton

**The Forgotten Isles**
*Impressions of Travel in the Balearic Isles, Corsica and Sardinia*

ISBN/EAN: 9783337209278

Printed in Europe, USA, Canada, Australia, Japan

Cover: Foto ©Andreas Hilbeck / pixelio.de

More available books at **www.hansebooks.com**

GASTON VUILLIER

THE

# FORGOTTEN ISLES

IMPRESSIONS OF TRAVEL IN THE

## BALEARIC ISLES, CORSICA

AND

## SARDINIA

*Rendered into English by*

FREDERIC BRETON

AUTHOR OF "THE TRESPASSES OF TWO," "GOD FORSAKEN," "A HEROINE
IN HOMESPUN," ETC.

*WITH 167 ILLUSTRATIONS BY THE AUTHOR*

LONDON
HUTCHINSON & CO.
34, PATERNOSTER ROW
1896

# TO THE READER

*O*N *the day after leaving Marseilles, Algiers, or Oran, the traveller by sea often perceives on the horizon the cloudy outline of certain dim, mysterious islands—they are Majorca and Minorca. Further off, against a pale, diaphanous sky, he can distinguish the snowy peaks of Corsica, or follow with his eye the long, monotonous undulations of the coast of Sardinia.*

*In all probability, the traveller's knowledge of the Balearic Isles does not go beyond what he learnt at school. He remembers, perhaps, that the Roman armies recruited slingers in the Balearic Islands, or that the Arab conquerors of the archipelago brought with them the secret, long since lost, of manufacturing a rare kind of pottery of blended colours—of gold, azure, and flame. He knows also that kings reigned at Majorca, and that the most Christian people of Aragon rescued the islands from Mussulman hands.*

*Corsica perhaps is more familiar, and the wild beauty of its scenery is linked with stories of blood-feuds and adventures with bandits. But he knows absolutely nothing of Sardinia, an abandoned land, with which even its Italian masters are unacquainted. Yet a visit to these* FORGOTTEN ISLES *is a revelation.*

*Palma can show marvels of art and superb monuments, while the grandeur of the* sierras *and* barrancos, *the friendliness and simplicity of the people, and the soft, equable climate, render a journey through Majorca a dream of enchantment.*

*Minorca is less beautiful, but it still preserves interesting traces of the Aragonese and Catalans.*

*Iviza and Formentera, the remaining islands of the group, sleep as they have slept for five hundred years, cradled by the guttural psalmody inherited from the Moors, and only waking to love or to draw the knife.*

*In Corsica, the impression is different. In the immensity of its forests, the solitary traveller still hears the* lamenti *of bygone generations and shivers with the pity of death, or crosses the moor in peril of robbers; and, in the cloud-swept solitude of the heights, seats himself at the humble hearth of soothsaying shepherds, poets of the peaks, who recite Tasso and Ariosto to the accompaniment of the pastoral instruments played by shepherds and rhapsodists from the remotest antiquity.*

*To visit Sardinia is to turn back the pages of history. Here the Middle Ages are revived; the costumes of other days have preserved their pristine beauty, and the black coat of the nineteenth century brushes familiarly against the velvet doublet of the fifteenth.*

*This introduction will suffice for the following record of a journey to these* FORGOTTEN ISLES, *whose names are so familiar, but whose features are so unknown.*

# CONTENTS

## Part I.

### *THE BALEARIC ISLES.*

## CHAPTER V.

## CHAPTER VI.

## CHAPTER VII.

## CHAPTER VIII.

# Part II.
# CORSICA.

## CHAPTER I.

## CHAPTER II.

## CHAPTER III.

## CHAPTER IV.

## CHAPTER V.

## CHAPTER VI.

# Part III.

## SARDINIA.

## CHAPTER I.

## CHAPTER II.

## CHAPTER III.

## CHAPTER IV.

## CHAPTER V.

## CHAPTER VI.

# LIST OF ILLUSTRATIONS

# Part I.

# THE BALEARIC ISLES.

Palma de Mallorca.

## CHAPTER I.

A Night at Sea.—*Palma de Mallorca.*—*San Alfonso.*—*The Ayuntamiento.*—Visit to the Corpse of a King.—The Cathedral.—Churches of San Francisco and of Monte Sion.—Recollections of Raymond Lully.—The *Lonja.*—The Climate —The Moncades.—Bellver.—Raxa.—Majorcan Houses.

OFF Barcelona, on board the *Cataluña*, 5 p.m. Wind south-east ; sea fresh. The sun was setting in crimson clouds. Its rays still lit up the city, reddening the roofs of the buildings, gilding the topmasts of the vessels moored in the stagnant waters of the harbour, and illuminating the octagonal towers of Santa Maria del Mar and the gigantic figure of Christopher Columbus, whose statue, on the top of a tall column, commands the bay and points to the infinite ocean.

Night fell as we gained the open sea, and, leaning on the stern rails of the vessel, I followed with my eyes the phosphorescent track in our wake, which gradually faded away in the shadow of the Spanish coast,

3

where a faint reflection in the sky indicated the position of the city which we had just left.

Shortly before dawn, after a slight tossing in the Gulf, I opened my eyes, and through the porthole of my cabin saw the indented coastline of the island of Majorca, *Balearis Major*, as it was called by the Romans. The sun had not yet risen, and the lofty silhouette of the island was vaguely outlined against a pale sky, in which the stars still shone with a mellow but fading brilliancy. One of the sailors on deck, whither I soon ascended, told me that we should reach Palma in three hours' time. Shortly afterwards, threading the narrow channel separating the rock from the land, a passage apparently enclosed on all sides by tall cliffs, we passed the lighthouse surmounting the rocky islet of Dragonera. As the daylight grew, the features of the coast began to be distinguishable, and at the far end of the oddly shaped little creeks between the jutting headlands clusters of cabins, scarcely differing in colour from the arid rocks around them, marked the site of some small fishing hamlet. This channel, known as the Friou, is perilous to navigation, being as thickly sown with reefs as the entrance to a modern naval harbour is with torpedoes. In fact, the whole of the south-western coast which we were following presents an iron front to the sea, bristling with bayonets of rock, and so precipitous that the mariner cast ashore would stand but little chance of scaling his way to safety.

The sun rose just as we entered Palma Bay, and its rays fell full on the capital of Majorca, which with its waving palm trees and Arab monuments has an aspect more Eastern than European, except for the number of windmills lining the coast, and recalling familiar landscapes in Holland or south-eastern England.

Naturally enough, the arrival of the steamer, *el vapor*, is one of the great events of Palma, and the quays were alive with people. A shoal of small boats gathered round our vessel, while, to the imminent risk but apparent indifference of the crowd on shore, numbers of *galeras*, small carriages drawn by mules or horses, galloped up and down for no motive seemingly save the bravado of display. On every side were light, colour, and motion, a vibration of sheer life under a spotless blue sky in a city bathed in sunlight.

As soon as I had disembarked, one of the aforesaid *galeras* quickly conveyed me to the *fonda*.

It seemed but a few days since I had left the dull landscapes of the north under the sombre sky of chill October, and here, at Palma, I found the warmth and brilliance of a bright summer's day. I eagerly left my room as soon as possible, therefore, to enjoy the bright freshness of the morning and see a little of the interior of the town.

The narrow streets, built apparently with the express purpose of retaining the heat, were very animated. It was Sunday. The bells were ringing, and the Majorcans, men and women, high and low, with a not inconsiderable sprinkling of soldiers, were thronging the streets, most of them on their way to mass. The pavements were strewn with foliage, the houses were beflagged, red hangings fringed with gold were displayed from the windows, and illuminations were being prepared for the evening.

It was the festival of San Alfonso Rodriguez.

But a placard on the walls arrested my attention :—

### PLAZA DE TOROS DE PALMA.

#### GRAN CORRIDA

##### LA SEÑORA MAZANTINA CAPEARÁ, BANDERILLARÁ

##### Y MATARÁ UNO DE LOS TOROS.

The art of varying pleasure is well understood at Palma, and a bull-fight is sandwiched in between the morning mass and the evening procession.

Towards three, o'clock in the afternoon I took my seat on one of the stone tiers of an immense circus, a unit in an impatient crowd as vehement of expression as any gallery of " gods " in a transpontine theatre. Higher up, in the more select places, the waving of innumerable fans, coloured and gilded, dazzled the eye like the shimmer of insects' wings.

After the usual preliminaries, the gates of the *toril* opened, the bull appeared, and a young woman, the Señora Mazantina, as announced in the programme, came to play the perilous part of toreador.

Despite its novelty, I confess that the spectacle which followed aroused my indignation, for it was indeed barbarous and repulsive. The crowd, intoxicated by the sight of blood, placed no restraint on its excitement, gesticulating and yelling like wild beasts, while the poor animal in the arena bellowed with pain as each new *banderillera* pierced its quivering flesh. The woman, who was dressed in spangled tights, showed a pale face under her raven-black hair, but she assumed an air of bravado which hardly concealed her nervousness, and finally mounting a horse, rose up gallantly in her stirrups to pierce the maddened bull with her lance.

After three bulls had been despatched by the *espada*, and their carcasses dragged by mules round the arena amid the plaudits of the spectators, a fourth and last animal entered on the scene. The usual play having been made with *banderilleras* and lances, the Señora Mazantina advanced to give the *coup de grace*. But the short sword, held by a trembling hand, slipped to one side. The bull fell upon the unfortunate woman, and, in the twinkling of an eye, both were rolling in the dust.

I did not wait to see more, and hastily left the building. I learned afterwards, however, that the *señora*, though carried off the arena in a swoon, had not been seriously injured, the dying bull not having had sufficient strength to do much harm.

As I left the *Plaza de Toros*, the bells of all the chapels and churches of Palma (the number is said to be thirty-six) were ringing their loudest to announce that the procession in honour of San Alfonso Rodriguez had left the church. I mingled with the crowd, most of whom had been spectators at the barbarous spectacle of the bull-fight, and marvelled at the tortuousness of the human conscience to see these people devoutly fall on their keees and cross themselves in adoration of the God whose laws of kindness they professed to observe.

The street at this moment was a wonderful avenue of purple, verdure, and gold, encumbered with improvised side altars bearing pictures of the saint, gross caricatures probably in San Alfonso's own estimation, but devoutly surrounded by lamps and candles, and enframed in green branches. The flags and hangings were more numerous than in the morning, the windows were curtained with coloured cloths, and the doorways were hidden by sheaves of palms, while underfoot was a thick noiseless carpet of aromatic plants. The sound of chanting and blasts of trumpets heralded the approach of the procession, and the people formed in line on either side of the thoroughfare. Immense images of saints loomed up above the heads of the grave mace-bearers of the municipality who preceded the *cortège*. These images, of unlikely anatomy and consumptive complexions, were carried on stands borne on the shoulders of four men. Several held in their hands religious emblems, but most bore a nosegay of artificial flowers.

The crowning figure was that of San Alfonso himself, modelled lifesize in wax. He was carried in a crystal chair, but was more impressive than attractive. The face was of a corpse-like hue, and the thin ivory-coloured hands were piously folded on his breast. The pretty and coquettish Majorca girls, with rosaries in their hands, crossed themselves, as the image passed, with an air of compunction somewhat out of keeping with the sidelong glances they bestowed on the young men in their vicinity.

The procession over—and it grew monotonous before the bishop brought up the rear—I was not sorry to return to my hotel and end a well-filled day with a good dinner and a better sleep.

On the next morning I had the good fortune to fall in with an acquaintance who offered to be my guide to the sights of Palma. I could not have had a better conductor. Señor Sellarès was interested in every form of art, and no one could have been a better judge of what was likely to please an artist.

We went together to the *Ayuntamiento* or *Casa Consistorial*, passing on our way a shop where was exposed for sale the flesh of the bulls killed on the previous day. The meat certainly did not look appetising, but was eagerly purchased by the poor, to whom no doubt its low price compensated for any deficiency in quality.

The *Ayuntamiento* (Town Hall) is a fine building, recalling the Florentine style by the extraordinary prominence of the roof, which projects nearly nine feet, and is supported by richly carved buttresses and caryatides, who seem to bear their burden with pain and difficulty. The general style of the architecture is that of the sixteenth century. In the interior the sessions-hall is the only apartment of any size. Above the seat of the President there hangs a portrait of the Queen Regent Christina, by a native artist, and along the wall a series of paintings of illustrious men of Majorca, among whom, by a contemporary artist, figures the King *Don Jayme I., el Conquistador*, who is said to have taken prisoner a hundred Moors with his own hand, this being merely a casual incident in a career of prowess. In a neighbouring room there is a picture by Van Dyck, *The Martyrdom of Saint Sebastian*, but I failed to see the portrait of Hannibal, which I was afterwards told hung in the same gallery. The Majorcans relate that Hamilcar, on his way from Africa to Catalonia, stopped at one of the promontories of the island, and that it was there, near a temple dedicated to Lucina, that his wife gave birth to Hannibal. As we came out of the *Ayuntamiento* we heard a formidable rumbling of drums.

A Tamborero.

"Those," said my guide, " are *los tamboreros de la sala* (drummers of the municipality)."

They fulfil the function of public criers, march at the head of all civic processions, and announce the decisions of the *Ayuntamiento*.

On January 1st in each year they perform serenades, assembling before the houses of all the leading inhabitants, and persevering in a formidable rub-dubbing without interruption until they receive a contribution. Unhappy, indeed, those families who delay to pay tribute, for the noise becomes so deafening that they are compelled to disburse with all speed, if they wish to preserve the drums of their ears intact.

Formerly the town possessed the helmet, saddle, and standard of Don Jayme I.

On December 31st, the anniversary of the great victory which ended the dominion of the Moors, the portrait of *el Conquistador* was formerly exposed on a daïs in front of the *Ayuntamiento*, surmounted by the standard, and surrounded by the framed portraits of eminent men of Majorca. At night this exhibition was illuminated. On the same day was also displayed an immense stuffed lizard, which, according to tradition, once ravaged the island, depopulating the villages near the marshes, which served as its base of operations. The remains of this terrible saurian disappeared some years ago, and the standard, helmet, and saddle of Don Jayme were transferred in 1830 to the arsenal at Madrid. The staff of the standard still remains at Palma, however, and on the last day of each year is decorated with leaves and ribbons, and solemnly conveyed by the magistrates to the Cathedral, where its arrival is announced by a salvo of artillery, and the playing of the Royal March by the band, while the clergy of all the united parishes intone a *Te Deum*.

Since my arrival, I had noticed with not a little curiosity all the women and girls of the place busily occupied in threading rosary beads on small cords. These beads, of enormous size and various colours, were composed of sugar or crystallised fruit. It appears that it is the custom in Palma and other towns and villages of the island to give children one of these sweetmeat chaplets on All Saints' Day, with the object, no doubt, of initiating them into the pious practice of the rosary. I wanted to give one of these sweet and sacred comestibles to little Francisco, the son of my friend Sellarès, but the father cried out aghast, the little fellow having in the previous year devoured the whole rosary in one day, and suffered violent internal pains in consequence. Some days afterwards I saw the entire juvenile population of Pollensa, girls and boys, marching along with their rosaries trailing to the ground, proud of possessing such fine ornaments, which they every now and then lifted to their lips for a suck on the sly.

"I will show you something curious in the Cathedral to-night," said my friend Sellarès to me one day.

On first entering the harbour I had been struck by the imposing aspect of the edifice as seen from the sea, and had frequently expressed a wish to visit it by day. But on one pretext or another my friend had always postponed the matter, and now when we did go it was by night. The great nave looked immense in the obscurity. A few Majorcan women were kneeling on the flag-stones and telling their beads, pausing at the end of each decade to fan themselves. Two or three men also were praying fervently. Far off in the lighted chancel the Cathedral chapter was chanting compline. Presently the chanting ceased, the tapers were gradually extinguished, and the canons, departing in silence, disappeared one by one in the shadows of the lofty pillars. Some one approached us and whispered "Come!"

We obeyed the summons. A priest and a friend of Sellarès joined us. Torches were kindled, and presently we found ourselves in front of a sarcophagus of black marble surmounted by a sceptre, a sword, and a royal crown. On one side of the monument I saw graven in the marble the words, "Here rests the body of the Most Serene Señor Don Jayme of Aragon II., King of Mallorca, who deserves the most pious and praiseworthy memory in our annals. Died the 28th of May, 1311."

"Open," said Sellarès in a low voice. A key was inserted in the marble, one of the sides rolled back, and disclosed a coffin, which the assistants dragged out. The body of the king was under our eyes, draped with ermine, the large mouth open, and the eye-sockets deeply sunken. Big drops of candle grease dropped by previous visitors seemed like tears frozen on the rough face, as if the corpse were aggrieved by the curiosity which disturbed its last repose. In the light of the torches the crown sparkled and the sword flashed, as if a few rays of glory still hovered over the remains of royalty. After a few moments the coffin was pushed back into the tomb, the key was turned, and we retraced our steps across the dark and silent nave, till we saw the stars in a deep purple sky, and the white houses of the town silvered by the moonlight.

I was not sorry for the change. There had been too stern a moral of human mutability in the spectacle of the great king, who once commanded these seas, and whose power extended over the whole of Aragon, now at the mercy of the first sacristan who chose

Night Visit to the Tomb of King Jayme.

to earn a few pence by exhibiting the poor remains to gratify the curiosity of the tourist.

Some days later I again visited the Cathedral in the morning. Its appearance was forbidding and gloomy, like that of all Spanish cathedrals, and the only striking feature was the double row of seven massive pillars supporting the roof. The choir being in the centre of the nave spoilt the perspective. Behind the high altar an old altar-piece in carved wood was relegated to dust and darkness, though in a perfect state of preservation. The carved statuettes of

Doorway of the Church of Monte Sion.

saints on either side of the centre-piece were painted and gilt like the illuminations in an old missal. When money was required to complete the church, the nobles were given the privilege of graving their escutcheons on the key-stones of the vaulted roof in consideration for one hundred Majorcan pounds, or on the roof of the side aisles for fifty pounds. The revenue derived from this appeal to vanity must have been considerable, to judge by the number of such coats-of-arms.

The edifice was completed in 1601, four hundred years after its foundation by Don Jayme, *el Conquistador*, in fulfilment of a vow made by him to the Virgin during a severe storm which imperilled the safety of the fleet sent to conquer the island.

In harmony of line and delicacy of execution nothing could surpass the great doorway facing the sea. Gothic art, it has been said, has never excelled this achievement in combining correctness of proportion with freedom of expression. Statues, stone canopies, chiselled like delicate em-broidery, folded draperies, garlands of delicate flowers, capricious interlacing of ma-son-work, festoons, columns, foliage, figures of holy doctors, all combine to make a mar-vellous whole and produce a masterpiece of artistry in stone.

It is unfortunate that it has been found necessary to wall up the doorway, owing to the violence of the sea-wind, which used to work havoc in the church, blowing down the pictures and over-turning the sacred vessels. Among the treasures of the Cathedral reliquary are six silver seven-branched candle-sticks, the pediments of which

Tomb of Raymond Lully.

are in the form of a satyr. There are also a relic of the true Cross, three thorns from the Crown of Christ, a piece of the tunic, portions of the veil and chemise of the Virgin, and one of the arms of St. Sebastian. These precious relics were brought to Palma in 1512 by an archdeacon of Rhodes, named Manual Suria.

Close to the Cathedral is the *Palacio Real*, a characteristic building said to be partly of Roman and partly of Moorish con-struction. It is surmounted by a Gothic angel facing the sea.

Among the numerous churches of Palma special interest attaches
to San Francisco, in that it contains the tomb of the great Ramon
Lull (Raymond Lully), the famous mystic, who was at once a
prolific writer, a theologian, a physician, and an architect.  His tomb
is one of the most remarkable funeral monuments of the latest period
of Gothic architecture.

Raymond Lully was born at Palma in 1235.  He soon displayed
a leaning to the profession of arms, and entered the service of the
Infante Don Jayme as a page.  After a youth of wild dissipation,
his parents, in the hope of bridling his passions, persuaded him to
marry.  His conduct, far from improving, however, became worse ;
and one Sunday he outraged all conventions by entering the church
of Saint Eulalia on horseback in order to see a lady of whom he was
enamoured.

Another of his adventures is worthy of record for the sake of its
savour of the poetry of pity and death.  He was in love with a
young girl, and because of his love he became a chemist.  The girl,
while avowing the return of his passion, resisted all his entreaties.
Not knowing the cause of her coldness, he redoubled his solicitations,
until she suddenly tore aside the vest covering her bosom, and
showed her breast eaten away by a cancer.

He, horrified, but not despairing, devoted himself to special
studies, and, so it is said, succeeded in discovering a cure for the
disease, but beyond that the legend does not go.

Later in life, however, like many another wild youth of the
Middle Ages, he strove to atone for his early wildness by penitence
and study.  After selling his property and making provision for his
wife and children, he made pilgrimages to Montserrat and Santiago
de Compostella, and then withdrew to the summit of Mount Randa,
to devote himself to meditation and work.  Here he wrote several
books, the fame of which caused him to be summoned by King
Jayme II., then at Montpellier, in order to teach Arabic, which he
had learned from one of his slaves, to thirteen Franciscan friars at
a new missionary college founded by the king at Miramar.  From
here Raymond Lully went to Genoa to translate an Arabic work, and

to Tunis to preach the Gospel and confute the Mahommedan doctors. He visited Rome and then Paris, and was a missionary preacher in the Levant and in Africa. Here he was finally stoned to death at the gates of the town of Bougie by the Mussulman inhabitants.

The body was recovered by some Genoese fishermen, who intended to take it back home with them. But when they thought they were about to enter the port of Genoa, they found that they were in reality off Majorca. They shaped a fresh course accordingly, but their boat, arrested by a mysterious power, did not advance a cable's length in despite of the favouring wind which filled the sails. Having landed on the island they recounted the miracle, and ultimately interpreted it as a sign that they were to deposit the body in its native soil. The remains having been disembarked, they continued their voyage without further obstacle. The monks of San Francisco having claimed the body as belonging to their community, it was temporarily interred with great pomp in the sacristy, and subsequently transferred to the tomb where it now rests.

Such was the strange and singularly chequered career of the great master of mysticism, for whom the inhabitants of the Balearic Isles have almost as much veneration as for a canonised saint.

The nave of San Francisco is large and well proportioned, but has been much spoiled by a so-called " restoration."

The convent of the same name adjacent to the church is the largest in Palma, and formerly consisted of two cloisters occupied by one hundred and fifty monks. Later in its history the building became the residence of the political governor. It is now a prison ; and when we entered the enclosure, some of the *presidaros* (prisoners) were strolling about in groups smoking cigarettes, while others were makings mats and brushes of broom. I was surprised at their number, but Sellarès hastened to inform me that they were all sent to Palma from Spain, there being no malefactors in Majorca, just as there are no ferocious animals or venomous reptiles. The traveller can traverse the island by night or day in the wildest and most savage districts, and not only will he be unmolested, but will everywhere receive the most hospitable welcome.

Doorway of San Francisco.

In the lower part of the town near the quays stands a massive rectangular building, whose walls are mirrored in the calm water of the harbour. It is the *Lonja* (formerly the Exchange). It is described as one of the finest Gothic monuments in Spain, but externally, except for its ecclesiastical windows, it strikes the average observer as not unlike a county gaol. The interior, however, is remarkable as one of those problems of architectural quaintness which the artists of the Middle Ages loved to display their skill in solving, setting themselves difficulties for the mere pleasure of overcoming them. The interior consists of a single hall of vast proportions, the flat, vaulted roof of which is supported by six slight columns, fluted spiral-wise. The hall is now used for the masked balls during Carnival time, and can accommodate twelve thousand persons without overcrowding. This alone testifies to the extent of the shipping and commerce of Palma before the discovery of America altered the destinies of all the seaports in Europe.

The Balearic Isles were for a long time one of the most flourishing commercial centres of the world— a prosperity which was due neither to local industry nor to the wealth of the inhabitants, but to their geographical position midway between the coasts of Africa, Italy, France, and Spain.

Under the peaceful reign of Don Jayme I. the commerce of Majorca assumed immense proportions, and the port of Palma was crowded with

Interior of the Lonja.

vessels. In the fifteenth century the Genoese merchants were so numerous that they had a special Exchange, and occupied a special quarter of the town, now inhabited chiefly by the descendants of Jewish converts to Christianity. In the archives of Madrid are to be found sumptuary laws of that period which testify to the

2

luxury and opulence of the inhabitants. Majorca was one of the great markets of Europe, and one of the chief centres of the Indian and African trade. There was scarcely a noble family which did not maintain at least one galley. But the discovery of the Cape of Good Hope changed the route for Asiatic products, and the expulsion of the Moors from Spain did much to ruin the prosperity of the Balearic Isles.

Nowadays the commercial relations of the group do not extend beyond the Mediterranean coasts of Spain, Africa, and France ; and the principal exports consist merely of oil, almonds, oranges, lemons, and capers, which go to Marseilles, wine to Cette, and pigs and vegetables to Barcelona.

Majorca is the largest and much the most fertile of the islands. The soil is so rich, the climate so soft, and the natural scenery so beautiful, that the ancients called the group the *Eudemones*, or Land of Good Genii, and also the *Aphrodisiades*, or Islands of Love. The population is relatively twice as dense as in Spain.

Palma, which contains over sixty thousand inhabitants, is said to have been founded by Quintus Cæcilius Metellus, surnamed Balearicus. It is related that when he first attempted to land on the coast, he was obliged to place an awning of skins over the deck of each ship to protect his men from the projectiles of the slingers of the island. All the old authors refer to the dexterity shown in the use of the sling by the inhabitants. Dameto, a local historian, wrote even as late as 1731, that the address and skill displayed in the use of this weapon were such that the leaden balls used as projectiles melted in the air from the very violence with which they were thrown !

The climate of Majorca is milder than that of Valencia, which is in nearly the same latitude. At the same time, temperature varies according to situation ; and on the mountains, which extend from north-east to south-west along one side of the island, it is often comparatively fresh when the plains are baking.

My friend Sellarès sometimes said to me when he saw my eagerness to visit the sights of the island, " When you've eaten four

The Castle of Bellver and the Terreno.

or five *encimadas*, you will begin to be in tune with Majorca. You are still far too nervous and active. At Palma we always have plenty of time; we are never in a hurry, or, if we are, we hasten slowly. We are always in good health, our existence passes without effort, our wants are moderate, and we grow old after long enjoying the sunshine and the marvels of our isle."

The *encimada*, of whose sedative properties Sellarès spoke so highly, is a kind of dripping cake, generally served with chocolate. I found them difficult of digestion, and I daresay they do tend to intensify the physical and intellectual torpor already induced by the climate. My stay in Majorca was not long enough to permit of my enjoying the benefits of this native confection, and, not having plenty of time, like the Majorcans, I begged Sellarès to accompany me to the famous pine tree of the Moncades, for which purpose I hired a *galera*.

These carriages are very light and graceful. They are drawn

mostly by mules, and, whether climbing or descending hills, always go at full speed.

After passing the quays, we followed a dusty road to Terreno, a sort of seaside resort much affected by the townspeople during the hot weather.   Every house stands in its own garden, shaded by the traditional fig tree and diversified with flowers.   The town is surrounded by a dense forest of Syrian pines, through which the road ascends to the gloomy castle of Bellver, which I visited on the following day.   The sea-view from this point is very extensive, and in clear weather the rock of Cabrera, of melancholy memory, is visible on the horizon.   Terreno is connected with Palma by a tramway, and a man can have his sea bath in the morning, go into business, and return home in the evening.   He can even come back for his midday siesta, for the journey into town only occupies a quarter of an hour.

After passing Terreno, which was deserted at this time of year (November), we followed the coastline for a long distance.   The sea was always with us, but here was none of the bleakness associated with seaside landscapes in northern regions.   The waves broke in silver fringes on sandy creeks, or, further out, washed in unbroken blue round some projecting reef, but the rich vegetation grew almost to the water's edge.   The air was scented with wild rosemary, cytisus, myrtle, and lavender, while heather plants of every tint of rose and tall as garden shrubs waved their supple stems in the warm sea-breeze.

After a two hours' drive the coachman drew up, got down from his box, and with true southern politeness, hat in hand, requested us to do him the favour of alighting.

Right in front of us was the famous pine of the Moncades, on a stretch of link land bordered by the sea.   It was here that Don Jayme the Conqueror disembarked with his comrades in arms, and on September 12th, 1229, first gave battle to the Infidels.   It was here, on the same day, that the Moncades, two brothers belonging to an illustrious family, and lieutenants of the king, met with death and undying honour.   It was to commemorate this that the giant pine was solemnly consecrated on May 5th, 1887, when a portion of the ceremony consisted of the reading of the passage in the Chronicles of Catalan describing the death of the two heroes. A full description of the strange but touching spectacle, when mass was said under the open sky, with the sea for organ and choir, to a congregation of peasants, poets, and artists, was given at the time in the *Revue Felibrienne.*

On our return journey we followed a more inland road through the forest on the shoulder of the mountain, and visited the château of Bendinat, which belonged to the Count of Montenegro. The origin of the name is worth recording. After the great battle in which the Moncades fell, Don Nuño, a lieutenant, led the king, who had tasted no food all day, to a country house, where his majesty dined to such good purpose that being satisfied he said, *Be hem dinat* (" We have dined well "). Some indeed allege that the king spoke in irony, his country fare not having been prepared for royalty ; but, be that as it may, the royal phrase gave its name to the place.

The Castle of Bellver, referred to above, has also the interest of association, for it was here that Francis Arago was imprisoned for two months in the *homenaje* tower. In 1808 the illustrious astronomer came to Majorca to pursue his work in connection with the terrestrial meridian. For this purpose he kindled some fires on a lofty hill above Bellver. The inhabitants of Palma, curious and suspicious, thought that signals were being made to the French fleet ; and as Spain was then at war with France, hurried to the mountain in order to put the treasonable signaller to death. Warned by a friend, Arago descended towards the town and met the infuriated crowd ; but as he spoke the language of the country with perfect facility, he was not recognised, and took refuge on board a boat lent by the Spanish Government to the scientific mission charged with the measurement of the meridian. The crowd soon learnt where he was, however, and became so threatening that the captain, refusing to be responsible for the scientist's life, lent him a small boat, in which he reached Bellver fortress, only getting away from his pursuers by the merest chance. After two months' imprisonment he succeeded in

Staircase of Raxa.

escaping in a fish-
ing boat to Al-
giers, where fresh
vicissitudes a-
waited him.

The Castle of
Bellver, built to
defend the en-
trance to the Port
of Palma, is a
curious relic of
the military archi-
tecture of the
Middle Ages. Its
lofty walls are
flanked by four
towers and as
many turrets.
The interior is
composed of a
circular enclosure
arranged in two
tiers, with two
galleries above.
The lower of
these, with plain
arches, is almost
Roman in its severity of type, but
the upper, with its rich mouldings and
trifoliated bays, recalls the carved
cloisters of the sixteenth century.
Two bridges connect the fortress with
the famous isolated tower of *homenaie*,
or homage, in which Arago was confined. The tower had already served

as a place of imprisonment for several personages of note, among them being Jovellanos, dramatic poet and minister of Charles IV. After the wont of so many captives, Jovellanos employed his leisure in carving on the walls a chronicle of events, choosing for subjects the deeds of which the walls had been the silent witnesses—murders, fights, treasons, and mysterious dramas, in all of which the Christians were cutting one another's throats. He wrote from his experiences of Court intrigues. The Castle is also the tomb of the unfortunate General de Lacy, who was shot within its precincts.

Another castle of interest in the vicinity of Bellver is the seat of the Count of Montenegro, which contains a notable collection of arms and tapestry, formed by Cardinal Antonio Despuig, an intimate friend of Pope Pius VI., and an uncle of the then count. There is also an immense library, in which the cardinal gathered together all that was remarkable in the bibliography of Spain, Italy, and France. The collection of works on ancient art, and particularly coins, is said to be unique. It was in this library that George Sand was implicated in an accident for which the Majorcans still hold her responsible. Among the treasures of the collection was a fine manuscript nautical chart of 1439—a wonder of patient and careful design, and enriched with many quaint miniatures. It belonged to Amerigo Vespuzzi, who purchased it at a high price, the Spanish inscription on the map testifying that it was bought by him for the sum of one hundred and thirty gold ducats. When the map was being shown to the French authoress, a servant, with more politeness than discretion, placed a very full ink-pot on a corner of the parchment to keep it open on the table. The manuscript being generally rolled, and the weight being insufficient to retain it in place, however, the parchment suddenly reverted to its usual position, with the result that the inkpot was upset, and the contents spilt over the face of the map. The chaplain, who was showing the treasure, lost his head completely, and, seizing a wet sponge, proceeded to clean the manuscript, but with such superfluous energy, that he wiped out the original as well as the new ink, obliterating at one fell sweep seas, islands, and continents.

The map is now preserved in a frame under glass, and has been removed from the castle library to the *alqueria* ⌐(country house) of Raxa, where there is a museum of antiquities belonging to the same proprietor. This *alqueria* is charmingly situated in a shady valley surrounded by mountains. In the time of the Moors the name was Araxa, and the adjacent property formerly belonged to the famous Arab, Beni Atzar, whose name it still bears. The principal staircase of Raxa, bordered by statues and antique fragments, the whiteness of which is relieved by the darkness of cypresses and greenness of pines, is one of the most striking features in the gardens round the house.

When lying awake in my room at the *fonda* in Palma, I often heard the monotonous tinkling of guitars in the distance, and at long intervals a simple song like an Arab chant. Earlier in the evening the voice of the *serenos*, or watchmen, intoned an old melody handed down for centuries :—

A - la - ba - do se - a    di - os    las  do - ce  de  la  no-che  no-bla- do.

The first phrase is certainly of Moorish origin, the Mahommedans always commencing their discourses with similar praise to the Deity.

In Palma, the *serenos*, who number about fifty, perambulate the city the whole night through, chanting the time and the state of the weather. They aid the sick and help belated travellers, fetching the doctor, if necessary, for the former, and assisting the latter to find a lodging. They signal to each other with whistles, and in an emergency can assemble together in a very short time.

Passing through the town one day with the landlord of the *fonda de Mallorca*, I was much struck by the Jewish types standing about in the doorways or serving in the shops.

"They are Jews !" I exclaimed.

"Don't speak so loud !" said the landlord. "We are in the Jewish quarter, but the inhabitants are all Christians now. For a long time after their conversion they were compelled by law to say their prayers aloud, for fear lest they should mutter blasphemies under the semblance of fervour."

The Jews were horribly persecuted at Mallorca in the Middle Ages. In the monastery of St. Dominic, now destroyed, the walls of the cloisters were decorated with frescoes representing the tortures to which these victims of religious intolerance were subjected. At the foot of each painting was inscribed the name, age, and date of execution of the person de-picted. Some of the pictures were marked by a representa-tion of cross-bones, indicating those whose ashes had been exhumed and thrown to the winds. I saw a list, printed by order of the Holy Inqui-sition in 1755, of the names, professions, and offences of the persons sentenced in Majorca between the years 1645 and 1691. They in-cluded four Majorcans, one a woman, burnt alive for Juda-sm ; thirty-two others im-prisoned for the same "of-fence," who died in the Inquisitorial cells, and whose

Moorish Bath-house.

remains were afterwards burned ; a Dutchman accused of Lutheranism, a Mahommedan, and six Portuguese, besides some sixty others, who were released from prison on retractation of their errors. Several of the persons accused who managed to escape were burned in effigy.

Notwithstanding the prolonged Moorish occupation of the Balearic Isles, the traces of Arab architecture are comparatively few. The only noteworthy relics in Palma are the porch of the Templars' Church and a bath-house in a private garden. On the other hand, every lover not merely of architecture, but of the picturesque, will

find much to please and interest him in the ancient houses of the
Majorcan Knights. Two of the *patios* or interior courts of these
buildings are exceptionally beautiful. They are those of the Olezza
and Sollerich Palaces. Nearly all the more interesting houses of
Palma appear to date from the beginning of the sixteenth century,
but the Renaissance architecture is in almost every case modified
by Moorish tradition. Above the ground floor there is but one
storey and a very low garret. The entrance from the street is an
arched doorway without ornament. Light enters the vast rooms of
the first storey through lofty windows, divided by columns of a
slenderness entirely Moorish, and one could easily believe that they
had been taken from some ancient Moorish palace like the Alhambra
at Granada. Some of the columns, though six feet in height, are
not more than three inches in diameter; and the fineness of the
marble of which they are made, and the tasteful chasing of their
capitals, all point to Arab origin. The topmost storey is a gallery,
or rather a succession of windows, close together, and fashioned after
the pattern of those surmounting the ancient Exchange or *Lonja*.
The projecting roof is supported by artistically carved beams, and
besides affording a protection from rain and sun, produces the most
striking effects of light and shade, both by reason of the long
shadows which it throws upon the house, and because of the contrast
between the brown timber-work and the pure brilliancy of the sky.
The staircase, carved with great taste, is situated in a court in the
centre of the house, and separated from the street entrance by a
vestibule, the roof of which is generally upheld by columns with
sculptured capitals.

Landscape at Soller.

## CHAPTER II.

At Miramar.

The Giant Olives.—The Carthusian Monastery of Valldemosa. — Souvenirs of George Sand and Chopin.—Miramar.—An Enchanted Coast.—The Garden of the Hesperides.—Soller.

A T seven o'clock on a fresh sunny morning in November I left Palma for Valldemosa and Miramar. The streets were still silent, for the people of Palma are late risers, and we drove through the fortified gate at the back of the town without having encountered a single wayfarer.

The white road unwound itself like a ribbon across the plain towards the mountains, which were half hidden by thickets of almond trees. Pale pink in the light and transparent

27

azure in the shadow, the distant hills seemed so translucent that it was
hard to believe they were not the effect of a mirage. But as we
advanced and the sunlight fell more strongly on their bare summits,
the shadows came out more distinctly, indicating where the slopes
fell steeply into the ravines or ended abruptly in rocky cliffs. The
road led past white houses overshadowed by waving palms throwing
a blue shadow. The flat roofs supported galleries from which hung
bright red and golden festoons of pimentos, interspersed with huge
bunches of maize drying in the sun. Hedges of cactus, or the thorny
cochineal plant, separated the gardens from the road. The plain had
the appearance of an immense orchard. The Majorcans, working
with their mule teams under the almond trees, were singing the wild
melody of some ancient *malagueña*. At intervals we passed large
reservoirs full of water, forming part of an intricate system of
irrigation established centuries ago by the Arabs. Orange trees,
with vivid green foliage and golden fruit, and pomegranate trees,
from which the ripe seeds of the half-opened fruit fell in ruby
showers, bore witness to the richness of the soil. Contrasted with
these were the silvern trunks and bare, twisted branches of the fig
trees, still bearing last season's figs—figs of the Christian, as they are
called in Majorca, to distinguish them from the fruit of the cactus,
known as the figs of the Moor.

After two and a half hours' rapid driving we reached the mountainous region, and entered a deep glen. Habitations became rare,
but the road was still bordered by rich foliage and bright flowers,
including the caper, the myrtle, the *stepa blanca*, with its starlight
blossoms, and the pretty little flowers known here as *lagrimas*
(tears).

The almond trees disappeared, and gave place to the olive.
These trees, which are of great age, and are said to have been planted
by the Moors, assume the most fantastic forms. Most have a huge
trunk, ending suddenly in a slender plume of branchlets. Others
are twisted like gigantic gimlets, or, like immense serpents, seem
to be fighting fold to fold. Some again resemble hideous monsters
with giant hands and grimacing faces, horrid with wens and nameless

excrescences. Some seem to be running away in terror. The roots writhe as if in pain, while the trunks seem furnished with troll-like faces, fixed for ever in a malicious grin. Altogether, these extraordinary trees are more like the monstrous vegetation with which the imagination of a Gustave Doré would provide Dante's Inferno, than the symbol of peace and content.

I visited them once later on by moonlight, and, in spite of myself, I shivered at the sight of their gaunt figures vaguely apprehended in the chill radiance. They seemed to be moving, and the night

Cartuja de Valldemosa.

breeze rustling in the leaves sounded like spectral whispering, while ghostly eyes appeared to glimmer through the trembling shadows of their long arms.

Beyond the olive trees the glen became a gorge, where the road was strangled between lofty summits, and an invisible rivulet clattered under the fallen boulders. I was told that in winter this rivulet becomes a raging torrent, which often renders the road impassable.

Such an approach heightened the smiling aspect of Valldemosa, with the vari-coloured clock tower of the old monastery, and its white houses among palms and cypresses, brightening the sun-warmed slopes with their joyous colour and rich vegetation.

The monastery was formerly occupied by fifty monks, and all strangers and wayfarers could stop there for three days and nights, during which they were lodged and fed at the expense of the community, a special building being reserved for their use.

The *cartuja*, which was originally a fort, was built by the king, Don Sancho, and was specially renowned for its falconry. The building was given by King Martin to Don Pedro Solanes, who transformed it into a Carthusian monastery, which existed until 1835, when all religious houses were suppressed in Majorca. It was in the deserted monastery of Valldemosa that George Sand and Chopin passed their winter in Majorca. And while the rains beat upon the windows, and the winter winds wept in the sombre galleries of the ruined cloister, the musician, already sick of the malady which eventually proved fatal, noted down the sad, complex harmonies in which his thoughts found expression, while the authoress wrote *Spiridion*—a gloomy book full of the feeling of the storm and of turbid philosophy.

Ill fortune dogged them even in this retreat, and the Majorcans treated the strange pair with scant courtesy ; though perhaps they found consolation in the natural beauty of their surroundings. Yet— such is the irony of fame—even their names are scarcely remembered in Valldemosa. I asked in vain which rooms they occupied. No one, not even the most aged inhabitant, recollected having seen the couple. I learnt subsequently, however, that the piano used by the composer is still religiously preserved by an inhabitant of Palma.

From the *cartuja* one, as it were, plunges into space. To the south the mountains roll down to the glittering plain, where Palma gleams like a point in the luminous immensity, and far beyond the sea flashes like a sword-blade in the sun. Northwards, however, the sea is close at hand, and, when the wind blows from that quarter, the murmur of the waves is plainly audible.

On passing the last houses of Valldemosa we reach the top of the ridge, and after traversing some cultivated fields we suddenly perceive the open sea at our very feet.

This is the north coast, the most picturesque portion of the island, and the most characteristic of Majorcan landscape. Above the *hospederia*, a sort of free inn, established by the Austrian Archduke Ludwig Salvator for the shelter of visitors and wayfarers, is a hermitage still occupied by a monk of savage aspect, worn out by privations, consumed by the ardour of faith, but still ready for all conflicts—a typical illustration, in fine, of the mediæval ascetic. No sound troubles the quiet of this solitary place, save the eternal dirge of the waves, or perhaps the fluttering of the wings of some bird of prey.

On leaving the *hospederia* the road follows the flanks of the mountains along a lofty cornice of rock, and leads to Miramar.

The North Coast.

The situation of Miramar is remarkable. It is perched upon an enormous rock overhanging the sea, which stretches like a piece of crinkled blue satin far below, at a depth almost terrifying to behold. The coast is jagged and rocky, full of crumbling crevasses, precipices, and steep declivities—*escarpada y horrosa sin abrigo ni resguardo*, says Miguel de Vargas.

These coasts, bristling with perpendicular rocks of blood-red colour, where wind-distorted pines seemed to be drawing back as if in affright from the abysses which they overhang, witness terrible storms. Many ships have been lost on this dreaded shore, and often not even a single piece of wreckage has remained to bear witness to their fate.

There was little hint of these terrors, however, on the fine day on which I saw the place. The warm air was balmy with the perfume of aromatic plants, only prevented from being overpoweringly sweet by the wild savour of the proximate brine. The sun gilded chestnut and pine, tall heath-bells waved in the wind, birds sang in the leafy shade, saffron clouds passed slowly across the sky or caressed the mountain tops, the sea slept silently beneath—a blue expanse stretching to a horizon of heat-haze. The archduke has preserved Miramar in its pristine wildness. A few rough paths have been cut in the rock, but no one is allowed so much as to break off one of the dead branches which whiten on the trees or crumble on the steep slopes. Owner of vast forests, the archduke buys his own firewood. Trees live, grow old, and die without being touched. The hoary rocks remain as they have been for centuries. Moss covers and re-covers their sharp angles ; and in winter, when the wind howls and the sea gnashes its teeth at the crumbling cliffs, huge boulders fall unceasingly into the ravines below.

The sun was setting and empurpling the spires of the pines, when by a zigzag pathway I ascended to the travellers' rest-house or *hospederia*. There, whoever passes may seat himself in content. By a pleasing custom—still observed, I am told, in the Holy Land—he will find a table covered with a white cloth, plates, a glass, a wooden fork and spoon, fresh water, salt, olives, bed, oil, and a fire. At night an antique copper lamp with several burners sheds a weird, flickering light. The women charged to administer hospitality receive the traveller with smiling courtesy, and lead his mule to the manger or his carriage to the coach-house. They will cook in oil the onions and pimento which the poor man brings in his wallet and eats with his brown bread, or roast the game provided by the more well-to-do traveller.

The sleeping accommodation is the same for all, consisting of a pair of scrupulously clean sheets, and in winter warm, soft coverlets. This free shelter and hearth may be enjoyed for three days, at the end of which the traveller, whatever his station, must give place to another. No money must be offered for the services rendered, for everything is a free gift, and the proffer of a donation would be resented as an insult. What a lesson in kindliness is this hospitality for countries priding themselves on their superior civilisation, where the poor and the wanderer must generally go without shelter, and is unable to seat himself by any fireside! One sleeps well in the silent and lonely *hospederia*, especially when the day has been spent in clambering down precipices and scaling rocks.

The sun was already high when I awoke, and I hurried to revisit the sea and the woods, and to breathe again the delicious air, redolent of the wild scents of the sierra and the sharp savour of the sea. My morning walk led me to a cliff crowned by a watch-tower, now deserted, but inhabited up to within a few years ago. The raids of the Barbary corsairs rendered these watch-towers a matter of necessity on all the Mediterranean coasts, and the promontories of Majorca bristle with them.

A code of signals was invented by a Majorcan astronomer, by which the towers were able to give notice to each other and also to the neighbouring islands of Iviza, Cabrera, and Dragonera of vessels passing near the coast, together with their destination and port of origin. As I sat on a mossy rock in front of the tower I thought of the by-gone centuries, when these coasts, now so untroubled, were the constant witnesses of murderous scenes, and when the inhabitants lived in a continual state of terror. I seemed to see the watchman

3

kindling his nocturnal beacon, which was answered from cape to cape, till the alarm reached Palma, while, on the opposite side, the answering flare of Soller called the attention of Pollensa, and awoke the lonely bay of Alcudia and Cape Pera. I heard the distant murmur of the call to arms, and the dissonant peal of the alarm bells mingling with the shouts of the terrified people, *Moros, moros en la mar!* (" The Moors, the Moors on the sea ! ")

The Creek of l'Estaca.

But, coming to myself, and looking round me, I saw nothing but the sunlight streaming through the trees, heard nothing but the singing of the birds and the far-away murmur of the waves. After breakfast at the *hospederia* I shaped my steps to Miramar, whither the archduke had returned on the previous day. He welcomed me with the cordiality of a brother artist, and invited me to lunch, at which I met the rector of the institute of Palma, Don Francisco Manuel de Los Herreros, to whom the archduke owed his first introduction to Miramar. Their first meeting was at sea, twenty years ago, when the archduke, heart-broken at the terrible death of the princess to whom he had been betrothed, was seeking to forget his grief in travel. Originally, the archduke had no idea of acquiring so large a property as he now possesses, and selected merely Miramar and the land immediately round the house. From the first he gave orders that the natural features of the landscape were not to be interfered with. But one day it happened that a Majorcan was felling an ancient tree on some adjacent property. The man was within his right, and the only means of stopping such an act of vandalism was for the archduke to purchase the peasant's plot of land. This he did at a high price. The result was that all the peasants in the neighbourhood commenced felling their trees, and the archduke continued to buy their land, until he had expended

The Sea Road.

many thousands and secured a vast estate.

After lunch, we all mounted mules to ride to San Masroig, the residence of the archduke's private secretary. The road ran at the base of lofty cliffs along the margin of the sea, and in some places was protected by stone embankments to prevent it from being washed away.

Suddenly the eye was caught by a long promontory of red rock pierced by a yawning orifice, through which the sky could be seen on the further side. It was the *Foredada*, a tunnelled cliff, under the arch of which the osprey still builds its nest.

From this point onwards the road climbed the cliff sideways, by a kind of stony stairway, so steep in many places that even our mules found it difficult to keep their footing. As we ascended higher and higher the boulders beneath seemed to diminish to the size of mere pebbles, and even the *Foredada* appeared flat on the sea, like a cape in a map, outlined with a band of blue.

At length we reached a plateau, and entered a grove of olives, where we dismounted at the gate of San Masroig. Here I took leave of the archduke, and, entering a galera, drove off along the road to Deá and Soller, passing a band of handsome work-girls wearing immense straw hats, which helped to set off their brown complexions and dark eyes.

After driving for several miles along a ledge high above the ever-present sea, we turned sharply to the right, and entered the valley of Deá.

Work-girl of Miramar.

The landscape changed in character, and everything indicated that the inhabitants were very industrious, being compelled to wrest their fields from the virgin rock. Nevertheless, the scattered houses were surrounded by shady gardens, where the ripening oranges gleamed in the trees. Palms and olive trees flourished, and, in many respects, the village was the counterpart of the hamlets that nestle among the foothills of the French Pyrenees.

Deá had become a thing of the past, when, on reaching the summit of a hill, I perceived at my feet the beautiful valley of Soller set like a gem in the heart of a lofty chain of mountains,

A Peasant and his Wife.

the lower slopes of which, with the plain at their feet, were covered with verdure ; and even where I stood the air was heavy with the rich perfume of flowers and fruit. The country was one vast garden—medlar trees, lemon trees, apple trees, palm trees, almond trees, banana trees, cherry trees, fig trees, peach trees, and apricot trees floated, as it were, on the sea of orange trees which covered the plain, with here and there a house gleaming like a white foam-fleck on the waves of foliage. It was the garden of the Hesperides. So fertile was the soil that a single tree has been known to bear as many as two thousand five hundred oranges, and a bunch of grapes has been cut weighing twenty-two pounds. Majorca is popularly supposed to be covered with orange trees, and a sailor serving on the line between Marseilles and Algeria once told me that he could smell their perfume twenty miles out at sea. This must have been the effect of his imagination, for, as a matter of fact, the Balearic Isles, especially Majorca, produce very few oranges. The district of Soller is the only exception ; and even here the production has fallen off considerably, owing to the trees being attacked by disease.

The evening shadows were slowly creeping up the mountain slopes as we drove rapidly down the zigzag road, and when we reached the town the last rays of the setting sun were reddening the peaks of the Puig Major of Torella, the loftiest mountain of the island, which rises to a height of nearly five thousand feet. A few oil lamps which flickered in the wind were the only lights in the dark, narrow streets. I was so tired with my journey that I fell half asleep with my elbows on the table when dining at the *fonda.*

Next morning I visited the harbour, which is about an hour and a half's walk from the town. It is surrounded by steep hills, and resembles a vast pond, being apparently landlocked, as the narrow strait on the north connecting it with the sea is indistinguishable. It was from here, according to tradition, that St. Raymond of Peñaffort crossed the sea to Spain, with no better boat than his cloak, when he was fleeing from the king, who, deaf to his counsels, persisted in living irregularly with the Lady Bernegwela. The king had given orders to all the boats not to take on board priests or monks, but the saint, trusting to the faith which conquers all things, threw himself into the sea, and was safely conveyed to Barcelona. To this day the sailors point out the rock on which St. Raymond stood while evoking the protection of Heaven.

In 1398 the women of Majorca organised a naval force, called the Holy Army, with the object of delivering the Mediterranean from

The Hermit of Miramar.

Moorish corsairs. In May 1561 the pirates attacked Soller, but were defeated through the energy and courage of two women, Francisca and Catherina Casanovas, in memory of whose exploit a nautical feast is held each year, called "The Feast of the Valiant Women."

Soller was one of the most important towns of Majorca. The population exceeds eight thousand persons. Its women enjoy a great reputation for beauty, which is justified by their appearance. Their features are regular, and their expression is one of perpetual

tranquillity. Their dress is charming, consisting of a [skirt, a short apron, and a black bodice with elbow-sleeves, over which a band of the chemise folds back, and is fastened by bright-coloured glass buttons. Their heads are covered by a *rebosillo*, a sort of muslin cowl which leaves the neck and shoulders unconcealed.

The men of Soller possess a remarkable talent for improvising verses in the Majorcan dialect, and the most eloquent members of the Balearic Bar are natives of Soller. It was here that I saw for the first time the ancient Majorcan costume, which is not unlike that of the modern Greeks, supplemented on Sundays and feast-days by a hat with a wide brim and a cloak with long sleeves.

The "Rebosillo."

Roman Bridge at Pollensa.

## CHAPTER III.

From Palma to Pollensa.—Yuca and its Majolica Ware.—Pollensa.—The *Campo Santo*.—Don Sebastian.—Majorcan Dances and *Malaguenas*.—The Sanctuary of Lluch.

A MINIATURE railway crosses the greater portion of the island, and a branch line at Enpalme connects the capital with Manacor on the east.

The speed of the trains, as might be expected, is not excessive, and the number of stations is legion. A well-merited tribute must, however, be paid to the courtesy of the officials. The ticket-collector never enters the carriage without respectfully greeting the travellers, and thanking them for the honour of inspecting their tickets. Moreover, every man is anxious to impart information, and the stranger need never lack a guide.

Looking from the windows of his compartment, the traveller is struck by the immense forests of almond trees, the blossom of which in early spring gives the plains of Majorca the aspect of a vast flower garden. Beyond the almond thickets the low country is dominated by the mountains, on the rocky escarpments of which one catches glimpses of old ruined sanctuaries. The first stopping-place of importance is Benisalem, a town of three thousand inhabitants, founded in A.D. 1300, surrounded by rich vineyards and fruit gardens. The church is built of marble and jasper procured from adjacent quarries. There are also lignite mines in the vicinity.

We next pass the little town of Lloseta, climbing the slope of a hill, facing the lofty, scarped crests of the Sierra del Norte. The antiquity of the place is proved by the medals and other objects of Phœnician, Carthaginian, and Roman workmanship which have been found in the locality.

A little further on the train reaches Yuca, one of the chief towns of the island, with a population of six thousand, and the principal centre of the manufacture of Hispano-Moorish ware. Windmills crown the surrounding hills, and contrast strangely with the palm trees which overshadow the gardens. In the old parish church is another of the uncorrupted bodies which so often form one of the holy treasures of Spanish churches. The remains in this case are those of a holy nun who died in the odour of sanctity.

The name *Majolica* ware, applied haphazard to a large class of Italian earthenware, is generally derived from Majorca. Scaliger, who wrote in the first half of the sixteenth century, speaks in high terms of the vases manufactured in his time in the Balearic Isles, and compares them to the finest china porcelain, of which he evidently considers them an imitation, for he writes :—

" It is difficult to distinguish between the imitation and the genuine article. The imitation ware made in the Balearic Isles is not inferior either in form or brilliancy, and is even finer in elegance of form."

The railway ends at the station of La Puebla, whence there is an omnibus service to Pollensa and Alcudia. La Puebla is not an attractive place. Its streets are straight and symmetrical, but terribly monotonous and dusty, and the surrounding country is flat. The people, nevertheless, are kind and hospitable. The stranger, gazing curiously through the doorways to catch a glimpse of the *patiô* within, is invariably invited to enter, and is offered refreshments.

The Majorcan manner of speech has a melodious charm, especially in the mouths of the women, whose voices are charmingly fresh. They seem to be speaking always in the major key, and the words, of farewell, which one hears at all hours of the day, are perfect musical phrases.

"*Bona nit tengua! Es meu cô ne basta per li di, adios!*" ("Goodnight to you! My heart will not let me say farewell!")

I reached La Puebla in the afternoon, and hired a carriage to Pollensa.

"*Vamos!*" said the driver, and we slowly drove away. Nobody is in a hurry here! We shall reach our journey's end at the appointed time.

It was night when we arrived at Pollensa. The streets were dark, narrow, and tortuous, the only lights being the glimmering lamps placed before the casual niches containing pictures of the Madonna or some favourite saint.

In the public room at the *fonda* some Majorcans were sipping anisette, and several were twanging their guitars.

After dinner I went into the church, close to the inn, but the service was not calculated to ensure a cheerful evening. Under the shadow of the immense nave knelt a number of men and women holding lighted candles. Otherwise the gloom was unilluminated, but beyond the flickering glare of the candles I faintly discerned a catafalque, while unseen priests in the choir-stalls chanted the Office for the Dead. The sorrowful psalmody, combined with the darkness, was well designed to impress the congregation with a wholesome fear of their latter end, but did not add to the pleasure of living, except, perhaps, by sheer force of contrast.

It was quite a relief next morning to walk abroad in the sunlight alongside the flashing waters of the Pollensa torrent. The stream is spanned by a picturesque Roman bridge, and in many places overhung by large, black carob trees, beneath the shade of which

At the "Wall of the Dead."

women were busily washing their linen, notwithstanding the fact
that it was the festival of All Saints.  On this day the Majorcan
fishermen do not put to sea, being convinced that if they cast their
nets the haul will consist of human bones.

The commemoration of the dead, customary on All Souls' Day,
is extended over several days in the Balearic Isles.  The first is
devoted to a visit to the cemetery, or *Campo Santo.*  Thither I
followed a crowd of women clad in black with rosaries in their hands,
and men wearing the national costume, together with girls and
boys, but all silent and devout.  The cemetery was very different
to the familiar graveyards of home.  Not a monument, not a stone
was to be seen ; not even a fading wreath pointed the moral of the
grass of the field.  There was merely a vacant space of turf, planted
here and there with dark cypresses, and enclosed by bare walls.
On the walls were some numbers.  These alone indicated the place
of sepulture.  As of old, at Jerusalem, the Jewish mourners used to
recite their prayers of sorrow before the wall, so here, at Pollensa,
the grief-stricken women knelt on the bare ground before the naked
masonry, with never a single kindly memorial to comfort their
soul.  On this second day of November alone, a few black lanterns,
surmounted by a cross, were placed at intervals along the wall, on
benches draped with sable cloths displaying the design of the skull
and cross-bones.

The setting sun reddened the melancholy rampart against which
the yellow flame of these lugubrious corpse-lights flickered in the
wind, while the wavering shadow of the cypresses fell athwart the
praying women like immense mourning veils.

A sort of grim procession made the circuit of the *Campo Santo,*
the black-robed women pacing slowly along with bent heads, chanting a funeral hymn, which they interrupted at intervals in order to
fall prostrate on the ground, with their faces towards the death-wall,
The pathos of these intervals of silence was strangely punctuated
by the contented twitterings of the birds going to roost in the
adjacent woodlands.

As I was returning to dinner at the *fonda,* after nightfall, I met

a genuine funeral procession. A cross-bearer in a large surplice
led the way, followed by acolytes with torches and chanting
priests. The coffin was carried by bearers, and the members of the
deceased's family brought up the rear. What surprised me was
the great rapidity with which the procession passed, priests, bearers,
and mourners almost running, as if in indecent haste to get rid of
their burden. The effect produced by the *cortège* in the dark,
narrow streets was fantastic to a degree. The lurid glare of the

Street in Pollensa.

torch flames, the
resounding
voices of the
dirge chanters,
and the un-
seemly and disorderly haste of the mourners, gave the solemnity
a spectral, preternatural appearance. It was a blood-curdling
legend in action—a troop of accursed beings driven before the wind
of the celestial vengeance, or hurried to doom by some diabolical
curse.

Yet it was only a pauper funeral. The body would be conveyed
to the cemetery mortuary, to lie there all night with uncovered
face, watched by two guardians. Only on the evening of the next
day would the remains be sealed up in the Wall of the Dead, the

delay of twenty-four hours being a precaution against premature burial.

But from these matters it is a relief to turn again to the town and its charming environs.

Pollensa is one of the oldest towns of Majorca, and the site was formerly occupied by a Roman colony. The antiquity survives,

Cascade of the Cala de Molins.

however, more as an atmosphere than in the concrete form of masonry.

Under the guidance of Don Sebastian, one of the priests of the parish, I made an excursion in the direction of Cape Formentor, to the *calas* (coves) of San Vincente and of Molins. Two mules and a driver came to the *fonda* after breakfast, and we were soon seated on the sheepskins which did duty as saddles, and making our way

4

up a shady road towards the hills, fording on our course several swift and stony mountain torrents. These safely passed, we came out on the bare hillside, and after riding for an hour and a half across a waste of grey rock and detritus, suddenly breathed the strong air of the sea, and found ourselves on the summit of a wedge of lofty cliffs, which separates the two creeks.

The Cala de Molins is the outlet of a stream which falls over the rocks in a fine cascade, and at high water it is difficult to distinguish the foam of the torrent from that of the waves.

The Cala de San Vincente shelters a few fisher-huts, but the coast is wild and rocky, and there is only one narrow channel by which boats can enter the creek.

The country to the north of Pollensa is a lonely, mountainous region, being the wildest part of the semi-circular range which protects the great plain of Majorca. These mountains, which, between Valldemosa and Lluch, contain so many charming woodland scenes, are here bare and arid, with wide views over sea and land. Some of the precipices are fringed with waterfalls, one of which, the *Font de Fartaritx*, has the singular property of falling only in the height of summer, when all the springs are dried up, while in winter it shrinks to nothing. One of the loftiest summits in this desolate region is crowned by the ruins of a fortress, known in the country as the *Castillo dels Reys*. The path to the ruin is steep and stony, and hard to find ; indeed, it bids fair soon to be obliterated by falling boulders, and near the summit the visitor must pick his way as best he can through a wilderness of naked rock, scrubby brushwood, and dwarf palms.

Some assert the castle to be of Roman origin, and the Saracens regarded it as impregnable. The Moors, under their chief, Xuayp, took refuge here, after the capture of the capital by Don Jayme. In 1343, when Palma and all the other strongholds of Majorca had sworn fealty to Don Pedro IV., the standard of Don Jayme still floated on the Castillo dels Reys, and the power of the governor, Arnaldo de Eril, wasted itself in vain before the lofty walls, now dismantled and ravaged by every wandering wind.

A special expedition, provided with battering-rams and other engines, was necessary to reduce the place to submission; and even then the soldiers of Don Jayme, after a three months' siege heroically resisted, only surrendered to the power of famine.

As a view point, this lofty summit is superb. On every side is a rolling wilderness of wind-swept summits and giddy abysses, a land of flying shadows and lonely stretches of sunlit rock.

A Majorcan "Jota."

The hostess of the *fonda* at Pollensa had remarked that I often spent hours listening to the guitar-players in the public room, and one evening she organised a festivity in my honour, inviting the best musicians and finest dancers of the town to take part in the performance. Young men came with their guitars, and girls dressed in their best, and escorted by their families, arrived in goodly number, while the sides of the apartment were lined with spectators, who overflowed into the neighbouring passage. Two guitars and a violin performed the overture, the theme of which was a popular Majorcan air.

A girl and a boy, with castanets, then danced a *jota* to a guitar accompaniment. As performed in Majorca, the *jota* has neither the fire nor the voluptuousness of the Spanish dance, but it has a primitive charm of its own which defies analysis.

After the dances came songs. Majorca cannot be said to have a national literature, but there is plenty of fugitive poetry in the form of songs and ballads which are still sung by the mountaineers.

These pieces, called *malaguenas*, are chiefly remarkable for their energy of expression. I noted down a few specimens on this evening at the *fonda*. They are to be heard everywhere—in the mountain solitudes, on the sea, along the dusty road—sung by shepherds, fishermen, and muleteers. At night, too, one may often hear them used as serenades to the tinkle of the guitar in the dark *patios*. Like all primitive ballads, they are imbued with sadness, and are remarkable for their vigorous expression of passion. The following is a literal translation of four verses :—

> "I know not why, mother,
> But the flowers in the cemetery,
> When the wind shakes them,
> Seem to weep.

> "I asked a wise man
> Of what illness I should die,
> And he told me 'Of love';
> Woman, I have loved thee!

> "If blood were sold,
> And I were rich and thou wert poor,
> I would take from thy veins
> What would mingle with mine. . . .

> "Dost thou wish to see if I love thee?
> Open one of my veins,
> And thou wilt see my blood
> Corrupted by suffering."

In another stanza comes a charming conceit :—

> "A star is lost from the sky
> And shines there no more;
> It has fallen on thee, love,
> And gleams on thy brow."

## BARCAROLLE.

> "I sail o'er the sea night and day
> To the sibilant shock of the breeze,
> While my light bark drifts swiftly away
> In search of some strange foreign shore
> Where men live without love.

" Far from thee, I may forget!
See thee no more save haply in dreams!
In dulcet peace and rest of soul,
Loving no longer, content shall be mine."

The melody to which these words are wedded is full of the languor of the southern night and the lilt of the southern sea.

Altogether, Pollensa is one of my pleasantest memories, and the mere sound of a guitar always recalls to me my pleasant evenings in its hospitable *fonda*.

Between Pollensa and Soller, in the heart of the hills, lies the venerable sanctuary of Our Lady of Lluch. Its miraculous origin recalls the story of Lourdes.

Five hundred years ago, a young shepherd, one of those who remained in slavery after the conquest of Majorca, wandering in the mountain pastures at twilight, suddenly perceived a blinding radiance fall athwart a pile of rocks. At first, he was nailed to the spot by terror, but as the light began to fade he warily approached the scene of the marvel, and perceived on the rock a stone image of the Virgin with the Infant Jesus in her arms. The figures were black, but the vestments wherewith they were clothed gleamed with an embroidery of golden lilies.

News of the miraculous find quickly spread, and a commission, composed of members of the clergy, lawyers, and some of the chief inhabitants, came over from Palma to investigate the matter. Whether they came to scoff history does not relate, but they did remain to pray, and the Virgin was solemnly declared patroness and queen of Majorca.

The pilgrims who visited the place became so numerous, that Don Guillermo de Como, the lord of the manor, had a house built for their reception. This house was subsequently enlarged and erected into a college, under the direction of a prior, with the obligation of educating twelve choir-boys, natives of Majorca, who were to be taught vocal and instrumental music, the Castilian and Latin Grammar, and a little theology.

On feast days and in times of pilgrimage, these boys to this

Water-carriers at Pollensa.

day sing hymns in the Virgin's honour, to the sound of musical instruments.

Pilgrims and travellers can at all times profit by the hospitality of the monastery, for here, as at Miramar and Pollensa, entertainment is a free gift, every wayfarer being entitled to three days' lodging, fire and light, with table service, including the use of oil and olives.

From Lluch there is a mountain path to Soller, passing through a stern landscape of forest, pierced at intervals by the blanched and rugged summits of the sierra. The journey on mule-back takes five hours, and is mostly by perilous paths cut along the precipitous slopes of deep ravines.

At Our Lady's Shrine.

Entrance to the Caves of the Dragon.

## CHAPTER IV.

Manacor.—The Caverns of the Dragon.—The Black Lake.—*Lasciate ogni speranza.* —Lost in the Darkness.—An Enchanted Lake.—The Caverns of Artá.

"A Spinster of the Predio."

I REACHED Manacor by the branch line from Enpalme.

After Palma, Manacor is the most populous town of Majorca, but it is purely a business centre, and its buildings are not worth notice. The country round is a vast plain, and, with the change of scenery, the character of the inhabitants also alters. No longer does one see the form of the skin-clothed shepherd silhouetted against the broken skyline of the cliffs. No longer does one hear the dreamy tinkling of guitars in the

58

dusky *patios*. The hospitable and leisurely mountain-folk, with their old-world songs and quaint customs, are of the past, like the patriarchal manners which they perpetuate.

Here, in the towns of the plain, the matter-of-fact resumes its sway. The people hurry to and fro about their business, drays are being laden with barrels bearing the trademarks of well-known foreign firms, pigs are being driven from the railway station to the port for shipment to Barcelona. The people are less courteous, the children more sullen  They do not fall on their knees to kiss the hand of the priest as they do at Pollensa. They have a greater idea of themselves. They have seen many foreigners ; some have been to Marseilles or Algiers ; they are in business ; they are making money ! Money, not manners, is the ruling principle.

Hence, there is less to interest the traveller or the stranger than there was in the mountains—at least, that is to say, above-ground.

But there is much that is quaint and curious, and even terrifying, *underground*. There, in silence and darkness, the forces of nature have for centuries been hewing and shaping an architecture more sublime than was ever conceived in the wildest dream of the Gothic craftsman.

The caves of the *Drac* (the Dragon) and those of Artá, near Manacor, are some of the finest in the world.

I could not, therefore, leave Majorca without having seen them. Accordingly, one spring-like morning in mid November I left the *Fonda Femenias* at Manacor and hired a galera to convey me to the caverns. My friend at Palma, Señor Sellarès, who knew of my intended visit, had previously taken the trouble to spend three days in the caves in order to photograph them by magnesium light, for to hope to obtain an interesting or truthful presentment in a mere sketch would be indeed a vain project.

The road from Manacor leads past the harbour, a busy little creak, speaking well for the commercial prosperity of the town. Further along the shore is a musical stone, which when struck by a stick gives out harmonious and remarkably prolonged vibrations.

A rock in a neighbouring bay is said to be encrusted with fossilised human remains, whence it is called *S'homo mort.*

The caverns of the Dragon lie on, or rather beneath the estate of Don José Moragues, whose *casa de campo* (country house) is not far from the entrance to the caves. The latter are closed by a strong door, lest imprudent visitors should attempt to enter without a guide, and lose their way in the maze of passages.

My guide, having kindled lamps with reflectors, divested himself of his coat and waistcoat, and invited me to do the same.

A hot and oppressive atmosphere ascended from the depths of the caverns, and made me feel ill at ease.

"You will grow accustomed to it in time," said my companion, as he handed me a lamp and a thick stick.

We were as yet only in the vestibule of the caves, and still enjoyed a sort of twilight, but we soon came to a wall of rock in which yawned a dark fissure. This was the real entrance, and it required little fancy to imagine written on the portals the fateful words of Dante :—

*"Lasciate ogni speranza, o voi che entrate."*

Just such an entrance would lead to an *inferno*, a rock-bound doorway, rigid, chill, and dark.

The name of *Drac* (Dragon), given to these caves, would seem to point to an old belief that the place was once guarded by one of the monsters, but I did not hear any legend to this effect.

After following a narrow gallery, we emerged upon a spacious cave known as the *Salon de Palmera* (Palm Tree Saloon). The floor is uneven, and littered with huge blocks of stone, in the midst of which rises *la Palmera*, a tall slight column, like the trunk of a palm tree, while delicate stalactites, hanging from the roof like pendent foliage, complete the arboreal resemblance. There is a second column of larger diameter and greater variety, but it lacks the elegancy of the *Palmera.*

We continued our way, passing two immense stalagmites resembling two idols squatting on their haunches—images of the

The "Palmera."

infernal deities of the dark world which we were exploring. But Christianity has penetrated even underground, and our next halting-place was a grotto known as the "Cave of Bethlehem."

"Take care," cried the guide, "there is water in front of you!"

I turned my lamp on the ground, but saw nothing, and was about to advance, when the guide's strong arm barred my further progress, while at my very feet he stirred with his stick a liquid surface,

Las Arañas.

which I had not perceived. It was indeed water, but water so colourless and transparent, that even when warned it was difficult to credit its existence.

Avoiding this, we pursued a tortuous course through a maze of narrow, dark galleries with low-pitched roofs.

At times it seemed impossible to breathe, and with the oppression of the body came a corresponding oppression of spirit. My guide, who had been watching me for some time out of the corner of his eye, observed, "Few people escape the instinctive fear which you

now feel, and not a few persons have been too afraid to venture
further than here. But there is no cause for fear. Even if our lights
go out, there are lamps and matches hidden in certain niches in the
rocks and sheltered from the damp. It was not so always, but—
I may speak of that later."

Thus reassured, I summoned up my energy and continued the
journey. We passed *el Fraile* (The Friar), a stalagmite resembling a

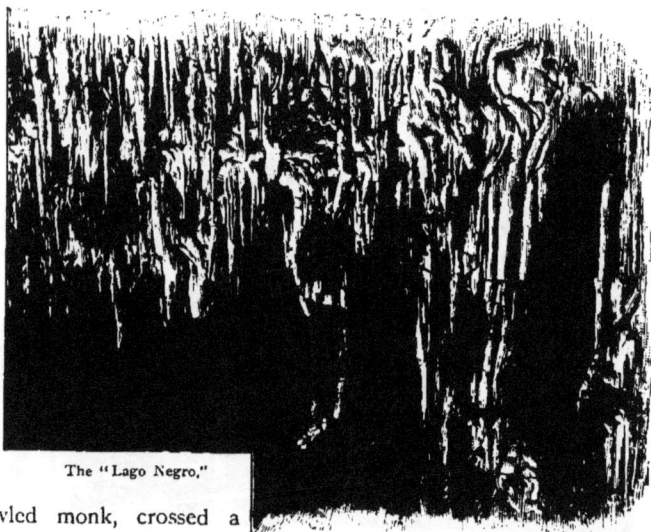

The "Lago Negro."

cowled monk, crossed a
section known as *la Carbo-*
*nera* (The Coal-mine), where the walls blacken the hands like coal ; and
coming beneath *las Arañas* (The Lustres), immense clusters of stalactites,
hanging from the roof like chandeliers, emerged upon a promontory
jutting out into the little *Lago de la Sultana* (Lake of the Sultana).
At this point my guide left me for a few moments, clambered over
the scarped rocks, disappeared round a corner, and presently stood
with his lamp amid the opposite stalactites. The effect was wonderful. Before me stretched a still, transparent sheet of water, flashing
fantastic reflections of the columns and crystal filigree work with

which it was surrounded. Talk of mountain solitudes! What were they to the loneliness of this subterranean tarn, whose waters had slept in darkness for unknown ages! Suppose strange beings of the early world still survived in these recesses! Suppose some half evolved human creature——

But such speculations were cut short by the return of my practical guide, who led me to the *Cueva de los Salchichones* (Grotto of Sausages), a shop of the Stone Age, from the roof of which hung strings of petrified sausages and dried cod.

Beyond this came another lake, the *Lago Negro*, the largest and most impressive of the lakes of the Dragon. Its motionless waters were lost in obscurity. Huge pillars rose on every hand from pediments of black rock, other slighter columns hung to the surface of the water, and were reflected in an unbroken line by the incomparable purity of the liquid mirror. The stalactites were of every shape and size. In one place, they formed a feudal castle, complete with turrets and battlements; in another, the pillared rows suggested the idea of an organ raising its stone pipes against the walls of a subterranean crypt, awaiting some demon-musician or Apocalyptic Wagner to touch their keys, and break the awful silence with more awful sounds, which should rouse the dead and summon them for judgment to this new Hall of Minos. But the stillness was unbroken, and oppressed the nerves more terribly than any noise. Such silence, such immobility, such sinister torpor, seemed to make one lose perception of time and space.

There are very few visitors who do not feel the strange impression produced by these underground solitudes.

My guide, however, told me of an Englishman who bathed in the lake, and in order to dry himself danced about naked on the rocks, pretending to play the violin, with his umbrella for instrument and his walking-stick for bow. The natives even now cannot speak of his unseemly levity without a shiver.

"But," say they, "nothing is sacred to an——Englishman!"

Next to the Black Lake comes the *Cueva Blanca* (White Cave), entered with difficulty through a narrow fissure. This cave is almost

5

blocked up with boulders, however, and the path is full of pitfalls, so that one often has to hold fast by the rock-staples to escape falling. Beyond this, the cavern has not been explored, and, to tell the truth, the way does not look inviting, leading apparently to the very bowels of the earth, and beset with crevasses and tunnels, dark with the horror of the unknown.

It was a relief to turn one's back upon this dismal region, and, after a few more windings, to arrive at the foot of *el Dosel de la Virgen del Pilar* (The Shrine of the Virgin of the Pillar), a splendid natural monument at one extremity of the so-called *Salon de Descanso* (Waiting, or Resting-Room). This part of the cave is known as *el Teatro* (The Theatre). From here, we enter the *Cueva de los Catalanes* (Cave of the Catalans), a lofty rock-room, covered with fine stalactites, in a corner of which rises *el Descanso de los Extraviados* (The Resting-Place of the Lost), a monument eighteen feet high, and one of the finest specimens of the natural architecture of the cavern.

It was while sitting at the base of this that my guide told me the story to which he had referred earlier in our exploration.

"Now that you are no longer nervous I can tell it you," said he. "The caves in which we are now, and of which we shall have soon reached the greatest known depth—for much still remains to be discovered—were scarcely known at all before the adventure of which I am now going to tell you. One morning in April 1878 two gentlemen of Barcelona left Manacor at daybreak, and at six o'clock entered the caves, accompanied by a man who had offered his services as guide. They intended to be back by noon, at which hour they had ordered lunch at the *Fonda Femenias*. They had been exploring the caves for some hours, when one of them noticed that they had returned to a place which they had already passed. Fearing that the guide had lost his way, they begged him to lead them back to the entrance. He tried to reassure them, but was evidently ill at ease, and, after vain wanderings through the labyrinth of passages, admitted that he had missed the path. The travellers were in despair. Their chief preoccupation was to economise their light as far as possible, in order not to be left in darkness. They placed different objects along the track they were following, in order to be able to retrace their steps, if necessary. But all was in vain ; they only wandered still further away. They ascended and descended ; rested and went on again, often stumbling, and sometimes falling into invisible pools of water. The silence, the darkness, the strange forms of the stalagmites, the rigid columns, the black orifices of bottomless abysses, the suffocating air, the fear of dying of hunger and thirst, stimulated their failing strength, and with feverish haste they staggered on for hours, bruising themselves on the sharp rocks, but always haunted by the hope of seeing at length the faint ray of daylight marking the entrance.

"Towards midday, overcome by fatigue and hunger, they rested for a few moments, and listened, in the hope that, as they had not returned at the appointed hour, a search party might have started from Manacor. As they sat breathless |in the stillness, they heard what sounded like the distant blast of a horn.

Cueva del Descanso de los Extraviados

"They shouted in answer, and waited, but heard no answer. Again they shouted in desperation, but the sound of the horn grew fainter, and finally died away.

"In utter despair they wandered about for a few more hours, and ultimately sank down completely exhausted, near the place now called after them, *Descanso de los Extraviados* (Resting-Place of the Lost). As their lamp was on the point of expiring, one of the party wrote on a stone the words '*No hay esperanza*' ('All hope abandoned')."

"And did they perish?" I asked anxiously.

"No. At ten o'clock at night, sixteen hours after entering the cave, they again heard the blast of a horn, but this time the sound came gradually nearer, and presently they heard the voices of the search-party organised by Señor Femenias, the landlord of the *fonda*. In gratitude for their deliverance, they gave him a small piece of pottery with a half-effaced design but no date, which they had picked up in one of the galleries of the cave. This jar is still carefully preserved at the *fonda*. The Archduke Salvator offered a hundred douros for it, but Señor Femenias would not part with it. The pottery is supposed to date from the Roman occupation."

I was now rested, and taking up our lamps and staves, we descended a sloping gallery and entered the *Salon Real* (Royal Saloon), a vast hall surrounded by queer-looking galleries, with curiously wrought pilasters and glittering walls which looked as if they were frosted. The floor was covered with blocks and obelisks of stone, the largest of which is known as the *Trono de David*.

Leaving the *Salon Real*, the way still led downwards through narrow galleries, until we entered another vast hall, which seemed to be a realisation of the Arabian Nights. In the midst was a lake, the *Lago de las Delicias* (Lake of Delights). Here we were confronted by no gloomy cavern, but by a subterranean crypt of marvellous richness and an architecture of pale ivory. It seemed an ideal world with no existence except in imagination; for, notwithstanding the precision of the pillars and the firmness of the delicate tracery, every object was diaphanous, and apparently unsubstantial, like a fairy

Lago de Las Delicias.

palace in an Arab tale. My guide stirred the water, and the vision shivered and seemed to crumble away.

Then, once more the pool grew still, and was of such crystalline transparency that it appeared to have no substance, and resembled merely a dense atmosphere. My guide pointed out a stalagmite like a child, upstanding, with its head hanging down on its breast, and another resembling a vase supported by an elegant pedestal, festooned with strange plants. To the right the roof formed an immense arch, completely covered with white stalactites.

Beyond this Elysian lake we came to another of smaller extent but of great depth, called the *Baños de la Reina Ester* (Baths of Queen Esther). This was the limit of exploration in this direction, and we retraced our steps to the *Salon de Descanso*, and thence through a series of long galleries to the *Cueva de los Murciélagos* (Cave of the Bats), the floor of which is covered with a thick deposit of guano, left there by innumerable generations of bats. The bats have been frightened away by visitors, but the cavern still has some distinctive fauna of its own. The guano, for instance, is inhabited by a species of ant blind as deep-sea fish, and in the recesses of the caves dwell weird-looking spiders with immense legs. I was wondering where the flies came from to feed these spiders, when a tiny fly fell on my sketch-book. Like the ants, it was blind, for it blundered against the pencil which I held in front of it, having evidently not perceived the obstacle.

Pursuing our devious way, we entered the *Bajada de Purgatorio* (Descent of Purgatory), the roof of which is upheld by huge columns from which project malformed stalagmites of a pale, bone-coloured earth, not unlike fungoids, blanched by the absence of daylight.

A few moments later a pale light gleamed through a crevasse, and we re-entered the vestibule whence we had started. We were perspiring, and my guide handed me my coat and vest, and bade me wait for a good half-hour in this transition atmosphere before exposing myself to the outer air.

Another series of caves, named after the Archduke Luis Salvator, opens into the vestibule, but I did not have the courage to explore them. They are rarely visited, being dangerous to walk in and suffocatingly hot.

As I was about to enter the *galera* to return to Manacor, my guide took me to the adjacent coast, and showed me an immense opening in the cliff surmounted by a watch-tower. " That opening," he said, "places the caverns in communication with the sea. The water of the lakes is more or less brackish according as it is nearer or further from the sea. The level of the lakes falls when the wind is off land and rises when the sea-breeze blows."

From Manacor to Artá is a long drive, but the road is pleasantly diversified, and affords pleasing glimpses of the Mediterranean.

Near Artá are some gigantic architectural remains of the kind generally described in northern countries as Druidical. They are hidden in a forest of chestnut trees, and closely resemble the *nuraghi* of Sardinia. The Majorcan peasants call these monuments *claper des gegants*. They are of remote antiquity, and are supposed to have served as places of sepulture.

About an hour's drive from Artá, near Cabo Vermejo, on the slope of a precipitous cliff above the sea, is the wide entrance of the cavern called in the country *Cueva de la Ermita* (Hermitage Cave).

The caves of the Dragon are rendered remarkable by their mysterious lakes and the richness of the various rocky halls. These caves of Artá impress one by their size and Cyclopean grandeur of decoration. One point in their favour is that the air in them is far purer, and one does not experience the sense of oppression and even of fear which renders the caves at Manacor so fascinatingly terrible.

The caves of Artá have been known for several centuries. The chronicler Dameto, in his history of Majorca, written in the seventeenth century, speaks of some people who were lost in their recesses, and, unlike the explorers of the *Descanso de los Extraviados*, never again saw the light of day.

The caverns are of grandiose dimensions. Few stalactites are to be seen near the entrance, but they become more frequent as one goes further in. Among them is the *Virgen del Pilar*, an immense

Entrance to the Caves of Artá.

natural stone statuę. Beyond this one enters the *Sala de las Columnas* (Hall of Columns).

The most remarkable pillar, however, stands alone in a sort of crypt, where there is nothing to detract from its immense size and singular beauty. An Englishman is said to have offered to purchase it for twenty-seven thousand douros.

The most fantastic part of this subterranean region goes by the significant name of *l'Infierno*. It is a nightmare in stone. Tongues of petrified flame seem to lick the walls. An enormous lion squats in one corner, staring at unhewn tombs overhung by rigid cypresses. Strange forms of antediluvian monsters lurk half-seen in the obscurity. Many of the stalactites, when rapped sharply with a stick, emit musical notes,

Sala de las Columnas.

some like the vibration of a harp string, others like the deep resonance of a church bell. These latter are in an immense hall as vast as a cathedral nave.

On leaving Manacor I returned to Palma, in order to take the

steamer to Alcudia to visit the island of Minorca, just visible on the horizon like a faint blue cloud.

One word must be said finally in dispraise of a country otherwise so charming, and that is, that throughout the lowlands, and especially at Manacor, the mosquitoes are a perfect pest. Not only are they the terror that stalks by night, but even driving along the roads one encounters immense swarms, as pertinacious as midgets by a Scottish trout stream.

Sea Entrance to the Dragon Caves.

Entrance to Port Mahon.

## CHAPTER V.

A City of Tombs.—Port Mahon.—A White City.—Serenades.—Christmas Celebration. — Ancient Customs. — *Monte Toro.*—The *Talayots.*—The Chafers of the Angelus. — The Musical Cobblers.

THE ancient town of Alcudia, on the bay of the same name, lies on the slope of a hill about two miles from the shore. Its fate has been a strange one. After playing a great part in the history of Majorca, often disputing the title of capital with Palma, it fell on evil days, and was almost abandoned. A traveller who visited it at the beginning of this century described it as a city of

77

tombs. Its position between the two finest roadsteads of the island, however, is so favourable to commerce and navigation, that, in order to induce the people to settle there, the Governor offered a sum of money with a free grant of land and a house. In spite of this, however, the-town to this day is desolate and poverty-stricken.

Roman Gateway at Alcudia.

From Alcudia to Port Mahon in Minorca is a seven or eight hours' voyage, and often a rough one, the channel between the two islands being quite exposed to northerly and westerly gales. Water-spouts are frequently seen in the Straits.

The broken coasts of Minorca soon come plainly into view, surmounted by the *Monte Toro*, the highest hill in the island, whose cone-like summit resembles the Puy de Dôme in Auvergne.

After a rough time off the *Isla del Ayre* (Isle of the Wind), at the south-west corner of Minorca, we doubled the cape, and entered the calm waters of Port Mahon.

To the right rose a lofty promontory, breaking down to the sea in red precipices. It is called the *Mola*, and is the dragon which guards the harbour, being strongly fortified and well provided with guns. It is surmounted by an ancient watch-tower.

The spacious harbour winds into the land, like Falmouth estuary, with many secondary basins and back-waters. The Mahonese claim that all the fleets of the world could anchor here without being in sight of one another, and the safety of the harbour is borne witness to by the old proverb "*Junio, Julio, Agusto y Puerto Mahon, los mejores puertos de Mediterraneo son*" ("June, July, August, and Port Mahon are the best ports of the Mediterranean").

Opposite the Mola are the ruined fortifications of the once renowned *Castillo de San Felipe*. Beyond this came into view, one by one, the immense lazaretto commenced in the reign of Carlos IV., and still unfinished, the *Isla del Rey*, where the military hospital has been erected, the suburb of Villacarlos, and the islet of *los Ajusticiados* (Isle of the Condemned), where prisoners sentenced to death were executed during the British occupation. The *Isla del Rey* was also called by the British "Bloody Island."

The town itself rises on an amphitheatre of sloping cliffs, and as we approached the white houses shone like snow against the dark storm-clouds which had accompanied our steamer from Alcudia. A very noticeable effect was the transparency of the shadows cast by the buildings, against which the passers-by gleamed like spots of pure colour.

Mahon is marvellously clean. Even the very pavements seem to be washed and scrubbed every day. Each Saturday, both at Mahon and at Ciudadella and the villages of the interior, the housewives clean the outer walls of their houses with lime-water. They do the same on the eves of fête-days. It is an amusing spectacle to see the women, armed with brooms of dwarf palm and immense pails of lime-water, gossiping along the walls from early morning, while they scrub and wash as if their lives depended upon it, fastening their brooms to long poles, the better to reach the higher parts of the wall. Should a death occur in a house, the walls are not whitened for a week, a fortnight, or even a month, according to the closeness of the relationship, or the degree of grief felt for the deceased. In rare cases the walls are not touched for six months.

An incontestable proof that the cleanliness of the houses is not merely superficial is the complete absence of bugs, which are not known in the island even by name. The interiors which I visited displayed a cleanliness and almost prim tidiness scarcely to be found in any country in Europe, except perhaps in Holland. This love of order is seen even in the garrets of the peasants, where from floor to rafter not a vestige of dust is to be seen.

Villacarlos, the suburb passed in coming up the harbour, is the "sailor-town" of Port Mahon. It contains several deserted barracks, capable of accommodating three thousand infantry.

The favourite resort of the Mahonese is the village of San Luis, the people of which carry their virtue of cleanliness to the verge of fanaticism. The very roofs are whitened, and the side-walks are marked by a white line like a cricket crease. At sunset the houses take on a tint of pale blue, while the windows resemble plates of molten metal.

Port Mahon possesses three theatres—namely, an opera-house, a comedy theatre, and a hall of varieties. It has also a museum, but its churches are insignificant from an architectural point of view, and even the *Ayuntamiento* is a comparatively modern building.

The ancient fortified gate of Barbarossa is so called in memory of the sacking of the city in 1536. The fleet of Charles V. was expected. One day a squadron was signalled by the watchmen, and the people flocked to the shore. It was soon discovered, however, that the advancing ships were not the expected fleet, but the vessels of the corsair Barbarossa. The inhabitants returned in all haste to the town, and prepared to defend themselves. Barbarossa sent two envoys, who entered by the gate since known by his name. No sooner were the portals thrown back, however, than the pirate hordes rushed into the city, which was compelled to capitulate. The conditions of the surrender were not observed, however, and the town was sacked and the inhabitants were reduced to slavery.

Minorca was for many centuries a coveted possession, and consequently passed through many vicissitudes.

In 1536, as related above, Port Mahon was sacked, and two years later the island was invaded by the Turks. In 1708 it came into the possession of the British, only to be captured by France forty years later. Twenty years afterwards the Spaniards became masters of the island, but the British soon recaptured it, and remained there until the Treaty of Amiens finally surrendered it to Spain.

The Gate of Barbarossa.

Traces of the British occupation still remain in about five hundred words of the local dialect, in some children's games, and in the general use of sashed windows. The houses have, moreover, an appearance of British solidity and comfort, but it is to be regretted that the use of the national costume died out on contact with the more practical dress of the northerners.

The population of Mahon is about 77,000, but the town covers a larger extent of ground than this figure would warrant, nearly every house having its court and garden, and being tenanted by but a single family.

The Minorcans live a patriarchal life, and are much behind the times in many points. Thus in medicine they still follow the

therapeutic method of Dr. Sangrado, especially in the country.   Dr.
Colorado, a practitioner in Mahon, and an ardent advocate of modern

Wine-Carrier of Mahon.

scientific methods, told me that he found
it most difficult to overcome the old prejudices.

When he is called to a country
patient, he always finds ready on a table
by the bedside a basin and bandages,
and the sick person holds out his bare
arm to be cupped.  The patient's family
have great faith in blood-letting, declaring
that even if the patient dies he passes
away more tranquilly for the operation.

What is probably another trace of English influence is the absence of the usual
running gutter in the streets—a common
feature of French and Spanish towns.   The inhabitants are forbidden
by law to throw any slops out of doors, but must keep them for the
*carros dels Xuchs.*
These are low
barrel - s h a p e d
carts drawn by
donkeys, which
visit the houses
at certain inter-
vals.

The practice
of love - making
by serenade is
much in vogue
in Minorca, and
frequently of an
e v e n i n g  one

El Carro dels Xuchs.

comes upon a young man leaning against a wall, singing some ancient
love ditty to the gentle accompaniment of his guitar while his eyes

are fixed on a neighbouring balcony, where a female form is indistinctly visible in the moonlight.

The manner of paying court to a girl is peculiar. The young men are not received directly into the house, but the girl's family permit the maiden to hold conversations with her lover or to gaze at him from a window. When, as occasionally happens, unfortunate results follow, the parents scratch their heads, and wonder how accidents could occur under such restrictive conditions.

But scandals are rare. Minorca is a Christian land, and a country where the tradition of the family is a potent force.

At Christmas every house has its "crib," or mimic representation of the stable of Bethlehem. Some of these are very elaborate, including a sky displaying the star of the Wise Men, the three kings themselves, with negro attendants and camels loaded with gifts.

These *tableaux* are not confined to the scene at Bethlehem. Sometimes there is a panoramic representation of the entire life of Christ up to the final scene of Calvary. The anachronisms in these pictures are flagrant. The sea, for instance, is shown covered with steamers and gun-vessels.

Moreover, the scenes are not always religious. Sometimes a sportsman is seen shooting in close time. The report of firearms is heard, and a hare perhaps scuds across the mimic stage; gendarmes promptly appear to arrest the poacher, who, amid the plaudits of the spectators, escapes with his dog at his heels.

Another favourite device is that of a man seated beside a lake with his mouth open. Live fish jump from the water into his throat, and he blows them back again. At other times a trade is represented—a crowd of bootmakers, carpenters, or joiners are busily at work, the place of honour being filled by Saint Joseph, who saws wood.

Then comes the collection. An aged bedesman comes on the scene with a wooden bowl, and taps the ground to attract attention. The visitors hasten to contribute. If the coin be a good one, the collector places it in an alms box; if it be bad, he throws it angrily away among the audience.

Every evening, from Christmas to the end of January, the people go round from house to house, to see these representations, called *bethléems de pastous*.

At Christmas, also, every confectioner's shop has its *bethléem* of sweetmeats, the shopkeepers vying with each other in organising the most attractive "show."

The Minorca churches also have a special Christmas custom. On the morning of Christmas Eve the *calenda*, or martyrology of the day, is solemnly sung to the accompaniment of the organ, by a chorister attended by twelve boys, clothed in white, and carrying lighted candles, who are called *sibylles*.

Meanwhile a drink known as *la calente* (the hot drink), composed of brandy, sugar, and aniseed, is prepared in the sacristy, and subsequently drunk, with sugar-plums, by the priest, the chorister, and the twelve *sibylles*.

At Christmas, it is the duty of all children up to the age of sixteen to pay a visit of ceremony to their godparents. The children, with arms crossed on their breast, bow profoundly, and kiss the hands of their godfathers and godmothers, who then offer them cakes and presents of money.

From November to the end of January every Minorcan family has one pig or more fattening. The killing of these is an occasion of great ceremony, known as *Matansa de porc*. All the members of the family—children, grandchildren, uncles, aunts, cousins, etc.— assemble, often to the number of one hundred persons. White aprons and sleeves are fastened on the children, and while their elders are killing and preparing the pig, these little pork-butchers march through the streets, singing :—

> " *Faldaret defora,*
> *Faldaret dedins,*
> *Tanca sa porta,*
> *Y fiquet en dins.*"

The very little ones, who cannot follow the others, are given the animal's lower jaw, which they tie a string to and drag about the courtyard like a toy cart, filled with pebbles and other childish treasure.

Thus, when every one is busy, the children are conveniently and kindly got out of the way.

On the night following the death of the pig a singular game is played. A ribbon of paper, called *el tio*, is fastened to a man's back. Thus decorated, he walks slowly round the room, with his head down, his back arched, and his hands on his knees, wagging the ribbon like a tail. Another person follows him with a light.

The first sings in a mixture of Spanish and Mahonese :—

> "*No me lo encendras*
> *Lo tio de detras.*"

The second answers :—

> "*Si te lo encendre*
> *Lo tio de paper.*"

The lighting of the paper is a difficult operation, and the two men walk for a long time round and round the room, while the spectators crack their sides with laughter. The parish priest is invited to all these games, and would greatly offend his flock if he kept away.

Another quaint custom of a more poetical character is observed in spring. A company of field labourers, with guitars, *guitarons* and *mandourrias*, go from farm to farm by night singing Catalan songs. They stand before the doorway of the farmhouse, and prelude with muted strings. Then the guitar gradually grows louder, the other instruments join, and the voices of the serenaders, sometimes in unison, sometimes in parts, swell in volume, till the windows are discreetly opened, and when the songs are sung the spring musicians are invited inside the house to partake of refreshments. When they are satisfied, their knapsacks are filled with eggs, sausages, white bread, and a bottle of wine, and the party make their way to the sea, where they spend the following day on the beach, singing and feasting on the results of their night's peregrination.

This Easter observance was brought to Minorca by the Catalonians and Aragonese, who came with Alfonso III., in 1286, to conquer the island.

The numerous coins and medals found in Minorca bear witness to its successive occupiers. Many are of Phœnician or Carthaginian origin. Others bear the effigy of Macedonian kings, and some are Celtic or Iberian. Coins of all the Roman emperors have been discovered, as well as money from Athens, Ephesus, Sarnos, Nîmes, Marseilles, and the Spanish colonies of Rome.

The environs of Mahon are arid and rocky, and offer little to attract one. It was therefore with pleasure that I accepted an invitation from Dr. Colorado to spend the day at his country house on the lower slopes of Mount Toro.

This hill, which is some thousand feet high, rises nearly in the centre of the island. At the top is a monastery in ruins, which used to be a place of pilgrimage to which men and even women climbed barefooted. Some actually ascended on their knees, telling their beads as they went.

At the beginning of this century the greatest treasure of the monastery, then tenanted by Augustinian monks, was a rude sculpture, representing a bull hewing out a statue of the Virgin with its horns. The name of the mountain was said to be derived from this miracle, but a more probable etymology is that *Toro* comes from the word *Tor*, meaning elevation. The view from the summit is naturally extensive. The most striking feature is the steep, bare hill of Santa Agueda, which was one of the oldest military posts in the island. The Romans took advantage of so commanding a position, and at a later date the Moors made it a stronghold, where they held out for a long time against the forces of Alfonso III. The fortress, which still stood at the beginning of the century, is now a ruin, and what is left intact has been converted into a farm building.

The weather in Minorca is very changeable, and storms rise with surprising rapidity, only to pass away with equal celerity.

While Majorca, sheltered from the winds by the Catalan coast and its own Sierra del Norte, enjoys a mild, equable climate, Minorca, situated further out to sea, and forming a sort of breakwater to the

Gulf of Lyons, is exposed to nearly every wind that blows, and the changes of temperature are sudden and trying. It is difficult to speak of Minorca without referring to its archæological monuments —*talayots, navetas, taulas,* megalithic habitations, menhirs, cromlechs, *antigots,* etc. Of these, the first mentioned three are peculiar to the Balearic Isles. They are popularly supposed to be of Celtic origin, but it has yet to be proved that the Celts ever occupied Minorca.

The typical *talayot* is a cone truncated a short distance from its base, and formed of immense blocks of stone roughly planed on the internal surface in order to give greater stability to the structure. The stones are set in parallel rows, and each row consists of a single line of stones. The summit of a *talayot* is invariably a horizontal platform with no parapet, and

A Talayot.

not even a bed of soil to make it level. The only other structures of antiquity which they resemble are the *nuraghi* of Sardinia. The latter might well be perfected *talayots,* and it is perhaps something more than a coincidence that the ancient name for Minorca was *Nura.* The *talayots* are to be found in every situation—on the hills, in the valleys, near the sea or inland—in fact, wherever the materials for their construction were to be obtained. Some consist of a single chamber, and probably served as a dwelling-place or a temple. Others contain only a stairway to the platform, and were merely watch-towers. The simplest are filled with stones, and a few originally contained cinerary urns.

Several have external cells built at various heights against the wall, but without symmetry; and certain constructions are crossed by simple or bifurcated galleries with cells, and passages ascending to the platform. Two or three *talayots* have the shape of the segment of a circle or of an ellipse. At what epoch they were built can only be matter of conjecture.

The *navetas*—diminutive of *nau*, a vessel—are of the shape of a boat keel upwards. They are built in the same manner as the *talayots*. The prows of all the navetas point to the north, and we find again traces of elliptical shapes, suggesting ideas of the mysterious early religions in which the science of the infinite seems to have played so large a part.

Taula of Talati di Dalt.

The *taulas* have no affinity with any other known monuments. They consist of an immense square stone of slight thickness, erected vertically on the ground, in which it seems to be sunk to a very slight extent, while on the top of this uncertain support is balanced another stone of equal length and breadth, but thicker. The equilibrium is generally perfect, but in some cases, as in the *taula* of Talati di Dalt, the horizontal stone is supported by a third.

Round some of the *taulas* is a vast circle of menhirs, forming a complete cromlech.

Their use can only be conjectured, but most probably they were altars—a theory which is borne out by the fact that while most of the vertical stones are well chiselled, the horizontal slab is always found in its natural state, the ritual ordaining that no sacrifices should take place on altars profaned by the hand of man.

But of what the sacrifice consisted it is hard to tell, for the dimensions of the altars forbid the idea of human victims or even of animals of any size

The finest specimen of these strange constructions is at *Trapúco*, where there are also some *talayots*, and one of the inexplicable walls to be found in the country, known as *antigots*.

It was at *Trapúco* that I heard the Minorcan name for cockchafers —chafers of the *Ave Maria*; so called because they appear at twilight, when in this Catholic country every peasant stops to murmur a prayer as he hears the Angelus bell.

That same evening I visited the theatre, and learned, to my surprise, that many of the actors were bootmakers of Port Mahon.

The cobblers in Minorca seem to have a monopoly of music, for nearly all are singers or instrumentalists, and they number nearly five thousand, including apprentices. The boot trade is one of the most flourishing in the island, which annually exports nearly £200,000 worth of boots and shoes, principally to Cuba and Central and South America.

Yet will it be believed, that in this country of cobblers the fishermen go barefoot, while the work-people generally wear only a kind of rudimentary sandals called *avárcas*, which they make themselves, of untanned leather?

Among the smaller industries is the manufacture of fancy goods from shells, which are found in great numbers on the shores of the island.

Physically, the Minorcans have no special type. In the streets I often met quite English faces, little girls with fair hair and blue eyes, and young men with chestnut hair. The Spanish type is the rarest, for the Spaniards, who fill nearly all the official posts in the island, seldom marry or settle in Minorca. Hence, as in other Spanish possessions beyond the sea, the sympathies of the people are not with the mother-country.

Passing along the streets, I was often struck by the colour and strange shape of some of the paving-stones used for repairing purposes. They were much larger and darker than the others. I questioned the passers-by without eliciting any information ; and it was not until after I had left the island that I learned that these stones, which, it appeared, had vexed the souls of several learned geologists, were obtained from the deserted English cemeteries in the suburbs of the town.

A friend of mine had the curiosity to turn some of them over, and there, still plain to be seen, were the English inscriptions. The Mahonese had had at least the grace to turn the faces downwards. Many of the memorial tablets were sent out from England during the British occupation by the families of those who died in the island. No one walking through the bright, cheerful thoroughfares would have imagined that he was treading on tombstones.

An Oratory.

The Road to Béni Duénis.

## CHAPTER VI.

The Alcade of Ferrarias.—The Distorted Trees.—The *Barranco* of Algendar.—A Night at Subervei.—Ciudadella.—The Breath of the Devil.—Return to Majorca.—Cabrera.

At the Barranco of Algendar.

THERE is a daily diligence service between Port Mahon and Ciudadella, the second town of the island. The journey occupies about five hours, and in this time Minorca is crossed from one side to the other. I had followed this road on the occasion of my visit to Monte Toro, but as I had gone by night I had seen nothing. Moreover, the natural beauties of Minorca, which are numerous in proportion to its size, lie

91

near the coast, and the road cuts right through the centre of the island.

One bright day saw me on top of the diligence, passing through the old Barbarossa Gate on my way to the country. Passing the harbour, where a few ships lay moored in mid-stream, we came upon another British memorial in the shape of a monument to Brigadier Kane, a former English governor, who constructed the road which we were following. Beyond this lay stony fields, where a few lean cows were searching for the scanty grass, which only grew in occasional patches.

A little white town gleamed on a height where windmills were turning rapidly, and added to the sense of life and motion given by the clouds sweeping over the sky, and causing a procession of shadows across the wide, bare country. The town was Alhayor, the third in importance in Minorca. The streets are narrow and tortuous, and there is only one inn, which is not of the best.

After a halt of twenty minutes, during which the postillions and several travellers imbibed glasses of *anisado*, the odour of which was more than enough, we continued our way over the foothills of Monte Toro.

The next stopping-place was the village of Mercadel, a picturesque spot with a windmill amidst the houses. A stream ran through the centre of the hamlet, and as the water was red and the cottages were white, the effect was singular. The sickly complexions of the inhabitants, however, plainly said that the place was unhealthy, and I was told that in summer it is a hotbed of fever.

We clattered on along the well-made road. Troops of children, armed with reeds, made a formidable noise at the edge of a field.

"They are scaring away the birds," said a fellow-traveller.

"You should see them in harvest," added the postillion.

When the grain is ripening, boys and girls watch the fields, and utter piercing cries, at the same time beating their hands with dried reeds—*et sonitu terrebis aves*, as Virgil says in the First Georgic.

Leaving on our left the old English road, which at this point

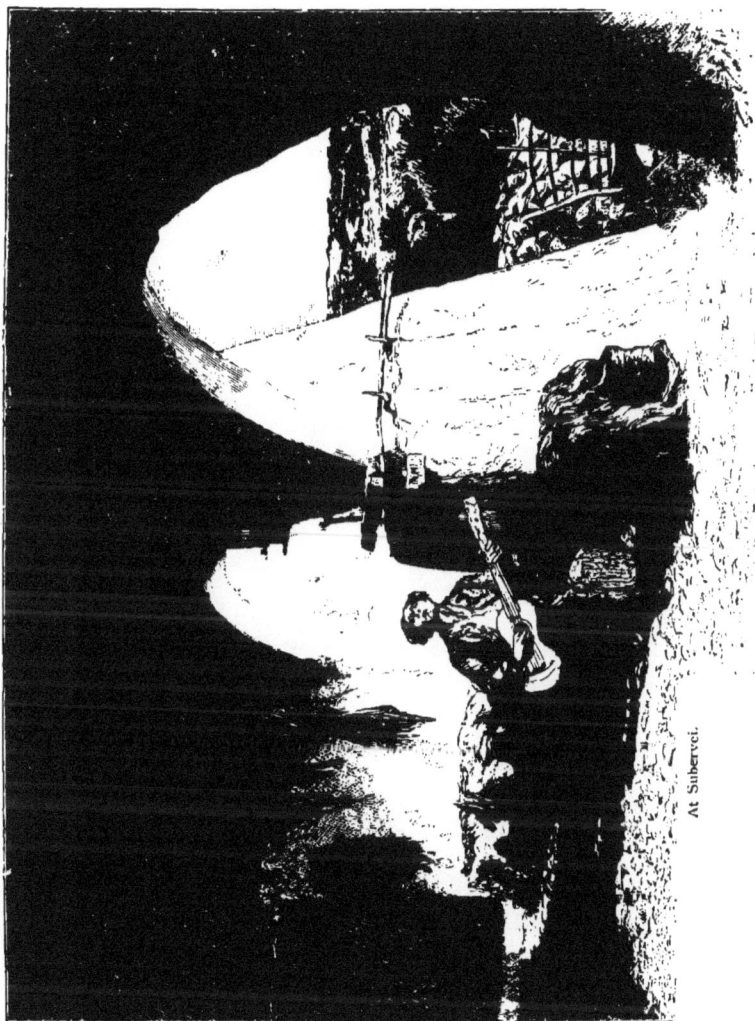

At Subervei.

enters the wild chestnut· woods of Béni Duénis, we descended between wooded heights into a fertile valley.

Beyond this came another ascent, and the diligence suddenly stopped before a roadside *posada*. My luggage was quickly placed by the side of the road, and the vehicle lumbered on up the hill, soon to disappear over the top of the slope.

The sun was setting. I was quite alone, and I looked ruefully at the miserable inn and the village dimly visible in the shadow of the valley below. But a moment later two boys appeared, one of them leading a mule, and asked me if I was the gentleman expected from Port Mahon. On my replying in the affirmative, they told me that they were respectively the son of the Alcade, and a messenger sent with a mount to convey me to Subervei, a *predio* near the *barranco* of Algendar, and the property of Don Rodriguez, a Mahon banker, who was to be my entertainer.

Before proceeding to Subervei I went down to the village of Ferrarias, to give a letter to the Alcade. Visitors are rare in this township, which lies in a low, unhealthy situation, and is the chief village of the poorest district in Minorca. The village children, for whom my arrival was an event, trooped after me to the Alcade's house, shouting as loudly as if I were a predatory bird to be scared away.

The Alcade took my letter with a grave air, put on his spectacles, and solemnly read the missive, interrupting his perusal now and then to run to the door with a stick to chase away the children, who seemed to entertain but small respect for constituted authorities. The official then offered me his services, and assured me that his house was at my disposal. I thanked him for his generosity, and reascended to the *posada*, where the young man with the mule was awaiting me.

We started away as night was falling, and climbed a stony path leading to a high tableland, with a distant prospect of the sea, over which the moon was rising, its disc enlarged and elongated, and of an orange-red colour, like the orb of a dying planet.

We were on an undulating plain, where the sun scorches in

summer, and in winter the wind blows coldly. Its aspect at the close of an autumn day was weird and sad.

The trees, exposed to the constant sea-gales, are all bent southwards by the northerly winds. Their twisted branches, of the ashen colour of the stone on which they grow, trail along the ground, while the naked roots protrude from the barren soil. They crowd up the arid slopes, struggling and grimacing, as if convulsed by some agony of apprehension. Their very foliage is hard and rough to the touch, like the dry skin of a sick animal.

A few consumptive-looking sheep wander over the stony soil in search of subsistence. Many die of hunger in summer-time, but with the autumn rains the slopes become again covered with fine verdure, and those which have survived are able to find pasture. They are pitiful objects as they wander with trembling steps over the stones—wild, solitary creatures, eluding the sight like spectres.

At times my mule, knowing the road which I could not discern, would suddenly halt. The guide would silently open a gate, and we would pass through a narrow opening, where my knees scraped against stone walls.

In the distance rose the dim crests of the mountains. Strange effects of light gleamed at intervals on the distant slopes. The wind rustled with a metallic clatter through the dry foliage of the distorted trees. The howl of the homeless dog of some deserted *predio* occasionally smote my ears.

It was a journey never to be forgotten.

The path grew worse and worse, and the mule stumbled at every moment, but presently welcome lights gleamed ahead, and I heard the homely barking of watch-dogs.

" Yonder is Subervei," said my taciturn guide.

They were the first words he had spoken since leaving the *posada.*

A last gate was passed, and we entered the courtyard of the *predio.* Friendly hands met mine, and I heard the traditional welcome, " *Bona nit, aqui ten vosté la seua casa* " (" Good-evening ; this house is at your disposal ").

The dogs limped about, barking furiously, but they could do

The Night Ride to Suberven.

no harm, their forelegs being fastened together with a chain, to prevent them jumping over the walls or attacking passers-by.

I followed the women, who preceded me carrying copper lamps of Pompeian shape with large smoking wicks. A table was spread in the *patio* with fresh water, bread, and hard-boiled eggs, frugal fare, but not to be despised after my hungry ride.

Early the next morning, one of the sons of the house guided me to the famous *barranco* of Algendar, which was the objective point of my journey.

After crossing an arid desert of stony mounds, we reached the edge of a huge crevasse which yawned suddenly at our very feet. I was about to dismount, but my guide caught my mule by the bridle and bade me keep my seat.

The *barranco* is a

Rio of the "Barranco" of Algendar.

miniature cañon, a fissure of verdure running across the sterility of the surrounding country.    On the uplands above, the sun scorches the cracking soil, and the keen wind forbids all kindly growth.    But down below in the *barranco* the air is always soft and warm, and cool shadows lie across orange trees, rose bushes, and flowering plants.

Passing through a narrow passage hidden between the rocks, we rapidly descended a steep path under over-arching trees through a sort of emerald twilight, pierced here and there by a shaft of gold.

A stream threads the bottom of the gorge, the precipitous red cliffs on either hand alternately closing in to make a place of shadow, and widening out to let the sun play on the green strath.    The waters murmur incessantly.    Here, it contracts to a mill-race, and after turning the wheel, expands once more to a placid stretch of scarcely moving water, which mirrors the oranges and roses on the bank.    Aquatic birds flash across the surface, and where they dive, break the still expanse into a whorl of quivering ripples.    On every side are orange trees, lemon trees, flowers, sweet perfumes, songs of birds, and beating of feathery wings, while palm trees wave their plumes against the warm cliffs that carry the eye to the unbroken blue above.    In Majorca we visited the Garden of the Hesperides. This was the Terrestrial Paradise.

Houses cling to the cliffs like swallows' nests, and where the ravine is bifurcated, a tall, isolated rock pinnacle rises like a cathedral spire.

For an artist the "subjects" are ready-made, though no palette could render the rich colours of the sub-tropical vegetation or the bright, almost crude, hues of the rocks.

I passed the entire day wandering through the woods or straying from mill to mill by the riverside.

When I returned to Subervei in the evening, I found the path completely changed.    At intervals, progress was barred by hastily built stone walls or immense tree trunks, while locomotion was hampered by bundles of faggots, heaps of dried weeds, or loose branches.    The foliage above our heads, however, was hung with

A Wedding Party.

coloured ribbons, and garlands of flowers and fruit, like the route of a triumphal procession.

While helping my guide to force a passage through the obstacles in our path, I asked him why the road should be thus barred, while, by a strange contradiction, it was at the same time decorated in so singular a manner.

" An old custom," said he. " To-morrow morning we expect one of my brothers, who was married to-day. Young men stationed in the vicinity watch for the coming of the bridal couple, and do everything in their power to make the road difficult. When the bride and bridegroom appear, these bushes will be set on fire, fresh walls will be built, and every sort of obstacle thrown in their way. They thus learn that the path to happiness is difficult, while at the same time their home-coming will be celebrated by garlands of flowers. The fruit symbolises the abundance wished to the married pair."

Another old wedding custom, now dying out, is for the young people of the neighbourhood to build a wall against the door of the house occupied by the young couple on the night after their marriage. Bride and bridegroom, on rising in the morning, are thus disagreeably surprised at finding themselves prisoners, and they are often not liberated until late in the day.

The old mule which took me to the *barranco* conveyed me back next day to the *posada* of Ferrarias, where I took the diligence to Ciudadella, which I reached the same night.

Ciudadella was formerly the capital of Minorca, but under the British occupation the seat of Government was transferred to Port Mahon. A certain rivalry still exists between the two towns, to the prejudice of the general interest. There is the same difference between them as, say, between Glasgow and Edinburgh. Mahon is the busy, prosperous trade-centre ; Ciudadella is the city of leisure and good birth. The bishop lives there, and in his train the higher clergy, the large landowners, and members of the old nobility.

Ciudadella contains some fine houses, but the streets are narrow and badly paved.

At Mahon, a garrison town, peopled by all classes and races, the inhabitants are obliging, amiable, and lively ; their ideas are more liberal and advanced than elsewhere. At Ciudadella the people are colder and more reserved, and their manners are solemn and sedate. The innkeeper hands you your soup with all the airs of a *grand seigneur*, and the chemist seems to pontificate as he gives you a seidlitz-powder. Your money is taken with the appearance of conferring a benefit on you.

A French traveller observes that this frigid manner is another trace of former British influence, but as a fact Mahon was the town most frequented by the English.

The harbour is small, being little more than a narrow channel bordered by rocks, difficult of access, and only accommodating ships of small tonnage. The situation of the town, as seen from seaward, is very picturesque, however, and the ancient ramparts built by the Moors add not a little to the effect.

At Ciudadella.

Old as the place is, it being traditionally said to have been founded by a Carthaginian general, there are no architectural monuments to speak of, and its chief attraction is a natural phenomenon in the environs, called the *Buffador*, or Breath of the Devil.

This is situated at the entrance to the harbour, near the dismantled castle of Saint Nicholas. Some twenty yards from the edge of the sea there is a narrow, round hole in the rock, of which the beach is formed.

I put my ear to the orifice, and heard a sound like deep breathing from below. Sometimes it rose to the volume of a gale of wind, and then grew feeble and stifled, like the last sigh of a dying man.

The opening being partially closed by blocks of rock, I begged the man who acted as my guide to clear them away. As he seemed loth to do so, I set him the example.

Instantly a violent blast from below drove clouds of sand and earth into our faces, while the unearthly rumblings grew louder and louder. In its way, this blow-hole was quite as noisy and conceited as an Icelandic geysir.

As we left, I noticed that the guide hastened to roll back the boulders over the orifice, and carefully mortared the interstices with pebbles. Only when this operation was completed did he seem at ease, and I then remembered the popular belief which attributes the subterranean noise to the infernal snoring of his Satanic Majesty.

Not far from the Buffador there is a church dedicated to Saint Nicholas, a saint held in great veneration by the sea-faring folk, who make frequent pilgrimages to the chapel. The walls of the interior are covered with *ex-voto* offerings—models of ships, pictures of the saint appearing to his clients in the heart of the storm, and all kinds of weird and fantastic objects.

The habit of placing such offerings before favourite shrines dates from remote antiquity. Horace, in his Fifth Ode, refers to the custom of hanging them in the temples ; and not infrequently those who had escaped a great danger carried a picture of the event, suspended round their necks, for the edification of their fellow-citizens.

Wandering along the shore, I came upon several beaches composed of innumerable fragments of red coral. The fishermen, I believe, often bring up whole corals in their nets.

The next morning I visited the church of the Rosary, which has a curious façade coated with lime ; and in the afternoon, I embarked on the little steamer, which conveyed me back to Majorca.

Due south of Majorca on a clear day, the horizon is broken by the rocky outline of Cabrera, the third of the Balearic Isles. A little steamer runs across at odd intervals, and I took the opportunity to visit the island, which is, however, little more than a rock.

The appearance of the place is not inviting. On all sides there is nothing but bare, sun-blistered rock, and an |old fortress on a height above the harbour adds to the grimness of the arid desolation. The historical souvenirs of the island are no whit more cheerful than its aspect.

On April 3rd, 1809, five thousand five hundred French prisoners of war were marooned on this rock, and left there without shelter or clothes, and almost without provisions.

These were the remnants of an army of nineteen thousand men, delivered to the Spaniards by General Dupont at the capitulation of Baylen.

They were marched, in the first instance, to Cadiz, but when they reached that city their number was already reduced to fourteen thousand. These were imprisoned on the hulks, but what with bad water and insanitary conditions disease soon broke out, and in a short time eight thousand were on the sick list. Their sufferings were terrible, and, to add to the revolting nature of their surroundings, the dead bodies had frequently to be kept on board for a week in the sweltering heat, before they could be thrown into the sea, as the tides often washed the corpses back into Cadiz harbour.

Finally the five thousand five hundred remaining of the fourteen thousand placed on the pontoons, were transported to Cabrera. The story of their existence on the island is at once horrible and touching.

The allowance of food per man was twenty-four ounces of bread and a few dried beans every four days. Some devoured their scanty allowance in a single day, and on the succeeding three, prowled about in the hope of robbing their more provident comrades.

There was but one spring of fresh water on the island, and the captives fought with each other like wild beasts to obtain access to it, until some of the wiser spirits established a guard over the well, and limited each man to a certain allowance.

No shipwrecked mariners ever passed a more terrible time than these prisoners. Many tried to assuage their thirst by sucking pebbles and shells to promote salivation. Others swam in the bay, but the salt water, while it cooled their bodies, only aggravated their agony of thirst.

Gaunt troops of famished men paced the island continually like lost souls, each suspicious of his neighbour, yet fearing to remain alone.

They had perhaps good reason for their fear, lashed to madness as they were by the famine fiend. Murder was not unknown, and in one instance a prisoner was found preparing to make a ghastly meal from the remains of a comrade.

The only humanising influence on the island was a solitary donkey, which happened to be wandering over the rocks when they arrived. This poor animal did good service in carrying water and wood for the sick, and soon became the pet of all.

But he also fell a victim. The boat which brought supplies from Corsica was several days overdue, and the position of the men became desperate. They had eaten everything they could find, down to rats, lizards, snakes, and shell fish. Many died of starvation, and others succumbed to terrible convulsions induced by eating poisonous weeds and even wood and stones. There was no help for it. Martin, as the donkey was named, was sacrificed, and his body cut up into four thousand five hundred pieces.

On the very next day the boat with provisions arrived, but many devoured all their bread at one meal, and fell victims to their imprudence.

Not a few instances were recorded of daring escapes on the part of individuals on canoes rudely constructed by themselves. In one case fourteen prisoners, after long and patient watching, seized a Majorcan fishing boat which adventured close to the coast, and compelled the fishermen to convey them to Tarragona, then occupied by the French.

Some forty naval officers succeeded in building a vessel of old barrels, with shirts for sails, the pitch being made from the turpentine secreted by the few pine trees on the island, and oil saved from their rations. But the project was denounced to the governor by a traitorous comrade, and the ship was confiscated.

On another occasion, when a Spanish vessel came into the harbour, forty-two men swam out and boarded it, threw the crew into the sea, seized the oars, and escaped to the mainland.

When first brought to the island, the prisoners were accompanied by their officers, who succeeded in maintaining some sort of discipline. But, later on, the officers and non-commissioned officers were taken to England, and the excesses of the men then became so frequent, that at last, in their own self-defence, they were compelled to institute a superior Council to maintain order. Its decisions were irrevocable, generally rigorous, and carried into effect as soon as pronounced.

The court was held in the open air, the judges sitting on stones arranged in a circle for the purpose.

It was a lesson in the evolution of order from anarchy.

Gradually a perfect colony was formed, in which trades and even amusements were zealously organised. A theatre was established in a disused reservoir, on the walls of which the captives wrote the legend " *Castigat ridendo mores.*"

Duels were frequent ; and as swords were lacking, the weapons used were scissors, razors, knife-blades, and even sail-needles fixed on the ends of sticks.

Their position in the matter of food became less intolerable as time went on, for the Spaniards, unaware of the death of three thousand prisoners, continued to send the same rations. Finally, on May 16th, 1814, after five years' captivity and abandonment, the few remaining men of the original nineteen thousand were taken off by a French transport.

In 1847 the bleached bones of those who died on the island were interred by the crew of the French corvette *Pluton*, and a monument was erected on the spot bearing the inscription : "*A la memoire des Français morts à Cabrera.*"

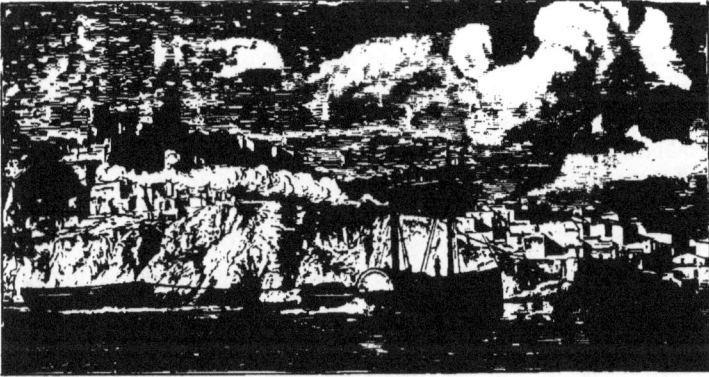

Iviza.

# CHAPTER VII.

The *Jayme Segundo.*—The City of Iviza.—
The Women of Iviza.—The Agua-
dores.—The Pescadores.—A Queer
Fisherman.—Country Remedies.

L OOKING from the crest
of the Majorcan sierra on
a clear day, the spectator
sees far to the south-west a
small net-work of dark blue
specks breaking the clear
turquoise of the
sea. They are the
Pithyusæ, the least
known and most
remote of the Ba-
learic group.

An old paddle
steamer, which
makes a service

109

between Palma and Alicante, calls at Iviza on the way, and I decided to avail myself of it to go to these distant and rarely visited islands.

In one respect, at least, the steamer reminded me of the old-fashioned penny Thames steamboat. There was no telegraph on the bridge, and the captain's orders were transmitted to the engine-room by a boy. " Stand by!" yelled the skipper. " Stand by!" repeated the boy leaning over the engine-room. " Half speed ahead!" from the skipper, " Half speed ahead!" from the boy, and so on through the gamut of modern nautical cries.

The *Jayme Segundo* forged bravely ahead, leaving a double track of foam across the sapphire sea. Brass-work and wood-work glistened in the sunlight, white gulls followed in our wake, the sailors sang at their work, children prattled merrily, and their seniors walked the deck with a self-satisfied air. No one would have guessed what a cranky old craft the steamer really was.

The shore loafers at Palma, however, indulged in much racy humour at her expense. " She is too delicate," said they, "to go out in winter, considering her age and long service!" Others declared that machinery doctors had inspected her thirty years previously, and had not given her six months to live. But, for all that, she made good weather on this occasion, and performed the crossing in nine hours, which was evidently considered excellent time—for *her*.

The mountains of Majorca faded away astern as the hills of Iviza and the precipitous cliffs of the islet of Tagomago arose in front. Towards sunset the town of Iviza came plainly into view. Its white houses, with flat roofs rising in tiers round an amphitheatre of rock, enclosed by copper-coloured ramparts, and surmounted by a cathedral and a sombre fortress, recalled the Kasbah of Algiers.

The crazy steamer, making a "spurt" for display, with a plume of black smoke streaming from her iron funnel, rounded the light-house of Bótafoch with much commotion, and proudly entered the harbour, amid the enthusiastic cheers of the population gathered on the mole to witness her arrival—the sole distraction of their uneventful days.

After the customary struggle with rival porters, who each seized upon a separate article, I reached the *fonda* with my train of bearers, all of whom, especially the man who carried my umbrella, kept mopping their brows to show me how heavy their burdens had been.

I was shown to a bare-looking room with white-washed walls, decorated with coloured supplements from French illustrated papers. On the bed was a wonderfully worked quilt, representing the Blessed Virgin upborne by angels, round whom was the inscription : "*Nuestra Señora de la Aurora, venerada en la villa de Benejama*" ("Our Lady of the Dayspring, venerated in the town of Benejama ").

The town of

Vincenta.

Iviza, with seven thousand inhabitants, possesses only one hotel, and even this lacks all comfort, in spite of the sonorous name of the landlord, José Roigt y Torres. He was familiarly known as *el Cojo* (Hoppy), from an infirmity in his gait. I can see the man now, with his enormous head and his ugly eyes blinking under lashes as thick

as horsehair, balancing his ungainly body on his deformed legs as he coursed round the table with the gestures of a performing bear, stopping to expectorate at my very feet, and panting like a wild beast, his breath reeking of vile tobacco.

And then the dishes of Heaven knows what meat, floating in oily sauce, which he shoved under my nose, saying each time—

" Now, this, Señor, is simply delicious ! "

He must have grinned to himself at my alarm at the meats and beverages which he brought me or sent by an old hag, disguised as a servant, named Vincenta.

" Ventana Comasema."

As I ascended the staircase my nostrils were assailed by the nastiest of smells, and I had to close the door of the *comedor* in all haste.

The moon was just rising over the sea, and I asked Cojo to open the window, but no sooner had he done so than ·I repented my rash romanticism. The odour from the harbour was worse than the smell on the stairs. I had been warned in Majorca that I should find Iviza a dirty place, but I had not anticipated such a universal infection.

After dinner 1 went for a moonlight ramble through the town. Here, as at Palma, the lamps are only lighted when there is a bright moon, and on dark nights they are not used at all.

Making my way up a steep ascent, I passed under a fortified gate with a portcullis, and entered a labyrinth of narrow alleys.

From all the windows and balconies staffs protruded, and I thought that preparations were being made for some festivity ; but I afterwards discovered that the staffs were connected by ropes, on which linen was hung out to dry in front of the houses. I scarcely met a soul in the whole course of my wanderings, and the silence of the streets was funereal. I was glad to get back to my room at the *fonda*, but the mosquitoes soon inspired a feeling of regret.

I had several letters of introduction to prominent citizens, including the *alcade*, the dean of the cathedral, and one of the canons, Don Torres y Ribas. The latter called on me at the hotel, but I was out at the time, admiring a wonderful window of Moorish architecture, the *Ventana comasema*. I stopped shortly afterwards to look at an escutcheon on the front of one of the houses, when I was accosted by a young ecclesiastic, with a pale face and large, dark eyes, half veiled by the long upper lids. It was the canon himself. We walked up the hill together to his house near the cathedral and episcopal palace. On our way we passed the *castillo* inhabited by the military governor, an old fortress with a battered keep and crumbling ramparts, which afford an asylum to nocturnal birds. It seemed an anachronism to see a modern sentry pacing up and down before such a building.

The Old Curia.

The episcopal palace stands hard by, and just opposite is the ancient *curia*, or court of justice, with a fine doorway, combining the Gothic and Moorish styles, surmounted by an escutcheon displaying the arms of Aragon.

In front of the *curia* is a small terrace, from which the island of Formentera, the *Pithusa Minor* of the ancients, can distinctly be seen.

I told the canon of my wish to visit the islet, between which and Iviza small sailing boats pass daily. The priest, however, strongly dissuaded me from making the attempt.

8

" It is an arid rock," said he, " containing two bitter lakes and
three fortified churches, like those you will see in the environs of
Iviza.  For the sake of these, it is not worth while risking being
detained on the island for several weeks in dulness and misery.
The wind is favourable now, but if it should change while you were
there, it would be impossible for you to return."

I owned the wisdom of his advice, and reluctantly abandoned my
plan of visiting the lonely islet.

The canon lived with his mother and a charming young niece
named Pepita, but at the time of my visit the household was in mourning.  An epidemic of diphtheria had been raging in the island, and
only a fortnight previously another of the canon's nieces and her two
little girls had been carried off within a few days of each other.

The women of Iviza lead a dull, confined life.  It is not considered
proper for a woman to go much out of doors, and, except to pay
visits of ceremony or to attend church, they rarely leave their dark,
silent houses.  The heat in these narrow streets in summer is
suffocating, but there is no shady public prómenade as in other
southern towns, and of an evening, when the women of France, Spain,
or Italy flock gaily to the public gardens or boulevards, the señoras
of Iviza merely open the shutters and sit on the balcony to enjoy
the cool breeze blowing in from the darkening sea.

In respect of its silence, Iviza resembles an Arab town.  There
are no *serenos* to tell the hours of night, as at Palma or Mahon,
and the tinkle of the guitar is never heard beneath its melancholy
balconies or in the shadows of its dark courts.  Only the sea or
the wind wakes the echoes of this ancient town, buried under the
prejudices of a bygone age and an alien race.

The cathedral of *Santa Maria la Mayor*, which the canon made
me visit, offers nothing of interest from an architectural point of
view.  A low Gothic doorway near the sacristy and a painted altar-
piece of primitive design, are all that remain of the original structure
of Don Jayme *el Conquistador*, who ceded the Pithyusæ to Don
Guillermo Mongriu, Archbishop of Tarragona, on condition that he
delivered the islands from Moorish dominion, and erected a Christian

The Aguadores.

church, in which mass would be said daily for the repose of the souls of those who fell in the enterprise. The sacristy and the church fittings betoken extreme poverty.

In the *Sala Capitular*, the only furniture of which consisted of a few leathern arm-chairs covered with dust and gnawed by rats, the canon showed me a portrait of Carlos III., the king who in 1782 changed the title of *ciudad* (city), conferred upon Iviza by his predecessors, into *villa ó real fuerza de Ibiza* (town, or royal fortress of Iviza). This picture had been "restored" with comic effect. The king's face, of a bright, brick-red colour, with eyes

A Street in the Maritime Quarter.

like a prawns, seemed to be jumping out of the dark back-ground like a Jack-in-the-box.

There is a splendid view from the belfry. To the north a wide plain dotted with white houses extends to a range of wooded hills. Westward, the land, chequered with salt lagoons, slopes down to the sea, on the horizon of which, far to the south, rise the long shapes of Formentera and the rocky islet of Espalmador. To the east is the garden-encircled bay of Iviza, and at one's feet the town, flat-roofed and white like an Eastern city.

Fair as the town and gardens appear, they are, nevertheless, veritable hotbeds of disease. Fever is endemic at Iviza. Besides such obvious causes as putrefying vegetable matter, stagnant water, filthy streets, drained by gutters which are no better than open sewers, there is no doubt that the confined and sedentary life led by the people helps to foster epidemics. Another custom favouring infection is, that when the death-bell rings, all the children of the neighbourhood are gathered together in order to give the last kiss to the face of the corpse, no matter what disease was the cause of death.

The inhabitants wonder at the persistence of fevers, but one has only to visit the old, maritime quarter of the town, with its damp, dark houses, and ill-smelling, narrow streets, without air and almost without light, to see the primary causes of the unhealthiness of Iviza.

The very flowers and fruit that grow so luxuriantly on the rich, decomposing soil, are poisoned in their germination.

In some streets of the upper town it is nothing unusual to see chickens, pigs, and even sheep, tethered to the doorways, where they are reared on vegetable and other household refuse.

Nevertheless, the upper town is clean compared with the repulsiveness of the maritime quarter.

I should probably not have stayed in Iviza longer than I could help, except that I was virtually a prisoner, as the steamer for Palma only calls once in ten days, and not as often as that in rough weather.

The only means of communication between the upper town, or fort, and the harbour district, which is outside the ramparts and of more recent origin, is through the ancient fortified gate of *las Tablas*, built, as its inscription attests, in 1585, in the reign of " Philip II., Catholic and most invincible King of Spain and the East and West Indies."

Hither, at early morning, come crowds of market-folk with baskets of fruit and vegetables, and the *aguadores*, or water-carriers, who are indispensable at Iviza, where, except for the rain-tanks in a few private houses, the only water supply is an old well near the harbour.

In the niches of the gateway are two marble statues, dating from Roman times, one of a senator, the other of a priestess ; but both are mutilated.

I entered into conversation with one old *aguador*, whom I asked

The Old Water-carrier.

to sit for his portrait. He informed me that a previous visitor had taken the portrait of himself and his donkey while they were in motion, climbing a hill. That señor, he added, had a little machine in which there must have been a devil, for it was beyond human power to do such extraordinary things.

During my stay I noticed that all the children, not even excepting the infants, were perpetually smoking cigarettes. I learned that this had been prescribed by the doctors of the town as a precaution against the prevailing epidemic of diphtheria.

The only industry which I noticed at Iviza was the manufacture

of earthen jars.  In Roman days, and long afterwards, the cups made
at Iviza were reputed not to be able to contain poisons, the earth
of which the ware was made having the quality of neutralising all
venomous substances, so that the most dangerous liquids could be
drunk from them without fear.  This belief gave a great impulse to
the manufacture and sale of these goblets, which became important
articles of export, and were much sought after.

The history of Iviza is little known.  It is supposed by some
to have been first colonised by the Phœnicians, and according to
others by the Carthaginians, who gave it
the name of *Ebusus*, signifying unfruitful.
Most probably, it was in turn overrun by
the same invaders as occupied the other
islands of the group—Phœnicians, Carthaginians, Romans, Goths, Vandals, Arabs,
and Catalans.

One is struck by the distinctly Arab
character of many of the faces one sees
in the country districts of the island.
This is far less apparent, however, in the
town, the people of which look down upon
the country folk as savages and barbarians,
the inhabitants of the upper town being
in their turn disdainful of the occupiers of

Fisherman mending his Net.

the maritime quarter, though these latter deem themselves far superior to the country folk.

The *pescadores* (fisher folk) are a class apart.  They spend most
of their time on their *faluchos* (feluccas), cruising along the coast
of the island and the north side of Formentera.  Unlike the fishermen of other countries, nearly all are clean shaven.

The coasts of the Pithyusæ swarm with fish, of which there are
no less than one hundred and forty species ; but the weather is so
uncertain, that even in the best seasons the fishermen are in a
state of poverty.  Moreover, means of transport hardly exist, so
that many a good catch is wasted for want of a market.

The notary of Iviza, though of another trade, was perhaps the most expert and certainly the most original fisherman I ever saw. A perfect diver and swimmer, he would suddenly plunge into the water, and come to the surface holding one fish in his mouth between his teeth, and another in each of his hands. With his high colour and flowing white beard, he more resembled a sea-god than a prosaic man of law. He was always accompanied in his walks abroad by a large, gaunt harrier, of the breed for which the Balearic Isles, and especially Iviza, used to be famous. They are slender, half-starved looking creatures, like the heraldic dogs which one sees supporting a coat-of-arms. There are plenty to be seen in the streets of the town, but I was told that they were treacherous.

The climate of Iviza is warmer and more equable than even that of Majorca. Rain is also less frequent. The islands of the archipelago differ as much in climate as in the character of their inhabitants. Majorca is mild and soft, Minorca windy and sterile, Iviza hot and fertile. In the first island the population is patriarchal, in Minorca it is cosmopolitan, at Iviza it is proud and haughty in the town, and rough and savage, but very hospitable, in the country.

The Notary.

The country folk employ many queer remedies. I asked a man one day the name of some large birds which I saw in the harbour.

"They are *garces*," said he. "These birds possess great medicinal virtues. We use their fat to make ointments, and the down between the tail feathers and on the breast, when placed on the skin of any man suffering from an hereditary complaint, will cure him completely."

To cure rheumatism, the people apply the branches of a resinous tree called *sabina*, which they heat before using.

The latter homely remedy is no doubt not a bad one, both the

warmth and the turpentine exuded by the tree having essentially curative properties.

Seal skin is supposed to facilitate child-birth.

Another queer cure is that resorted to in the case of mules suffering from colic. Pedro, standing on one side of the animal, holding a white fowl, passes the bird over to Pablo, standing on the other side, saying, " Take it, Pedro." Pablo passes it back, saying, " Take it, Pablo." And thus they continue handing the fowl to and fro, and exchanging names, after which pleasing and inoffensive operation they go their way rejoicing, convinced that the mule is cured.

Of Uncertain Temper.

Fortified Church of San Antonio.

## CHAPTER VIII.

San Antonio.—A Fortified Church.—Primitive Music.—Santa Eulalia.—Courtship and Gunpowder.—A Night Cry.—Love and Death.—*El joch del Gall.*

A "Cantado"

A DOUBLE rainbow spanned the bay, and, according to local weather lore, gave promise of a fine day, as my friend the canon and I drove into the interior on our way to San Antonio, on the opposite or western side of the island. Men working in the fields raised their heads as we passed, and I noticed that they wore a kind of apron of goat skin to protect their legs from the thistles and other thorny plants covering the ground.

We crossed a deep ravine, now dry and rocky, but in wet weather a raging torrent. The canon told me that only in the previous year, two women,

123

who took shelter on their mules beneath the arch of the bridge, were surprised by a sudden rush of water, carried out to sea, and drowned.

This torrent is named *el torrente de ses Donas.* Being dry for most part of the year, the bed is used as a path.

The *pagesos* of Iviza call torrents in general *torrentes roigs* (red torrents), owing to the crimson tint given to the waters by the soil through which they pass.

The road along which we were driving and the neighbouring fields were bordered with small white flowers with a strong scent, called *ramallets de la mare de Déu,* or *flores de la Virgen.* Mothers tell their children that on these spots the Mother of God dried the linen of the Holy Child, and the ground at once became covered with flowers.

An hour and a half after leaving Iviza, we came to the church of San Rafael. The villages here are not agglomerations of houses in one spot, but are scattered townships, of which a solitary church is the centre. Only on Sundays do the people of the parish gather together for service ; and if it were not for this weekly meeting, many of them would never see each other, the houses are separated by such long distances.

Many of the farms are fortified, and all the houses have an Arab aspect, overshadowed by tufted palm trees. The road is bordered at intervals by stretches of waste land, where flocks of black sheep browse among the furze. Copses of almond trees, fig trees, and olive trees grow round about the homesteads.

Turning to the right at San Rafael, we rapidly descended towards the gulf on which San Antonio is built, the *portus magnus* of the Romans. The white houses of the village are grouped round an ancient fortified church, opposite the island of Cunillera, or Conejera— in Spanish, the isle of conies—the precipitous, red cliffs of which are crowned by a lighthouse.

The church, dating from the thirteenth century, is practically a fortress. It is flanked by two massive towers, and the apse is supported by a buttressed rampart, from the embrasures of which old guns still point to the *cala de los Moros,* where the corsairs used to land. As soon as the watchmen signalled the pirates' approach, all the people of the village took refuge in the church, which was well supplied with provisions, and contained a well. The walls are nearly eight feet thick, and a machicolated parapet over the doorway enabled showers of projectiles to be hurled on the assailants.

The parish priest, to whom our visit was an agreeable surprise, made great preparations for our entertainment; and after much bustling to and fro of servants and messengers, a nondescript but gargantuan meal was spread for us at the presbytery, a small white house abutting on the church.

In the evening we went to hear the *caramelles de Natividad* (ancient Christmas carols), for which all the villagers assembled. These traditional songs were sung to the accompaniment of a *flautin* (a long flute), a *tambo* (tambourine), and a metal instrument like a triangle. The music was primitive to the last degree, thin yet plaintive, the sort of music which one imagines must have obtained among the pastoral peoples of the dawn of Christianity.

But these religious chants, and the love songs which I heard afterwards, all corresponded well with the character of the people, with their simple faiths and violent passions.

The midnight mass in Iviza is a striking spectacle. The church is brilliantly illuminated, and after the reading of the Gospel the priest sits with his back to the altar, while the notables, wearing their gala costumes, and with enormous castanets on their fingers, chant to the assembled people the glad news of the Saviour's birth, to the accompaniment of tabors and tambourines.

The music of Iviza differs greatly from that of the other islands, and, owing to the people having come into contact with no external influence since the time of the Moors, is much more characteristic. The improvisers of poetry, known as *Cansonés*, are numerous, while the *Cantados*, who do not themselves compose, sing old ballads to the monotonous accompaniment of the tambourine, which here replaces the guitar in popular esteem. The almost innumerable verses of the sentimental songs are frequently interrupted by heavy sighs on the part of the singer, who concludes each strophe with a kind of trill, producing a remarkable effect.

The costume of the peasants is dying out, and its use is now almost entirely restricted to old people. It consists of a red cloth cap, bordered with black, a white shirt with a high, stiff collar and ample sleeves with the cuffs turned back, and often a pleated front, a black silk waistcoat ornamented with two rows of pendent silver buttons, shaped like round bells, a short coat similarly decorated, and white peg-top trousers. On chilly days a large, brown, sleeveless mantle is added.

The women wear a black bodice with tight sleeves, ornamented with tiny gilt buttons, a bright-coloured shawl, and a long close-fitting skirt of a thick, closely woven material, with an infinite number of vertical pleats. A multi-coloured apron, embroidered with arabesque designs, and a large silk kerchief complete the costume.

They wear their hair in a single plait, hanging down the back, and fastened at the end by brown and yellow ribbons.

The great day in every village is the feast of the patron saint of the parish. His image is exposed at the door of the church, and, preceded by the *alcade*, the men, armed with old-fashioned muskets, march past in rank, each discharging his musket at the ground as he passes the statue. The hole caused by these discharges is often deep enough to conceal a man, and it is not by any means unusual for the muskets, which are generally loaded to the muzzle, to burst in the firer's hand. One frequently meets men mutilated from this cause, but such accidents do not in the least damp their ardour for firearms. May not this apparently senseless device of discharging guns for the mere pleasure of doing so be another Moorish trait, similar to the "powder play" practised to this day by the warriors of Morocco, when they wish to show any one special honour? The dangerous custom is now prohibited by law, but it is nevertheless still observed in the remoter parishes. Droll as it may seem, the firing of these same muskets plays a large part in rural courtship.

Some days after my visit to San Antonio, I drove out to the village of Santa Eulalia, where I was again the guest of the parish priest. The peasants had just come out from attending mass, and as I was talking to the clergyman at the door of his house, I was

Returning from Mass at Santa Eulalia.

startled by several loud reports. On my asking the priest what the sounds meant, he led me quickly to the foot of a little hill, where I perceived a girl walking slowly home from church. A young man

An Ardent Avowal.

with a musket was hurrying after her, and just as he overtook her he suddenly fired at her very feet, raising a cloud of stones and dust which almost hid her from view. But without so much as the quiver of an eyelash the girl continued to walk serenely on, and, the young peasant

9

placing himself by her side, they both continued their road chatting amicably together.

This, it appears, is the recognised form of salutation between man and maid throughout the island, and the girls make it a point of honour to betray no emotion at the firing, though they are always taken unawares ; for the lovers, wearing light *espardenyas*, creep up behind them as silently as panthers. After spending the evening at the girl's house, moreover, every young man takes leave by firing off his musket in the middle of the room, adding *"Buenas nôches"* (" Good-night "). This form of farewell shows that there is no ill-feeling towards any of those present.

But if the visitor says good-bye first, and then fires, if, in the Arab expression, he makes his powder speak, it is a defiance to a rival admirer. He then leaves the room, and waits outside the door. The challenge is invariably accepted, and fierce fights, and not infrequently murders, result.

The church of Santa Eulalia resembles a mosque externally, and the interior bears out the Eastern character. The porch, which is of unusual size, is like a Moorish corridor, and the roof is supported by rows of slender columns.

Sitting under an olive tree in the presbytery garden that after-noon, I was struck by the intense silence of the hot noonday. Not a breath stirred, not a bird fluttered, and the few rare insects of the country were sheltering under the stones from the insupportable sun-rays.

In the other islands, even on the hottest summer days, one always hears the low murmur of life, the distant neigh of a horse, the rustling of a branch, the buzzing of a fly, or the movement of an insect in the grass.

But in Iviza there is not a sound. The white, hot sky glares down pitilessly at an arid land where everything is mute. It is only when the evening breeze begins to blow in from seaward that the tension is relaxed and movement recommences.

At this cool hour, I accompanied the priest down to the village in order to see the peasants dance. On our way we looked in at a peasant's house. The interior was anything but homely—bare, whitewashed walls, a few rickety chairs and a table, and in the corner three shivering children with yellow parchment complexions.

" *Tenen las tercianas*" ("They have the tertian ague "), said the priest.

At Santa Eulalia, as at Iviza and throughout the island, fever is endemic, and malaria grips the people from their very cradles.

Dancing was already in progress on the *plaza* when we reached the village. To the sounds of tambourine and flute, the girls, with their eyes cast down, and their elbows against their sides, and their hands half uplifted in the attitude of a Hindoo idol, glided backwards and forwards or turned slowly in a sort of waltz. The men, with immense castanets (*castagnolas*) in their hands, gesticulated wildly in front of their partners, whirling round, kicking out their legs in every direction, and finishing with a leap in the air.

The symbolism was manifest. The man was courting the girl, who shyly withdrew from his advances ; he kicked out to drive away his rivals, and a joyous bound celebrated his conquest.

But twilight was falling, and the Angelus-bell pealed softly from the church. Every one uncovered, and the priest recited the " Angelus Domini," the peasants devoutly crossing themselves and giving the responses.

I got into conversation with the *profesor*, the schoolmaster, and with him slowly returned towards the church. I tried to discover from him the truth of the strange account I had heard at Iviza of the customs of the peasants, but I could see that he had a natural reluctance to disclose the darker side of their mysterious habits.

The white walls of the presbytery were gleaming through the dusk, when suddenly a strange, wild cry rang through the night— "*Hu-lu-lu !*" A similar cry sounded in answer from across a neighbouring gorge. It was as if two wild animals were calling to each other.

The schoolmaster shivered, and I felt his arm tremble against mine.

" Are you ill ? " I asked.

" No, Señor, but I can never hear those terrible cries without shuddering. Some one's powder has spoken. Often, at night, after one of those fatal evenings, the silence is thus broken by a cry of distress. That is all. But it means another body thrown into some ravine where it will be found to-morrow. The invisible murderer, his vengeance attained, slinks away through the woods, and is at home before dawn. Who can discover the assassin? His weapon has been hidden in some bush in the woods. There are no means of identification. Perhaps the police come from Iviza to hold an inquiry, but none will give them any information. The very parents of the victim would not give up the name of the murderer, even if they knew it. The victim himself, if he did not die immediately, would not say who had struck him. Only last year two young men were horribly wounded in one of these duels. They were found lying in the woods still grasping their terrible *navajas*. They were conveyed in a dying state to the hospital at Iviza, where they both succumbed without saying how they had received their wounds, and denying with their last breath that they had been fighting. Love! Jealousy! Revenge! It is the custom of the country. Even if tried at the Assizes, the prisoner is always acquitted by the jury. Listen! Here come some young men."

Some youths passed, and the few words they exchanged were uttered in a kind of head-voice. They change their voices like masqueraders at a carnival, and with such facility that it is impossible to recognise their ordinary tones. They all wear the same dress, they know every inch of the country, and are extremely active, so that it is labour lost to pursue them in the darkness. They disguise their voices not only in order to avoid being recognised themselves, but also to escape interrogation as to the persons they may have met on their way. Moreover, they do not greet each other when they meet after sundown. A greeting at night is regarded as a grave affront.

At carnival time the young men have a habit of going masked to the house of any girl whose lover is absent, and endeavouring to wean her away from him. The lovers themselves will sometimes adopt this expedient in order to test a girl's fidelity; and never is a maiden able to identify the man who has visited her, so completely is his ordinary voice disguised.

The Ivizan peasants strictly observe the external observances of religion, but here, as elsewhere, this does not prevent them having a very wide conscience, when there is question of deceiving their neighbour. At bottom, their faith is fatalism.

"*Dios lo ha dispuesto*" ("God has willed it so"), say they, when misfortune overtakes them or their family.

Withal, they are extremely superstitious. The gadfly brings good news ; the hoot of the howl is a sound of terror ; Tuesday is an unlucky day, and no work is ever begun on that day. It is fortunate to meet certain animals, the reverse to encounter others. Cats enjoy special consideration, and whoever kills one is bound to die in the course of the year.

The politeness of the people is extreme.

"Whose is that house over there ?" I asked the priest of Santa Eulalia.

"I inherited it, and it belongs to me, but it is yours also, Señor."

And when we came to the said house, the ecclesiastic exclaiming, "Well, we've reached the house at last," corrected the phrase, saying, "I beg your pardon—*your* house, Señor !"

One peculiarity of the peasants is that they have a horror of giving a direct answer to any question.

"Are you coming to to-night's party ?" I asked a man.

"It may be so, Señor, but it will be to accompany you."

These parties are called *vetlladas* (vigils), and are greatly in vogue. We left the presbytery one night to attend such a gathering. Our road was by rough pathways, where the stones, wet with dew, glistened like jewels in the moonlight. The priest was accompanied by several persons. From time to time one of the men would say in a low voice, "*Corazon ! Corazon !*" another would reply, "*Corazon ! Corazon*" ("Courage ! Courage!"), and the clergyman would add, "*Vamos con Dios !*" ("Let us go in God's name !")

The people are so accustomed to hidden ambushes that they never walk by night without encouraging one another by these words.

We proceeded thus towards a distant house
whose windows made squares of light against the
dark hillside. We soon heard the
sounds of tambourine and flute
and the barking of a dog.
"*Deú los guard*"
("God keep
y o u"),
said the
peasant,
ushering
us into
his house.
We sat
beside
the mas-
ter of the
house in
a corner
of the
r o o m.
T h e
young
people
conversed in low tones,
and occasionally a *Can-
tado*, in a strong nasal
voice, sang one of the weird
popular songs, with an in-
termezzo of flute and tambourine.

The daughter of the
house, wearing a gold cross
and many trinkets on her breast, sat to receive the homage of her
admirers. A young man was beside her with his back turned to the

Courtship.

"El Joch del Gall."

company. He talked in a low voice, and the girl occasionally pointed his remarks with a shrill laugh.

Presently, he rose and silently rejoined his companions, the vacant place being taken by another of the girl's admirers, who talked the same soft nothings, interrupted, as before, by the sharp hilarity of the maiden.

Thus, turn by turn, each man had his chance of paying court. If one of them remained too long, or the girl showed any marked preference for his company, the others signified their impatience by coughing and shuffling their feet till he moved. Should he persist in stopping by the girl's side, it is not unusual for the man who should replace him to make him pay for his temerity by a bullet or a blow from a *navaja* when he leaves the house. Sometimes he is torn away by force and hurled into the middle of the room, whereupon follows one of the terrible midnight duels in the woods, referred to above. In rare cases, all the young men divide into two hostile camps, and a general conflict ensues, with fatal consequences for one or more.

When the girl has finally settled upon her choice she is betrothed, and the lover carries her off, with the consent and support of the parents, who help to convey her to the lover's house.

Occasionally, the *profesor* told me, this kidnapping of the bride is not followed by marriage. Some girls have several such escapades, and return home without incurring any reproaches from their parents, and without impairing their chances of securing new admirers and finally marrying.

The evening gatherings generally take place on Sundays and feast-days, and sometimes during the week, on a Thursday. The courting and singing are varied by dances, among which *lou fasteig* (the flirt) is most popular.

Of out-door games, the chief is the *joch del gall* (game of the cock). It is practised in various ways. Sometimes the cock is fastened to the ground, and the young men take shots at the bird with stones, paying a fine of one halfpenny to the owner for every miss. As the distance from which they throw is considerable, the owner of the cock generally makes a good profit ; but sometimes, of course, a good aimer will hit, and win the prize at his first throw.

Another mode of playing the game is for the cock to be hung to the branches of a tree. The men, blindfolded, and armed with an old sword, then try to cut it down. I saw the game played in this manner at Santa Eulalia, and the way in which the men slashed about them without hitting the mark was extremely diverting.

The pastime is a cruel one, of course, but it is not worse than bull-fighting. It would be interesting to know if this game of

A Fortified Farm.

throwing stones at a cock is the origin of the word " cock shy," meaning mark or aim.

But to study all the quaint customs of the Ivizan peasants would require months of residence, and the time for my departure soon arrived.

Mounted on an ass, as in primitive days, and accompanied by the hospitable priest, I started back to Iviza town to catch the steamer for Palma. At a turn in the path, I looked back and took a last glance at the village with its white presbytery and old rampart-flanked church. In spirit, I seemed to hear again the wild scream which had made the *profesor* shudder, the dull report of the murderous musket, and the cry of distress which followed. I wondered if I should ever again visit this strange, half-forgotten people, with their barbarous customs and terrible superstitions. I said as much to the clergyman when he bade me farewell at the top of the hill.

" *Quien sabe ?* " was his wise reply.

# Part II.
# CORSICA.

141

Ajaccio.

Monte Cinto from Calacuccia.

# CHAPTER I.

*Ajaccio.*—Memories of Napoleon.—Suarella.—Sampiero's Wife.—A Wild Drive.—
Woodland Scenery.—The Forsaken Inn.

La Maison Bonaparte.

SMILES are not to be expected from Corsica. Despite its sunny blue skies and flowering fields, it is an island of tragedy. The men are grave and reserved : the sad-eyed women dress habitually in black ; the children do not play, except at fierce games, such as "robbers" or "soldiers." The people partake of the character of the country in which they dwell—wild, austere, stormy, and, in certain aspects, grand.

The Corsican race has never been softened by contact with more civilised peoples.   Tried by adversity, the Corsicans take a pride in preserving their old characteristics, fighting to preserve their moral independence, just as in bygone times they fought to maintain their civil liberty. They practise stern, antique virtues, are faithful to tradition and to their friends ; but on the other hand easily prone to take offence, and vindictive to a degree.   They seem to accept life as a torture to be

The Place du Diamant at Ajaccio.

endured, or, at best, a stern duty to be performed.   Poor and proud, eager for combat, they are yet capable of noble sacrifices.   The more one knows them, the more one appreciates their good qualities, but it is saddening to see so fine a race producing nothing of their own, even in a country where nature has been so lavish of her gifts.

In no part of the world are such varieties of climate to be found in  so  small  an  extent  of  country.   Leaving  the  coast  towns  at dawn, the traveller may in one day see tropical, temperate, and alpine vegetation, traverse the dense scrub called the *makis*, lose himself in virgin forests, cross fierce torrents, shudder in savage gorges, and climb cloud-swept summits, to the verge of eternal snows.

But nature alone has embellished Corsica. Of all the peoples attracted in turn by its beauty or geographical position, not one has left any permanent trace. Nor Romans, nor Goths, nor Arabs, nor Genoese have left any mark of art or civilisation. The great men who have appeared among the Corsicans themselves have all been men of action or combat,—Sampiero, adventurer and warrior ; Paoli, organiser, legislator, and soldier ; and Napoleon, the genius of war. Not one has been illustrious in science, literature, or art. The Corsicans are born fighters, and fighters they remain to their last breath. To go a-soldiering is the height of the young Corsican's ambition. When the troops march back from exercise, in the morning, at Ajaccio, they are preceded by crowds of street-boys, carrying sticks over their shoulders in place of guns, keeping step and holding themselves often far more upright than the genuine military article. When a battalion is quartered at a village, the people are only too anxious to give them food and shelter. The head of the family surrenders his bed to the soldier, and, if he has no other, will sleep himself in the wood-shed or out in the open air.

I remember being at a performance at the Saint Gabriel theatre in Ajaccio, at which one of the chief attractions was a lightning-transformation artist. Amid stolid silence, the comedian assumed in turn every character from Punch to the Pope of Rome. At length, suddenly buttoning his overcoat, and covering his head with the traditional marshal's hat, he folded his hands behind his back and assumed the historical attitude of Napoleon I., while, behind the scenes, a bugle sounded "boot and saddle." The effect was electrical, the entire audience rising to their feet and cheering as one man.

One September afternoon during the Franco-Prussian war, a

10

telegram reached Ajaccio announcing that the Emperor Napoleon III. had gained a great victory and had taken forty thousand Germans prisoners.   When the telegram arrived, it happened that a procession of the statue of Saint Roch was passing through the streets ; but no sooner was the news circulated, than devoutness gave place to wild enthusiasm.   The holy image was hastily put down on the roadway, and the crowd dispersed with shouts of joy.   The men fetched their

Tower of "Capitello."

guns, with which they continued to fire salutes during the remainder of the afternoon, and in the evening the town was illuminated. Even the clergy took part in the general demonstration, and poor Saint Roch lay forgotten for hours at the corner of the street where he had been set down.   On the morrow, however, an official despatch announced the surrender at Sedan.   Curses and imprecations then succeeded the cheers of the previous day.   Women became hysterical or fainted in the streets, which were soon littered with portraits of the Imperial family, thrown out of the windows by the enraged people. But the outburst of wrath subsided as rapidly as it had arisen, and the houses were soon draped with mourning. Black flags hung from every casement, traffic was stopped, the streets were deserted, and Ajaccio became like a city of the dead.

The name of Ajaccio is derived from Ajax, by whom the town is said to have been founded. But a better name would be Napoleonville, for the figure of the great Emperor confronts one at every turn. On the Place du Diamant you see him, accompanied by his four brothers. On the market-place he stands alone, robed in a Roman toga. Yonder, on the opposite side of the gulf, rises the *Capitello* Tower, where Napoleon was invested by the insurgent peasants under Paoli. For three days he remained alone in this tower, surrounded by enemies, and with no better food than the flesh of a dead horse. The birthplace of Napoleon, the *Maison Bonaparte*, is a common-place, barrack-like building, but it contains the wooden bedstead of Lætitia Bonaparte, and the sedan-chair in which the Emperor's mother, when overtaken by the pangs of labour, was conveyed home from the adjacent church. There are also an ivory cradle brought home by Bonaparte from Egypt in 1799, and the trap-door by which he fled in 1793, to escape from the followers of the insurgent Paoli.

The Town Hall contains some striking portraits of the Imperial family, and other relics are to be found at the museum in the *Palais Fesch*.

Apart from its Napoleonic souvenirs, the town of Ajaccio, notwithstanding its splendid situation, is not attractive. There are no buildings of interest, and the houses are like barracks.

Seen from the deck of the steamer, the town appears to be just emerging from a forest of olive trees, and advancing to the water's edge to admire its own reflection, though that is not much to boast of. But beyond the outline of its common-place houses, and old yellow fortress, rises tier upon tier of hills, culminating in snow-clad mountain summits. The Gulf of Ajaccio is one of the most beautiful in the world, combining the luxuriance of Sydney Harbour with the ruggedness of a Norwegian fjord. The old women of Ajaccio will tell you that from this harbour the witches, called *massere*, used secretly to cross the sea in an ill-found fishing-boat to the African coast, starting at sundown and returning at dawn with fresh bunches of dates. The old women know, too, that the *massere* still exist, and that, if you meet them at noonday in a solitary place, you will be seen no more alive ; with one glance of their small blinking eyes, the *massere* will have drunk up your soul.

The climate of Ajaccio deserves to be better known. The vegetation indicates a climate hotter than that of Cannes or Nice, but the air is remarkably dry, and, in winter, so bracing, that highly nervous people cannot support such constant stimulation.

The environs are charming, whether you ascend the heights inland, or confine your walks to following the coast-line towards the Iles Sanguinaires, along a delightfully shady road, where vistas of the sea are caught between the pines and olive trees.

Another pleasant resort is the beach, especially in the early morning, when the fishermen, great brawny fellows like Florentine bronzes, are drawing in their nets.

If you are at Ajaccio in Lent, do not miss the funeral of King Carnival, which is followed by all the boys in the place, beating a formidable requiem with sticks, on barrels for drums. Every day you will see penitents following ordinary funerals. While the women of Ajaccio cannot be called beautiful, their pale faces are generally distinguished by a certain nobility and energy of expression. They seldom go out of doors, however, and then generally of an evening, when they promenade on the Place du Diamant.

But Ajaccio nowadays is not Corsica. It is too cosmopolitan, too like other towns, though pleasing enough as a residence for the pleasure-seeker or the invalid. I only stayed a few days, therefore, and then started for the interior, making first for the Coscione, a wild, primitive district where the monotony of existence is relieved by bandits and vendettas

Accordingly, one morning found me in a light carriage, driven by a young Corsican named Antó, proceeding on the first stage of my

Fishermen Drawing their Nets.

journey. For about a mile and a half the road skirted the gulf, bordered by an avenue of trees, through which the eye caught flashing glimpses of a sapphire and emerald sea, where the white sails glided past towards the haven, and the gulls fluttered down upon the waves like a cloud of white butterflies. Now and then we passed a milkmaid, or a woman of Alata, wearing an immense straw hat.

After leaving the shore and crossing the *Campo del Oro* (field of gold), a small fertile plain formed by the alluvial deposits of the Gravona, we entered a narrow valley, and, at one plunge, seemed to pass out of civilisation. The country-side was deserted ; and if we did chance

Suarella.

upon a casual wayfarer, it was a Corsican on horseback, dressed in black velvet or clad in goat-skin, and holding his gun across his saddle. Wooden crosses were to be seen at intervals on the side of the road, and caused me an involuntary shudder, for each one marked the scene of a murder.

Then came a long rise of nine miles, in course of which we passed

close by the picturesque village of Suarella, where there is a huge
tree, on the branches of which a two-storey dwelling has been
constructed.

The immense circle of the valley below loomed dimly through
a heat haze, from which rose reddish hills streaked with perpendicular
shadows.

It was in the gorges behind Suarella, that Sampiero Corso,
ancestor of the Marshals d'Ornano, and one of the bravest com-
manders of his day, was treacherously murdered.

The son of a shepherd of Bastelica, Sampiero left Corsica as a
soldier of adventure, and having served under the famous John de
Medicis, won, in the service of France, during the reigns of Francis I.
and Henri II., the rank of *mestre de camp* and colonel. Bethinking
him of his native isle, then under the yoke of the Genoese, he
conceived the idea of wresting it from the Italians and incorporating
it with France. With this object he returned to Corsica, where the
entire population responded to his call to arms. After gaining some
successes, he went to the Levant, and, in his absence, some Genoese
messengers persuaded his wife Vanina to go to Genoa to obtain the
restitution of the estate of Ornano, which had been confiscated.
Believing that she was acting in the interests of her children, she
embarked with her youngest son on a felucca one dark night and
shaped her course for Italy. But she was stopped off Antibes by
a trusted friend of her husband and conveyed to Aix in Provence.
Sampiero on his return, believing that she had sought to betray his
children into the hands of the Genoese, had her arrested and condemned to death. The sentence was to have been carried out by
Turkish slaves; but the poor woman, throwing herself at her
husband's feet, said that, if she must die, she would rather that her
life were taken away by the man whom she had chosen for husband
on account of his bravery. The stern Sampiero thereupon tied a
handkerchief round her neck and strangled her.

A few years later, on January 17th, 1567, Sampiero fell into a
Genoese ambuscade near Suarella. Suddenly surrounded by enemies,
he drew his sword to defend himself, when one of his squires, named

Vittolo, bribed, it is supposed, by the relatives of Vanina, fired an arquebus at his back, and he fell, mortally wounded. His body was hacked to pieces by the Genoese, and his head was taken to the Governor of Fornari. When news of his death reached Genoa, the bells were rung and salutes fired to celebrate the event.

To this day, the name of Vittolo is a synonym for traitor, and no more grievous insult can be given to a Corsican than to call him by this name.

After passing the village of Cauro the road continued to ascend, and the carriage went so slowly that the mule-bells scarcely tinkled. The driver, in a guttural voice, sang an old *lamento* : —

> *" Nelle monte di Coscione nato ciera una zitella*
> *E la so cara mammona gli faceva la nanarella*
> *Adormentati parpena alegreza di mammona."*

    \*      \*      \*      \*      \*      \*      \*

A puff of wind carried away the remainder of the song. A lash of the whip made the mules shake their heads, and we reached the top of the pass of San Giorgio, where the air was cooler than in the suffocating valley.

Looking backwards, I caught a distant glimpse of one of the promontories of Sardinia, floating upon a sea as bright as molten metal. Before us, the road descended in rapid zigzags to the valley of the Taravo, where the white houses of Santa Maria d'Ornano gleamed amid evergreen holms.

After a brief rest at the inn, where I was served with some delicious *broccio*, I walked down to the hamlet, where the maiden-home of Vanina, the unhappy wife of Sampiero, raises its scarred façade beyond a broken drawbridge.

From Santa Maria d'Ornano to Zicavo, our next stage, the landscape is sombre and forest clad, recalling the pictures of Poussin and Salvator Rosa. The former artist is said to have worked in this district, and at Rome there are ten studies from nature which might certainly have been made at Ornano. It is a country of simple sweeping lines,—dark masses of woodland throwing opaque shadows, forest clearings strewn with fallen timber or threaded by amber-coloured streams, and, in the background, the broken slopes of verdant hills. It is the *lucus* of the Latin poets, the sacred woodland, where the shepherd plays his pipes as he watches his flocks, and the faun hides to peep at a sleeping nymph or a goddess emerging from her bath.

Daylight was fading as we crept up the steep ascent to Zicavo.

House of Vanina d'Ornano.

At Giutera the sunlight still lingered on the tops of the trees, but it was twilight when we crossed the Taravo, which murmured far below in a chaos of blanched rocks. The water at this hour gleamed like cold steel. The slopes of the hills looked larger in the shadows, and the trees were etched in ebony against a pale sky, in which one star was timidly beginning to shine.

The road grew steeper and steeper, and the mules panted heavily. Their hard breathing and the turmoil of rushing waters were the only sounds. Sharp rocks surrounded us like threatening armies. On one side was a deep gorge, where fallen trees hung their twisted branches over the edge of the precipice. Occasional gleams in the nether darkness seemed like reflections from the scales of some vast serpent.

"Where the deuce are we coming to? Where is the village, Antó?"

Antó smiled and pointed to a cluster of lights on the slope of the mountain.

"Yonder is Zicavo," said he, "and the serpent down below us there is the Molina torrent."

We plunged for a few moments into the darkness of a chestnut wood, and, as the trees fell back, saw the dull gleam of charcoal brasiers through open doorways. Wild-looking men, carrying guns over their shoulders, and bearing torches of resinous pine, came out to glance at the strangers. The weird yellow glare lit up their sallow cheeks and glittered in their black eyes. Yet each and all greeted us with, "*Bona notte.*"

We crossed a small square and drew up in front of the inn. Its aspect was not encouraging. In the darkness it appeared little better than a ruin, with yawning window-spaces and cloistral arches, from which hung tufts of wild grass. Nothing stirred, and no light was visible. The only sound was the lugubrious murmur of the wind in the chestnuts.

"Hi, Peretti, hi!" called Antó.

Thereupon a slow footstep echoed under the ruined arches, and a flickering light, held by a gaunt arm, vaguely illuminated a sort of stone balcony reached by rickety wooden steps.

Sheepfolds at Palaghiolc.

## CHAPTER II.

At Zicavo.—The Cascade of Camera.—Strange Superstitions.—Vampires and Demon Hounds.—Forest Fires.—*Schiopetto, stiletto, strada.*—The Vendetta.—The *Vocero.*—A Dance of Death.

WHEN the first sun-rays made me open my eyes next morning, I found myself on a truckle-bed in a sort of monastic cell. I quickly dressed and hurried downstairs to examine the outside of the inn. My eyes had not deceived me on the previous night. The building was indeed a ruined Franciscan monastery, turned to more modern, if not more practical, use as a hostelry. In what was left of the church I noticed some half-opened tombs. Bleaching bones lay here and there, objects of derisive curiosity to some black pigs, who were now grunting in the sacred enclosure which formerly echoed to the chants of the monks.

I spent the remainder of the day wandering about the village and its environs. The township of Zicavo, for it is more of a township than a village, consists of a number of scattered houses, perched upon the steep side of a mountain, but surrounded by gardens and orchards, and overhung by umbrageous chestnuts. The sound of falling water replaces the hum of industry, and wherever one turns one sees little cascades gleaming like streaks of quicksilver in the

156

shade of the rocks and trees. From the altitude of Zicavo the eye overlooks an intricate system of mountain gorges, where small hamlets nestle in the velvet of rich vegetation, while the prospect is bounded by a rampart of wild rocks. Savage, lonely, characteristic, Zicavo is in the heart of old Corsica, the country of vendettas, bandits, and strange superstitions.

The Molina, the stream which flows past Zicavo, is a perfect type of the mountain torrent, a rocky stairway for the hurrying water, where cascade follows upon cascade, with here and there a treacherous pool, almost too dark to reflect the trees upon the banks. To follow up the course of the stream is to make a voyage of discovery. Here, at the foot of a precipice, opens a cool, green grotto, whose verdant darkness is the home of all manner of capricious plants, dewy with the moisture dripping from the roof. Little flowers in tears, bend and rise again as the crystal drops fall and then roll off the petals, like the scattered beads of a broken necklace of pearls. From a fissure in the rock a jet of water is constantly playing and trickling back to the parent stream.

Continue the journey up the gorge and you come to the cascade of Camera, where the torrent falls from a height of some hundred and twenty feet, not in one desperate leap, but tumbling and slipping over a chaos of rocks, bluish in tint and burnished by the boulders which are rolled over its surface in times of winter flood. High above in the mist of the fall, a second cascade, but of forest, rolls down in green waves from the ridge of the mountain. The sunlight glitters and scintillates on leaf, rock, and water. A bare-legged fisherman springs from rock to rock, and at length brings to bank a shimmering, quivering trout.

On the 6th of August, after a day of suffocating heat, the mountains veiled themselves at evening in mufflers of mist. As the day waned the fog crept down to the ravines and blotted them from view, while the moon, at its rising, was dim and blood-red as in an eclipse.

I was standing outside, when the woman of the inn came up to me, saying,—

" I should not advise you, sir, to stand out like this in these evil fogs. They are peopled by *Gramante*."

I looked at her in surprise, but she gazed on me sadly for a moment, and then withdrew without a word.

"What are these *Gramante*?" I inquired of an old fisherman who was passing.

He bade me follow him to his house, where he made me sit down, and, as night had fallen, lighted a torch of pine.

" The murmur of waters," said he, " the hooting of owls, the flight of birds, the vague noises heard by night, the hum of evening insects, the shape of clouds, the sound of the wind, in fact, all the forms and all the sounds of nature have a meaning for those who know how to observe and understand. Our ancestors, who were ever on the watch, dwellers of the forest, learned to read the book of nature, and could even foretell the future. The present generation no longer dwell in such close communion with nature, and do not listen to her voice. In those clouds, now falling upon the mountain and about to enshroud the village, the evil spirits called *Gramante* are making ready to swathe themselves, and to come down with the mist. Do not expose yourself to their evil influence. The doors must be kept shut, and every one in the house must be provided with holy-water.

" Man is not alone on the earth," he continued. " Besides the animals, there are also the elements which suffer and weep, and beings which our senses cannot perceive, but which assuredly exist. Take, for instance, the *streghi*, or vampires. They are shapes like old women, which enter the house by night without being seen, and, fastening on the throats of little children, drink their blood. In the old days, the horrible creatures were sometimes seen, but nowadays they are invisible, and the death of the little ones is the only sign of their presence. ' Beware the *streghi* !' say the women of our mountains to each other at bedtime, and some keep under their pillow an old billhook or sickle to kill the vampires.

" The *Acciacatori* are equally dangerous, and their very name inspires terror. They are men, like you or I, who during the day

The Cascade of Camera.

follow their usual occupations, or walk abroad. At night they go to bed like the rest of us, but their body alone sleeps. Their spirit, horribly awake, hurries to wait in ambush by the cross-roads in some wild ravine, and there, armed with an invisible hatchet, it attacks belated travellers or wandering pilgrims, whose bodies are found next day, stretched on the ground, with their skulls battered in."

The *Acciacatori*, I thought, are probably merely peasants fulfilling a vendetta ; but the aged fisherman continued his recital of terror.

"You have heard of the demon hounds !" said he. "Sometimes furious baying is heard, and an invisible pack of hounds rushes into the deeps of the valleys. The baying grows fainter in the distance, then a cry of agony smites the listener's ear, and then there is silence. When the listener can recognise the voice which uttered the cry, it is an infallible sign of the death of this person. Sometimes, the baying of the hounds resembles the lamentations of the women who mourn for the dead, and it is a token that death will soon visit the village.

"The *Spirdo* is another presage to be reckoned with. If a person comes to meet you in the street and you mistake him for somebody else, it is the spirit, *Spirdo*, of the other which has manifested itself, and he will die within the week. Nevertheless, if the person coming towards you take a rising street or road, he will escape danger ; but if he descend, a fatal issue is inevitable."

I was told of many other strange beliefs in Corsica ; for instance, the drum heard at midnight, indicating the early death of one of the village-folk : the spectral voices which call those about to die : the spectres which go in procession at night from the cemetery, and recite the rosary at the door of the sick and the dying.

I heard many another story in the house of the old fisherman, tales of battle, of wonderful wild-sheep, wild-boar, or stag hunts on the neighbouring *Coscione*, of severe winters when flocks of mouflons (wild sheep) were driven by the snow to take refuge in the peasant's stables.

One of the most singular sights was to see the villagers watering

11

their gardens at night by torch-light. The people are very poor, and scarcely know the use of lanterns, instead of which they employ torches of resinous pine. In the old times, the peasants were even worse off than they are now. Thus at Zicavo, the men only began to wear shoes at the age of twenty, —and such shoes! mere soles of pigskin fastened to the feet by a woollen ligament. Even these were only worn in winter. In summer the men went barefoot.

It is recounted as a sign of immense wealth, that at a certain marriage - feast the bridegroom provided each of the hundred guests with a bag of barley for his horse. These nosebags, called *narpia*, are made of pigskin, which is in general use throughout Corsica, cow-leather being a rarity.

Girl of Zicavo.

The girls of Zicavo are undeniably handsome, and are very industrious. It is a pretty sight to see them filling their water-jars at the spring. They are usually grave of expression, but they have always a smile for the foreigner—the " continental," as they call him in Corsica.

The Corsicans quite worship springs. As in the West Highlands, there are wayside wells by every mountain path, and it is rare not to come upon some one resting in the vicinity. The horse's bridle is slung over a branch, the gun leans against a tree trunk, and the passing traveller or muleteer, or possibly bandit, has engineered a sort of channel with leaves. Some springs are reputed to have curative properties. This, on the homœopathic principle, cures dropsy : that is so cold that it freezes any object placed in its water. On the road to San Pietro di Verde (Saint Peter of the Greenwood) there is a spring at the foot of an ancient chestnut, of which every wayfarer religiously tastes. You may be perspiring profusely, but the water will do you no harm ; so say the country folk, at least.

Further on, a path winds through the valleys to a torrent, the bed of which is a litter of mossy rocks. This place is famous for its giant chestnuts, many of which measure twelve yards in girth.

The chestnut trees near the village of Zicavo are all gashed with axe-cuts or riddled with bullets. The trunks are used as targets by the young men, who always shoot with ball, the game of the neighbourhood being generally insensible to shot, for the quarry is usually either the mouflon or the wild boar, not to speak of the man-hunts, which are perhaps more frequent.

Many quaint superstitions are now dying out. The fire enchanters, for instance, are gradually being forgotten. These were witches, who laid spells, not only on fire, but also on water, animals, and even men. They could draw out the sting of a venomous insect. Robbers had recourse to them to enchant dogs, so that they should not bark when the bandits went by night to rob some outlying farm or wealthy household.

Belief in the *jettatura*, or evil eye, is still widespread. When a mother thinks that her child is *innochiato*, or struck by the evil eye, she calls in an old woman, expert in the art of conjuring the spell. The method of exorcism is quite dramatic. The old woman crosses herself thrice, mutters a secret prayer, lights an iron lamp, and pours water into a plate. Still muttering, she places the plate on the head of the child, plunges two fingers in the oil of the lamp, and lets a few drops fall in the water. According to the manner in which these fall, she tells whether the child is delivered or not from the spell.

The manner of discovering whether a child is suffering from worms is equally curious. The old wife places a ball of lead in an empty iron lamp, which is then placed on red-hot coals. When the lead is melted, she pours it out on a plate of water, crossing herself thrice and murmuring some cabalistic words. If the metal on contact with the water breaks up into small streaks, the child is suffering from a helminthic complaint. If the lead does not separate, it has some other disease, to be discovered by different means.

· Eggs laid on Ascension Day are carefully kept to safeguard the house from lightning, sickness, and other evils. When a storm comes, the people hasten to place these eggs in the windows to secure the safety of the house. An equal virtue resides in bread, blessed in church, on the feast days of Saint Peter, Saint Anthony, or Saint Roch. These loaves are displayed with the eggs during thunderstorms. They are also given to cure sick animals, and are thrown upon a fire to extinguish the flames.

A forest fire is an exciting event.

One afternoon I heard the tocsin ringing wildly, and looking out of my window, saw thick clouds of smoke rising from the slopes of the mountain above. Men were running from house to house to fetch hatchets, and hurrying away to the forest to render assistance. Voices rang from the heights, " *Al foco! Al foco!* " (" Fire ! Fire !"). They sounded as if the people were already being suffocated, and all the while the bell kept ringing the alarm.

I begged Perreti, the landlord, to find me a mule, and was soon following the villagers up the mountain path to the scene of the conflagration. After a wild climb of an hour's duration, alongside rushing torrents and on the brink of giddy chasms, I arrived opposite the burning mountain.

I could hear the crackling of the flames, and see the living trees twisting and curling as if in throes of agony, rising up in one desperate, final effort to survive, and then coming down with a crash and breaking to pieces in a shower of sparks and blazing

Giant Chestnuts.

fragments. A continuous roaring dominated all minor sounds, and columns of acrid, grey smoke rolled steadily skyward. In a clearing above, I saw men and women bravely fighting the flames, looking much like pigmies striving to do the work of a giant. But the intelligence of the pigmies triumphed, and a stream, diverted from its course, presently poured over the mountain declivity, raising clouds of steam, but gradually extinguishing the fire.

The day had been very hot, however, and the firing of the forest was not confined to one locality. That night, the sky was lurid with the glare from similar conflagrations in several directions.

Corsica loses thousands of valuable old trees every year by these fires. Between 1874 and 1886 a ninth part of all the timber in the island was destroyed, and between 1878 and 1886 there were ninety-one fires which devoured over two thousand acres of State forest.

But to return to Zicavo. Cloudless days succeeded each other with almost monotonous regularity, and each one disclosed some fresh charm in that book of nature which the old fisherman had spoken of as closed to the present generation, but which we moderns peruse in a more inspiriting fashion. The children of the village are very fond of bathing, and parties of boys were constantly to be seen disporting themselves in the quieter reaches of the torrent, where the sunrays, striking through the leafy branches, or reflected by the water, made strange play of shifting light on their glistening bodies. Their favourite resort was a sort of rocky conch-shell, framed in moss and glistening foliage. A tiny cascade, falling through a fissure, just rippled the calm expanse of the pool, the waters of which were so clear that the eye could follow to the very bottom the little bronzed figures, who used to throw themselves off the top of the rocks and tumble about in the cool depths like young tritons at play.

Sunset always lighted a pretty pastoral picture of flocks returning home. The goats were particularly handsome, with shining coats of all colours, from ebony blackness to purest white, with gradations of lilac and brown in between. The tinkling of the goat bells, the rustle of the torrent, the cry of belated birds, and distant calls from the mountains, all made a characteristic farewell to the sun sinking behind the rim of the forest. And as the light died away, the shepherds, shouldering their guns, descended the steep paths among the blocks of granite, now disappearing behind the roots of a giant chestnut, now standing out like martial statues against a primrose sky.

Few things impressed me more at Zicavo than the number of armed men I met on the mountain paths, and even in the streets of the township. The municipal councillors even brought their guns to the Town Hall, though leaving them outside while they attended the sittings of the Council.

The sight of these guns gave one a sensation, not of fear, for strangers are rarely molested in Corsica, but of an alien, melodramatic environment. Sometimes, at dusk, I would come upon a man lurking in the shadows, with eyes as watchful as if he were looking out for an enemy.

"When one has an enemy," runs the Corsican saying, "one must choose between the three S's—*schiopetto, stiletto, strada*: rifle, dagger, or flight." And again, "There are two presents to be made to an enemy—*palla calda* or *ferru fredda* : hot shot or cold steel."

When a certain justice of the peace, named Bonaldi, was acquitted of wounding a peasant named Franchi with a pistol shot, the prosecutor observed, "The jury absolves, but *I* condemn."

When a Corsican takes the law into his own hands and slays his adversary, he is spoken of much in the same way as other people talk of the victor in a duel. He is a man *under a cloud*, to be pitied, or even secretly admired for his courage, but never to be blamed. He has earned the absolute fidelity of his relatives and of his "clan"; if he becomes a bandit, he is fed, and protected against the ambuscades laid by the gendarmes. Every one is in league to save him from the grip of the law ; and if he should happen to be arrested, no stone is left unturned to secure his acquittal.

Their fighting instinct gives the men of Corsica a sombre expression ; but the women also, veiled by their black *messaro*, have a look

The Widow.

of sadness in their eyes, though these occasionally light up with a
cold brilliancy, like the flash of a dagger.

Visit the spring whence the women of the village draw water morning and evening. You are fascinated by their graceful attitudes and the harmonious folds of their dark draperies. Yet only last year this same spring was the scene of a bloody drama. A pitched battle took place between two hostile families, and in a moment four men bit the dust. The parish priest, who was passing, hurried to administer the last consolations to the fallen, but he was too late. They were already dead. Then the brave ecclesiastic stood up between the living, offering his breast to their bullets and daggers, and, speaking of the God who pardons, succeeded in preventing more bloodshed.

The murderers took to the bush, and as the families at feud counted many members, it was feared that other murders would follow. The most influential people in the country, the Abbatucci, the Colonna of Istria, and others intervened, however, and the members of both families were convened at the Church of Aullene. The bells were rung, the Blessed Sacrament was exposed, a *Te Deum* was sung, and the enemies signed a treaty of peace on the altar, in presence of a crowd of the country folk.

There was a woman at Zicavo who was always smiling. Gracious and bright, her aspect differed completely from that of her companions. Yet I learned that she always carried a dagger, and used to say to her brothers, " It is not for you to help in accomplishing my revenge. I am quite capable of doing it myself ! "

She had been widowed, and had a *vendetta* to fulfil. The knowledge of a mission to accomplish was an antidote to her grief. Her husband was not dead to her, as long as she had his death to avenge. From the subject of vendettas, the transition is easy to the matter of death.

At twilight, one August evening, I heard the bell tolling, and learned that a woman had just died in the village. A procession of women clad in black, wearing the *mezzaro* or *faldetta* on their heads, moved silently towards the house of mourning. Within that house, as soon as the last breath had gone from the body, the fire was extinguished, the shutters were closed, and the relatives uttered heartrending cries, tearing their hair and scarring their faces with their finger nails. As soon as the neighbours reached the house, some of the women set about getting ready the deceased's best clothes to dress the body, while others sang the *voceri*, chants of mourning im-

provised in verse. The singing continued till the Angelus bell rang, when the neighbours departed, only the relatives and intimate friends remaining in the house after nightfall.

It was formerly the custom to let three days elapse without rekindling the fire, opening the windows, or preparing any food, but this observance has been abandoned, at Zicavo at least, and nowadays a mid-

A Man of Zicavo.

night repast is served in the death-chamber itself. The table on which the body is laid out, however, is not used again for domestic purposes for the space of eight days.

At six o'clock the next morning, I heard the church bell again

tolling, and at once went outside. The valley was still obscured by mist, but the mountain tops were gilded by the first rays of the rising sun. I directed my steps to the house of mourning, and, through the open doorway, saw, by the paling glimmer of resinous torches, the body of the deceased woman laid out upon a table, clad in her marriage robes. She had died of consumption, and the emaciated, ivory-coloured face, now so full of majestic repose, seemed like a vision against the sombre walls of the interior. Presently the table was lifted, carried outside, and set down in front of the door, while some children carefully laid a few flowers on the body. It was a strange spectacle at that brilliant hour of reawakening life to see this quiet figure clad in a wedding garment, as if to celebrate her union with death, the face and hands rigid and yellow against the white sheet laid underneath, while grave women stood round, all clad in black, all motionless as statues, and some with their raven hair falling over their shoulders like funeral veils. Under the cold, bright sky of early morning, weeping eyes seemed redder, tears more bitter, and faces paler than by the mellow glow of artificial light. Inside the house, by the empty hearth, the candles were guttering out, and seemed to be shedding great tears of wax.

A *voceratrice*, with hair as dishevelled and face as pale as that of an inspired priestess of old, improvised a funeral hymn, interrupted from time to time by the sobs of the onlookers.

" Listen ! " said she, leaning over the body as she sang :—

*" Chi nô consulera mai,*
*O speranza di a to mamma,*
*Ava chi tu ti ne vai*
*Duve u Signor ti chiamma ?*
*Oh ! Perchè u Signor anchellu*
*Ebbe di te tanta bramma ?*

*" Ma tu, ti ripose in célu,*
*Tutta festa e tutta risu.*
*Perchè un n'era degnu u mondu*
*D'avè cusi bellu visu ?*
*Oh ! Quantu sara più bellu*
*Avale u Paradisu !" etc.*

"Who shall ever console us,
O thou, thy mother's hope,
Now that thou dost go,
Summoned by the Saviour ?
Oh ! why hath He, the Lord,
Desired thee so greatly ?

"But thou in Heaven now resteth,
All joyful and all smiles.
Was earth perchance unworthy
To hold so sweet a face ?
Ah ! More beautiful is now
Thy face in Paradise !" etc.

And while the *voceratrice* is singing, the women put their mouths to the ear of the dead and talk in a low voice, as if they were still heard, while, from time to time, they press their lips to the cold brow.

At intervals, new arrivals, raising their arms to the sky, uttered heartrending cries and threw themselves on the body in a frenzy of farewell. Thus interrupted by groans and sobs and sudden outbursts of grief, the *voceratrice* continued singing, until she was out of breath and signed to one of her companions to replace her.

The scene was painfully impressive, and no one could dispute that, however sober in their joys, the Corsicans know how to render death a terribly dramatic spectacle.

The contrast between the mourners and the brightness of nature added to the effect. The sunlight gradually spread in golden bands down the mountain slopes and the wooded highlands, till the ample rays embraced the entire valley. The sobs accompanying the doleful chanting were themselves accompanied by the twittering of birds and the cheerful chatter of falling waters.

At length the priest arrived, and grave men placed the body in the coffin to convey it to the church. The *voceratrices* gave one final scream of anguish ; and the lugubrious procession moved up the sun-flecked pathway, and paused beneath the dappled shadows of the chestnut trees.

Now for a time came silence, broken only by the low voice of the priest as he read the burial-service ; but no sooner had he concluded, than the relatives uttered piercing cries and threw themselves on the body, which they covered with kisses and strained fiercely to their breasts in a last embrace.

The lid was then nailed on the coffin, and the tap-tapping of the hammer seemed even more terrible than the wailing of the mourners. The latter spoke of the grief of the living, but the former of the helplessness of the dead.

No ! A Corsican funeral is not an inspiriting ceremony, and after a murder the scenes of despair are even more violent than that above described.

When a man has been killed by the bullet or dagger of an

enemy, the body, with the face exposed, is laid on a table ; his friends flock to the house, and the *gridatu* (mourning) begins.

At first there is a storm 'of grief, crossed, as if by lightning, by burning oaths of vengeance. Men draw their daggers and knock the floor with the butt-ends of their rifles, while the women wave their handkerchiefs and soak them in the wounds of the murdered victim. Presently a sort of vertigo seizes upon the assembly, and, taking hands, they dance round the corpse, jerking out the words of the lyke-wake dirge called the *Caracolu*.

Intense silence follows this frenzy. Then one of the women relatives of the deceased stalks forward and lays her ear against the chill lips of the dead, as if to receive his orders. Then, in a vibrating voice, she intones the *vocero*,—no solemn funeral hymn this, telling of human sorrow giving place to heavenly joys, but a battle-song, set to a clipped, breathless rhythm, which seems to keep time with the beating of her heart. She begins by addressing the relatives of the dead, and urges them to descend on the murderers like vultures upon their prey. The appeal for the *vendetta* has commenced, and its effect upon her hearers is like that of a tocsin. Rifles and daggers tremble in the hands of the men, and at nightfall a son or a brother goes forth on a mission of vengeance into the dark depths of the forest.

Sometimes, with a strange contrast, prayers are interwoven with the appeal for vengeance, like a scapular round the neck of a bandit, or the daggers of the Middle Ages, which often had the *Pater Noster* and *Ave Maria* inscribed on their blades.

At Zicavo interments are not confined to the cemetery, which, to tell the truth, is a dreary spot ravaged by winter rains—the *scumbapio*, or rains of the dead, as they are called. Burial crosses are to be met with everywhere : on mountain bypaths, under the chestnut trees, and on the borders of the fields, even by the highway side.

After a death the deceased's dogs often betake themselves to the grave, where they howl for days and scratch at the earth to get at their masters. Some of the poor animals cause such alarm in the village by their nightly baying that they have to be shot.

Not many years have passed since it was the practice in many parts of Corsica to throw the bodies into the charnel-pit, dressed in their best clothes, but without coffins. The charnel-pit of Zicavo was in the old ruined church opposite the inn, where I had seen the pigs rooting among the bones.

The pigs of Zicavo, it must be remarked, are not at all the mild domestic-looking creatures of ordinary farms. With their black, bristling crests and white tusks, they are more like wild boars. In order to prevent them getting into the gardens they all wear triangular iron collars, and pitiably ashamed some of the poor creatures look in these ridiculous necklaces.

he Pigs of Zicavo.

Sheepfolds of Frauletto.

## CHAPTER III.

Pastoral Life.—A Strange Encounter in the Forest.—Shepherd-lore.—Ossianic Verse.
—The Ghastly Horseman.—On the Incudine.—A Meeting with Bandits.—
Vengeance and Hospitality.

AFTER so many terrible impressions of death and violence, I
felt a longing for softer scenes. At the same time I was glad
that I had witnessed the wilder and more savage side of Corsican
character. To visit Ajaccio, Bastia, or Calvi, in fact, any of the
coast-towns, is not to see Corsica. To get at the real characteristics
of the country it is necessary to penetrate into the mountains, bury
oneself in the forests of the Coscione of San Pietro di Verde, or
to ascend the heights of the Incudine, Mount Cintho, or San Angelo.

On the slopes of these mountains are remote hamlets where the
people change almost as little as the eternal hills themselves, and
higher yet, towards the summits, are nomad, pastoral tribes with
special customs, which have not altered for centuries.

Corsica does not reveal itself to the traveller who merely crosses
the island ; manners and customs escape him, and he even misses
many of the sublimest landscapes.

Now, if one could only become a shepherd for a few weeks,
pass beyond the forest-border and climb to the cloud-swept heights,

176

where the eye may roam over the distant sea to the far-away outline of Asinara and the blue undulations of Sardinia, life up there, methought, would be a natural joy! To be awakened of a morning by the sound of the goat-bells, to walk the heights in the first freshness of dawn, and, from some lofty rock, see the sun majestically upspringing from the Tyrrhenian Sea. To stand thus, as it were, on an island in the sea of mist covering the lowlands, to be alone with the sun and infinite space, would be to have the sensation of being the firstborn in a new world.

The day is spent, perhaps, with a man, known in the lower world as a bandit. Such fine moral distinctions do not hold on this lofty plane, and you pass many hours very pleasantly in his company, having a stray shot at a stag or a wild boar, or stopping at a crystal stream to catch a trout, which, with a portion of roast kid, a draught of milk, and delicious *broccio*, will form the evening meal. And when the moon rises and the distant baying of farm dogs answers the roaring of the stags, pipes are lit, and you lie comfortably round the fire, while the shepherds recite whole stanzas of Tasso or Ariosto, and tell strange stories of wild superstition. Then, when your eyelids grow heavy, you wrap yourself about in your *pelone* or goat-skin cloak, on a bed of beech leaves, and sleep soundly on the lap of mother-earth, with your feet outstretched to the wood fire.

I made my first ascent of Mount Incudine in August. The nights were still warm, and there was every prospect of obtaining a clear view.

I was awakened before daybreak by a handful of gravel rattling against my window, and, on looking out, could just discern the mules, hitched to the broken arches of the old cloister, attended by the guide, who had his gun on his shoulder and a long fishing line in his hand. We were well provided with guides, for a young man from the village volunteered to accompany us for the mere pleasure of the expedition, while Peretti, the innkeeper, and his two sons also formed part of the escort.

Besides myself, there were also the doctor of Zicavo, and the advocate Bucchini, his brother. Both were rather late in arriving, for in Corsica, as in the Balearic Isles, what George Eliot describes as " fine, old-fashioned leisure " is not yet banished, and nothing is undertaken without due preparation and consideration, not even getting out of bed.

The sun had been up some time, when the cavalcade started, followed by a sumpter mule carrying provisions for two or three days, a very necessary part of one's equipment for an expedition to the mountains, where food is hard to obtain, while the appetite is sharpened by the bracing air.

Taking a short cut, we climbed an extraordinarily steep ascent, where even the rocks seemed only held in position by the twisted roots of the giant chestnuts. Having surmounted this, we regained the road, and a few moments later the falls of Camera flashed through the foam clouds, in the gorge beneath. In strong contrast with this luminous apparition, we next crossed the entrance to the savage gorge of Siccia Porco, an arid avalanche of boulders, and soon afterwards entered the chestnut forest, where the sunlight filtered through the leaves, and gave the trunks of the trees and the moss-grown rocks the sheen of green velvet.

On leaving the forest, still following the bridle-track, we crossed a bare plateau, whence we saw sparrow-hawks circling against the clouds, or gazed to the blue horizon of the distant sea. Beyond this, again came the forest, though, at this height, the chestnut and the ilex, or evergreen oak, had given place to the beech and the hardy English oak.

Here a characteristically Corsican incident occurred. We had just crossed a rocky torrent in the heart of the forest, and I was riding in front with the doctor, when five men suddenly appeared on the other side of a clearing. At the same moment we heard the click of the triggers, and all five levelled their guns at us. But, seeing that we were peaceable, they soon lowered the weapons, and advanced in silence, passing us by, without even the greeting customary between all wayfarers. The incident befell so quickly that we might have been shot, almost without being aware of it.

"What are they?" I inquired of the doctor. "Why did they aim at us?"

"I don't know," said Bucchini. "They are strangers to the district, and, as you saw, act instinctively on the defensive. Depend upon it they have serious reason to do so."

At midday, when the birds were silent and even in the shadow of the dense verdure there was no trace of coolness, we alighted at the humble hermitage of San Pietro, where we lunched on the greensward, seated round a spring at the foot of a beech tree.

The chapel of San Pietro was built about the year 1500, in reparation for a *vendetta* perpetrated on this spot. The parish priest of Zicavo says mass there every year on the 1st of August, and the shepherds and villagers assemble to dance *sub tegmine fagi* to the sound of pastoral instruments.

After leaving San Pietro, we entered the virgin forest, which has never been violated by the woodcutter's axe, and the recesses of which are known only to the bandit or the wild animals, which make it their lair. Not one young tree was to be seen : all were veterans, with long grey locks of lichen and mantles of rusty moss covering their knotty limbs. We wound in and out among the huge trunks and interlacing roots, like a small procession of larvæ. In some places, whole companies of these forest veterans had succumbed to old age, and their white skeletons littered the ground, which was deeply indented by the shock of the falling trunks, though the roots still gripped the boulders, like the talons of gigantic vultures. Dead silence reigned in this vegetable mausoleum, and it was with an instinctive breath of relief that we came out on the bare ground beyond, though it was but to exchange the dreariness of the untenanted woods for a desolation of stone and naked rock. Every crest and boss of the soaring heights in front of us seemed a landslip. On a denuded slope strewn with rounded boulders were a few huts, scarcely distinguishable in colour from the stones among which they were built.

"Yonder is Frauletto," said the old guide, pointing with his finger.

I looked, but saw nothing save the empty sky and naked rocks
—a wild waste place of implacable solitude, dominated by the bare
summit of the Incudine.   Below this, a few black specks slowly
moving among the *débris* indicated the presence of the flocks, and
at length I made out the cabins of the shepherds, the last inhabitants
of these summits.

Here, in the silence of the mountains, they support the torrid
sun of August and the sudden chills of September, fighting the
fevers which they frequently contract in the unhealthy plains below,
whither they are driven back by the frosts at the beginning of October. I have seen the mountain saeters of Norway and the "black-houses" of the Hebrides, but never a more miserable human dwelling than the huts of these Corsican shepherds ; and the romantic picture I had formed of their free life with wild nature, was soon chilled by contact with the stern reality.

Shepherds' Huts.

Inside the huts, the accommodation consists of a smoky hearth,
a bed of beech leaves, and a few blocks of unhewn wood to serve as
seats.   The walls are constructed of rough stones, between which
the wind whistles.   The roof, which is of planks, is covered by pieces
of rock to prevent it being lifted off by the northerly gales.   The few
household utensils, for cooking milk or making cheese, are hung from
a tree trunk in the centre of the *stazzo* (hut).

As in former days, the shepherds sleep on the ground before the
hearth, with a log for a pillow, and their *pelones* for coverlet.   Their

Shepherds on the Move.

dark clothes are woven of lambs' wool by their wives. The food of these patriarchal families consists of milk, *polenta*, and rye or barley bread, made in large quantities in advance, and dried in the oven to such hardness that it has to be soaked in water before being eaten.

The shepherds of the Coscione have retained all the beliefs and customs of their ancestors. Hospitality is regarded as a duty, and they are affable and serene in manner. The habitual contemplation of vast landscapes and mountain loneliness has rendered their expression grave and their look meditative, as if they, in their own way, had found the "inward eye, which is the bliss of solitude."

A Shepherd.

Their minds are haunted by innumerable superstitions. At eventide, by the glowing embers, the children listen with wide-open eyes to strange stories of hobgoblins (*folleti*), and shudder when they hear the casual cry of a passing *mal achelo*, or bird of evil omen, or the wail of the wind through the creviced walls.

The shepherds have great faith in omens. The appearance of weasels foretells rain, and a certain bellowing of the cattle is a sign of snow. Much is also signified by the stains and texture of the shells of the eggs laid by the fowls.

When disease breaks out among the animals, the shepherds hurry to Zicavo to obtain the key of the oratory of Saint Roch, which they throw in the midst of the flock, and the epidemic instantly ceases. They also sprinkle the cattle with scrapings from the church walls.

Monday is unlucky, and no sales are ever effected on that day.

The women believe in the evil eye, and also attach a malefic influence to the praise of certain people. Children may thus be suddenly struck by mortal illnesses; and then they are censed with the smoke of burning olive branches, or palms blessed on Palm Sunday. In times of doubt, the shepherds cut the throat of a buck, a lamb, or a kid, and examine the shoulder-blade of the victim, with which they practise divination.

Near the forks of Asinao, a quasi-sacred mountain close to the Coscione, terminating in three gigantic rock spires, the ancients assembled one night in the time of the First Empire and immolated a kid. The augur, after long examination of the shoulder-blade, exclaimed, "A line of blood crosses the east side. Women will weep and many fathers will bid a last farewell to their children." Strangely enough the prophecy was soon realised.

All the shepherds are poets and musicians. At noon, when the sun beats hot upon the mountains, they give the flocks their *merezzare* (midday meal), and, retiring to the shade, recite Tasso and Ariosto, or improvise poems, which they sing to their lyres, or, in default of these, to the accompaniment of pan-pipes or bag-pipes.

The following are two verses, very popular among the shepherds, which bear not a little resemblance to the style of Ossian.

| | |
|---|---|
| *" Fra l'orror di notte tetra,* | " Through the horror of the mirk night |
| *E tra il sibilo dei venti,* | And the whistling of the wind, |
| *Mesto al suon di antica cetra* | With the sound of my ancient lyre, |
| *Io qui accoppio i miei lamenti;* | I accompany my laments; |
| *Ma tu dormi, ed io frattanto* | But thou sleepest, and I vainly |
| *Alzo invano all' aere il canto.* | Spend my songs on the air. |
| | |
| *" Se la notte fosse priva* | " If the night were deprived |
| *Delle sue fulgide stelle,* | Of its gleaming stars, |
| *Dio potrebbe, o cara diva,* | God would be able, O beloved goddess, |
| *Colle tue luci si belle* | With thy two beautiful eyes, |
| *Adornare in un momento* | To adorn, in one moment, |
| *D'altre stelle il firmamento."* | The sky with new stars." |

The shepherds are the protectors of the bandits, and provide them with food. During my stay at Zicavo, the gendarmes of the neighbourhood were constantly concentrating on the hermitage of San

The Ghastly Horseman.

Pietro, but without effecting a single capture, although forty bandits were known to be hiding in the solitudes of the Coscione.

After visiting Frauletto, we went to the shepherds' village at Palaghiole, where we saw cheese in process of manufacture. I was surprised at the cleanliness of these humble dwellings.

From Palaghiole we descended through some woods to the banks of a torrent, where I stopped to gather some flowers while my companions rode on. Making a short cut across some common land to overtake the party, I came upon a most extraordinary and ghastly spectacle. An old man dressed in an ample goat-skin cloak was mounted on a horse, which was shivering all over and appeared terrified. The old man's seat was rigid, his head was held high, his eyes were closed, and his face was ghastly pale. It was a corpse.

A forked twig fixed to the saddle upheld his chin, and cords and pieces of wood kept the body in position. Close behind this grisly apparition came a small escort of shepherds, who were taking the dead man to his native village for burial.

It appears that this is the only means of conveying a body across this rough region, which is impracticable for wheeled vehicles.

From the Coscione to Zicavo, or Fium' Orbo, even a hand litter can only be used for a portion of the way, and on the steep mountain tracks a horse must perforce be employed. The poor quadrupeds appear painfully aware of the nature of their burden, and, though they hasten their pace, never trot or gallop. They go through such an agony of fear, however, as to be quite exhausted and unfit for further service after one of such journeys. The shepherds notice that the horses always stop at the spots where the dead man himself was in the habit of pausing to rest.

The sun was setting when I rejoined my party, and we hastened on, up the steepest ascent we had yet climbed. There was no path, and we had to pick our way over loose boulders and fallen tree-trunks, through the deepening twilight of the forest. Darkness had completely closed in when we reached the spot chosen by the guide for our camping ground, which was on the extreme verge of the forest-line, at the foot of the summit of the Incudine. Enormous blocks of granite enclosed natural rooms, sheltered from the wind, with the star-strewn sky for a decorated ceiling, and after lighting a fire of brushwood and making a hasty meal, we lay in a circle with our feet to the embers, and were soon asleep.

The guide woke us an hour before dawn, and leaving our mules in charge of some boys, we quickly scaled the last height in time to see the sun rise. An icy wind chilled us to the bone when we reached the top; and the warm colours of day were welcome in a twofold sense. A vague glimmer in the east announced the uprising of the sun, and the distant sea was growing pale, before flushing rosy-red. Gradually, an indistinct line on the eastern horizon indicated the coast of Italy. Southward, Sardinia came full in view, like a raised map, and I could distinguish the Gennargentu and the peaks of Limbara. Close at hand rose the forks of Asinao, and Sartène and Bonifacio gleamed on the edge of the plain beyond. Behind us was Ajaccio. Then came Mounts Rotondo and Renoso, the bulk of which hid a large part of the island, but northward the eye roamed free to where Cape Corse cleaved the sea like a wedge.

While we were admiring the view we were joined by some of the shepherds from Palaghiole, accompanied by two other men, both of whom were armed to the teeth.

One of them especially attracted my attention. He was a man of small stature, but proud bearing, yet with a singularly devil-may-care expression. He was curling his slight moustache, while a cold smile, which just revealed his white teeth, seemed stereotyped on his face. But his eyes were not still for an instant; and as he stood alone on the topmost peak, scanning the vast prospect, not a detail seemed to escape his glance. He and the shepherds with him had come out to shoot *mouflon*, a sport both as exciting and as tedious as deer-stalking; and quick, accurate sight is as requisite to detect the animals as it is to aim at them.

The man, I learned subsequently, was the redoubted bandit Giovanni, friend and comrade of Rocchini, the brigand chief executed some years since at Sartène. The man who was with Giovanni was also a bandit, but of less account.

The Gorge of the Taravo.

Leaving the hunters to pursue their stalk, we returned to our mules, and proceeded to the "moving fields" of Castel Rinuccio. These fields, which cover a wide plateau, consist of a surface of fine turf several inches thick, resting upon water. The soil rocks at each step one takes upon it, and produces a feeling of dizziness which is by no means pleasant. But flocks pasture on the rich grass fearlessly, and even the hoofs of the mules do not sink in. By putting one's ear to the ground, one can hear the gurgling of the water underneath. The shepherds even cut holes in the turf, and net small trout, which they grill on heated stones and eat with butter.

A few days after my return to Zicavo, I made an excursion with my friends, the Abbatucci, to the river Taravo, which, after a tumultuous course down the mountains, glides calmly and dreamily through a wooded granite gorge, which is spanned by a bold arch. I passed many quiet hours by this solitary torrent, which, like a human life, after a stormy youth, finds itself moving contentedly in its appointed groove.

The long Corsican summer was coming to an end ; morning and evening mists crept through the valleys, and every torrent and watercourse was filled with storm-rains. When the household fires were lighted at early morning, the village was veiled by a blue haze, in which the houses seemed to float like phantom dwellings. The hearth, which has no chimney, is in the middle of the single room, in order that the rising heat may dry the chestnuts placed on a sort of gridiron laid across the rafters, and the smoke having no other exit, filters slowly through the interstices in the roof and walls.

The month of November came in softly, *novembre del oro*, as the people called it, bringing an abundant harvest of mast and chestnut. Of an evening the melancholy *scumbapio*, precursor of northerly gales and cold, howled about the roof-tree ; but the doors were snugly closed, the charcoal fires glowed cheerily, and by the light of resinous torches the folk gathered round the hearth to tell stories of bandits and historic wars, when the Corsicans rose in arms and hid in their forests, to preserve their independence.

It was at one of these gatherings that I heard the following story.

The bandits, who generally work in pairs, cement their partnership by a common crime, which forms an indissoluble bond between them. Two bandits were once wandering in the woods round Zicavo, when one of them requested his comrade, with whom he had only recently associated himself, to give proof of his fidelity by shooting the occupant of a neigh-

Going to the Well.

bouring house. The other did so and took to flight, hotly pursued by gendarmes, Being hard pressed, the man took refuge in a house in the village.

"I have just killed an enemy," said he; "the gendarmes are on my track, and I demand asylum."

The hour was late, but supper was prepared and the master of the house gave up his own bed to the fugitive.

The next day had worn to night, when the bandit was roused by his host, who said: "You must make haste to leave before daylight, in order that no one may see you!"

The bandit then rose and followed the master, but, before they parted, at a spot some distance from the village, the fugitive's entertainer said: "You asked for asylum, and I opened my house to you : you were hungry and thirsty, and I gave you to eat and drink : you were weary, and I gave you my bed : but . . . the man whom you killed yesterday was my brother. Flee, then, from my presence ; for now that you are no longer under my roof, I will pursue you with my hatred."

The murderer began to stammer excuses, but the other interrupted him with, " I give you an hour in which to escape. After that, we shall be enemies. Be on thy guard, as I will be on mine !" Such is the duty of hospitality in Corsica, stronger even than the law of vengeance.

The Ravine of Bocognano.

# CHAPTER IV.

A Witch.—The Light of Busso.—Another Brigand Story.—Corte.—The Genoese.—
Ghisoni.—The *Christe Eleison.*—The Passes of Inzecca.—Eternal Oblivion.

The Mill of Niolo.

I T was not without regret that I left Zicavo, where I had seen and heard so much that was interesting, and where the very rocks and trees had become like friendly faces.

But it is foolish to lose one's heart, whether to men or things ; for farewell must be said sooner or later, and it is tempting fate to add even "till we meet again."

One evening accordingly found me back at Ajaccio, and the next morning I was in the train with a ticket for Bocognano on the line to

194

Vizzavone. Had I not seen and admired the valley of the Taravo, Zicavo, and the Coscione, the scenery might have more interested me. As it was, I found it sad and depressing. On every side, I beheld only scorched mountain slopes, black gorges, and withered trees. In the direction of Vizzavone, the flanks of some of the hills were still smoking with forest fires ; others were grey and naked, and covered with grey ashes, which, at a distance, seemed like a leprous skin. The tragic gloom of the sky enhanced the desolation, and the blanched, distorted skeletons of the trees, scorched by fire and drenched by autumn rains, seemed to be writhing in mute agony.

At Bocognano, where I left the train, I walked for the entire day across arid summits, overlooking yawning gorges, beyond which mountain rolled upon mountain, till the distant heights were lost to view in a canopy of heavy clouds. Stray gleams of light broke through at intervals and irradiated the corrosive, chemical colouring of the rocks, or suddenly revealed the depths of a dark ravine.

For an instant, the summit of the Monte d'Oro suddenly appeared across a gap in the hills—a dazzling vision of snow against a corner of blue sky, above the black pine-clad valleys.

Then twilight gradually fell upon the land. Fires gleamed here and there among the mountains, and the red glow of the burning *makis* crept down the hills in serpentine lines like volcanic lava, while columns of dense smoke spread outwards and upwards towards the darkening sky.

I was belated on the foot hills of the Monte d'Oro. A few distant lights indicated Bocognano ; but I had lost my way.

At this juncture I was passed by an old woman, whose head was covered by a thick veil, though her fantastic profile was distinctly outlined against the sullen sunset light. I hailed her, and she stopped. Her hooked nose, hawk-like eyes, and emaciated hands, crooked and knotty like the talons of a bird of prey, gave her the appearance of one of Macbeth's witches wandering across the blasted heath. Her voice was a shrill, quick cry ; and when she raised her arm to point out the village in the depths below, her *mezzaro* shook in the breeze like the wings of some bird of night.

" Follow me, follow me ! " said she, coughing and trembling from
sheer senility, as she walked ahead down the steep narrow path.
She had gone but a few paces when she came to a standstill, saying,
" Yonder is Busso ! Look for a moment, and you will see !

I turned my eyes in the direction indicated, but could only just
distinguish a few white houses in the shadows. Presently, however,
a vague, pale radiance hovered in the air above the village, slowly
increased in volume
and intensity, and
then, all at once,
disappeared. A
few moments later,
the light began
again, waxing gra-
dually brighter, and
then going out as
before.

The old crone
blinked at me fur-
tively from the
corner of her eye.

" What is that
light ? " I asked.

She sat down on
a stone by the way-
side, sighed, and
told me the story.

The Witch.

" Once upon a time, there lived at Busso a very pious lord, who
kept a monk as chaplain, whose chief duty was to say prayers when
the lord returned from the chase. The lord listened devoutly, standing before the altar with his gun in his hand, while his hounds
kept the door. Ah ! He was a mighty huntsman ! One evening,
he was belated, chasing *mouflons* ; and when he reached the castle
the prayers had been said, and the monk was in bed. Furious with
rage, the lord rushed to the chaplain's room and striped his sword

through the priest's body. From that time, the monk returns each night to the village, wandering about with a lighted taper in his hand, searching for the site of the chapel in order to say mass, as he did in the time of the old lord."

All the time she was telling this legend, the light kept waxing and waning, and on the following day I made inquiries which proved that I was not the victim of a hallucination. Many other people have had their curiosity aroused by this nocturnal phenomenon, but none has ever been able to determine the exact spot whence the light proceeds ; for it fades away as the village is approached, and can only be seen from a distance.

The night was very thick, and I had some difficulty in keeping pace with the old woman, who seemed to glide quite noiselessly down the steep, stony way, and only betrayed her presence by coughs and sighs. She disappeared with almost magic suddenness, and I found myself at Bocognano, where the lights of the inn made a friendly band of light across the dark street.

I rediscovered my old woman next day, and she proved to be really a kind of sorceress from Corte, skilled in making decoctions to ward off the fever of malaria or induce the less obnoxious fever of love, and learned in exercising the evil eye. I made her sit for her portrait, though, like other birds of night, she dreaded the daylight, and blinked like an owl when I made her sit in the sun.

Pentica, near Bocognano, is celebrated for the exploits of the Bellacoscia band of brigands—true mountain kings, to whom a prefect of Corsica once paid his respects, as did likewise a brilliant man of letters and a well-known member of the French Chamber of Deputies. These bandits, in spite of the heroic legend which has grown round their name, were four times condemned to death for murder or other crimes, and their only distinguishing characteristic was that they managed to snap their fingers at the law for nearly fifty years.

Pentica is now occupied by gendarmes, and the refuge of the Bellacoscia is unknown ; at least, so it is said, though as every one in the country befriends the bandits, it is not likely that any one would profess to know where they are, or imperil their safety.

The following is the thrilling story told by a lieutenant, who sought to effect their capture :—

"Xavier Suzzoni, of Nogario, was sentenced to several years' penal servitude for manslaughter. Being desirous, on the completion of his sentence, of returning to live in Corsica, he asked the mayor of his commune to give him a certificate, stating that his return need not cause fear to any one ; but the mayor, knowing the man's bad disposition, refused. A few days later Suzzoni shot the official dead. He then took to the *makis*, murdered two of his relatives, and swore implacable hatred against Jean Battesti, mayor of Nogario, who had declared his distrust of the ruffian. Suzzoni was joined by the brothers Antoine and Jacques Bonetti, called Bellacoscia, of Bocognano.

"Jacques Bellacoscia and Suzzoni arrived one night at Nogario, and sent word to the mayor that two people wished to speak to him. Battesti suspected a ruse; but being a brave man, armed himself with a dagger and two pistols, and proceeded to the meeting-place. The bandits were followed by a huge dog, an animal which has since become almost legendary. When Battesti, after a trivial conversation, wished to depart, two rifles were levelled at his head, and he was ordered to march in front of his enemies. He had no resource but to obey, and all three proceeded towards Mount Venaco, close to Pentica. On arriving near Corte, where Battesti had a brother, a parish priest, the brigands told a woman to inform the priest that the mayor was in their hands, and would only be released for a ransom of £120. Such a sum could not be collected in a moment, and the brigands and their prisoner waited forty-eight hours, at the end of which time they had exhausted their provisions, and were worn out by fatigue. Jacques Bellacoscia then ordered the dog to go and fetch a goat from a flock which was grazing on top of the mountain. The dog ran off, and soon returned with a young kid, which was killed, skinned, and eaten raw, without bread. On the evening of the second day, the woman returned with the ransom, and Battesti, being released, went straight to Corte and warned the police.

" As commanding officer at Vivario, I was informed of the crime, and immediately started in pursuit, with seven men. Supposing that the brigands had crossed the pass of Vizzavone, in order to reach Pentica, over the Monte d'Oro, I had this passage guarded. It was the depth of winter, and there was much snow. In fact, we were almost perishing from cold, when the famous dog arrived, acting as scout, and, having scented us, warned his masters by furious barking. As the brigands could not cross the mountains deep in snow, except by the gap of Manganello, between the Monte d'Oro and the Monte Rotondo, I decided to reach the spot before the bandits and wait for them. But this idea was frustrated by the enormous snowdrifts, and we risked our lives only to reach the gap a few minutes after the brigands.

" On the 2nd of January, having received information of the bandits' hiding-place, I started off at nightfall, with four men, carrying a week's provisions, and arrived at midnight at the barracks of Bocognano, where we waited in hiding till the following night. Thence we were guided by a man of the village to the summits of Sico and Tasso, near Pentica. There we camped in the snow till January 7th, when, on emerging at daybreak from the cave in which we had sought shelter, I heard the baying of a dog. At nine o'clock we heard a rustling in the bushes. It was a wild boar which the dog was chasing. We cautiously followed, and, two hours later, saw two men sneaking through the forest, and, a moment later, the smoke of a camp-fire rising above the trees. We hurried on, and soon came upon three men sitting round a fire, with their guns on their knees and a dog by their side. They were our four enemies. We at once began to surround them, but the dog signalled our presence by a sharp, dry bark. The brigands leaped to their feet, one of them exclaiming, ' *Sangue de la Madona !* ' saw my men, and fired. We replied with a volley.

" Being too low down to see well, I jumped on the trunk of a tree, and perceived one of the brigands making off to the mountain.

I levelled my rifle, but he hid behind a rock. Another bandit followed. I aimed again, fired, and saw him fall. The first brigand seized him by the hand, and, still under cover of a rock, tried to lift him. I fired two bullets, hitting him on the cheek and the right arm.

He dropped his comrade, w h o, struck by a ball, w h i c h  h a d entered the right ear and gone out by the left, was stone dead, and took to flight with his brother Jacques, at the same time setting the dog upon me. Not having properly reloaded, I shouted to my men, 'Fire on the dog! Fire on the dog!' One of the gendarmes, seeing my danger, rose up from his ambush, and the dog rushed upon him only to receive the muzzle of the rifle full in the chest and be blown to pieces. The man whom I had killed proved to be the notorious Suzzoni ; but the t w o brothers, Bellacoscia, made good their escape to the mountain fastnesses, where it was useless to follow them."

The Gaffori House.

Such is the narrative of the origin of the famous Bellacoscia brigands. When I left Bocognano the weather had cleared up, and

I took the diligence to Corte, the road to which is an almost unbroken descent. The driver of the diligence gave his horses their heads, and the journey was one dizzy whirl downwards, along the edge of precipices, round sharp corners, and neck-and-neck with the rushing mountain torrents, till, out of breath and with reeling brains, we pulled up at the foot of a short hill, and climbed to the village of San Pietro, where a second descent, skirting the shoulders of a mountain, brought us suddenly into Corte.

Corte is one of the quaintest towns in Corsica, with its gun-powder-grey houses clustering round the steep, vitrified rock, on which rises the ancient citadel. The place looks as if it had been but recently besieged. Many of the houses are little more than ruins, from the cracked stone walls of which the charred timber frames project like broken sword-blades, while the unglazed, shutter-less windows resemble yawning shot-wounds.

One of them, the *Maison Gaffori*, which is still occupied, is simply riddled with the shots from Genoese blunderbusses. In 1746 General Gaffori chased the Genoese from the city and invested them in the citadel. Through the perfidy of a nurse, they had captured the general's little son, and, displaying the child on the ramparts, they threatened to decapitate him, should the citadel be assaulted. Un-deterred by this, Gaffori continued the attack, and the garrison eventually capitulated, without, however, carrying out their threat of killing the child.

Four years later, in the absence of the general, the Genoese laid siege to his house; but his heroic wife threatened to blow up the building rather than surrender, and managed to hold out until her husband returned. Not long afterwards, however, General Gaffori was assassinated by his own brother, corrupted by Genoese gold. The widow led her son, the same child who had been exposed on the ramparts of the citadel, in front of the dead body, and made him take an oath to avenge his father's death. He was then only twelve years old ; but he remembered, and when he was grown up fulfilled his oath.

Such was one of the bloody dramas enacted at Corte during the occupation by the Genoese, who were so detested that, in 1729, the girls of the town swore never to marry as long as the enemy defiled the soil of the country ; in order, as they said, not to bear slaves as children.

Even now, the very name of the Genoese is cursed ; and several Corsicans repeated to me, with emphasis, the words of Dante,—

> " *Ah !  Genovesi, uomini diversi,*
> *D'ogni costume e pien d'ogni magagna,*
> *Perchè non siete voi dal mondo spersi !* " . . .

By a singular coincidence, this warrior-house of Gaffori, the scars on which are religiously preserved by the general's descendants who occupy it, was once the residence of the father and mother of Napoleon the Great, and it was probably between these walls riddled with shot, that Mme. Lætitia found herself about to become the mother of the soldier son who was to fill the world with his name.

Corte is surrounded on all sides by lofty summits, bare mountain crests, and scarped rock-needles, overhanging wild ravines, two of which are threaded by savage torrents, the Tavignano and the Restonica, whose pale green waters roll over blocks of polished marble, white as snow.

Having received an invitation to visit my friend M. Bianconi at Ghisoni, I left Corte one night by diligence for Vivario, the nearest station to Ghisoni. We reached Vivario at half-past four in the morning. The diligence stopped, set me down, and drove on, leaving me standing alone at the foot of a flight of stone steps, leading to a closed door, above which hung a dried branch rustling in the wind. That branch, which was the sign of the inn, and the twinkling stars, seemed the only animate objects in the chill loneliness of the waning night.

I picked up a stone, and rapped with it on the door. A few moments later, I heard heavy footsteps, the lock was turned, and the door opened. I entered a miserable hovel, lighted by a candle, which the innkeeperess held in her hand. Setting this down, she kindled a fire of faggots on the hearth, sitting by which, I dozed uneasily till dawn.

When I awoke, a few men were sitting at the table, drinking black coffee and cheap brandy, and the room was full of the acrid smoke of bad Corsican tobacco. They were Sardinians and Italians from Lucca, engaged as workmen on the railway. At daybreak flocks of goats passed, on their way to pasturage ; and shortly afterwards, I was told that a carriage had been engaged to convey me to Ghisoni.

As I left Vivario, I could not help noticing its primitive belfry, which is nothing but a plane tree, the bells being hung to transverse beams laid across the branches, with the ropes hanging down to the ground.

The road to Ghisoni sharply rises to the pass of Sorba, the head of which is some 4,200 feet above sea-level. On either side are dense pine forests, the trees growing to an immense height, the stems straight as pillars, though the branches are torn and twisted by the mountain winds, which rustle through the needles with a sound like that of falling waters. The descent on the opposite side of the pass is still through forest, but the pines soon give place to chestnuts, and the air grows milder.

Ghisoni lies in a sort of funnel, formed by the Sorba and a range of mountains, the serrated ridge of which recalls the splintered outline of the Cuchullins in Skye. Unlike the other mountains of Corsica, the nakedness of these Ghisoni hills is unrelieved by so much as a blade of grass. Grim and severe, the precipices and pinnacles rise abruptly from the valley, like the jagged outline of an iceberg. Livid or purple, according to the slant at which they reflect the light, the rocks have a primeval aspect, which is almost terrifying. Vertical fissures divide peak from peak, and the wildest peak of them all bears the strange title, *Christe Eleison*, " Christ, have mercy ! "

In revolutionary times a persecuted priest is said to have sought refuge in a cave at the foot of the highest crag, where he was sustained by the shepherds, who came in fear and trembling to hear the prohibited mass, which he used to celebrate with a rock for altar, and mountain and sky for church.

An adjacent peak bears the complementary title of *Kyrie Eleison,* " Lord, have mercy ! "

When out walking with M. Bianconi, on the evening of my arrival at Ghisoni, the quiet of the country road was suddenly broken by a formidable rumbling of heavy traffic, accompanied by the tinkling of myriad mule bells, and the outlandish oaths of Corsican carters.

The "Christe Eleison."

Presently, by the yellow glare of resinous torches, which made strange play of light and shade in the forest aisles, appeared a string of carts, each with a team of twelve or fifteen mules, bringing timber from the forest of Marmano, on their way to the passes of Inzecca, whence the wood is taken to Ghisonacce, there to be embarked on Italian vessels.

Early on the morrow we ourselves visited these same defiles of Inzecca, which are a series of narrow gorges where the road follows a precipice overhanging a torrent.

Leaving Ghisoni, we crossed a picturesque Genoese bridge, spanning a clear stream, which reflected the stern escarpment of the *Christe Eleison*, and soon reached the gorge of the Fium'Orbo, which

The Pass of Inzecca

has hewn out a course for itself through the solid rock, the surface of which is planed and polished by the action of the water. The gorge grew narrower and wilder as we advanced, and the sheer cliffs on either hand were fringed with pine trees, some seedlings of which had effected a lodgment between the rocks in the very bed of the torrent. Further on, we opened up a valley, where a picturesque village gleamed on the forest-clad heights; and after a sudden and unexpected glimpse of the distant sea, we entered the narrowest of the passes of Inzecca.

The road was a mere ledge along the side of an unscaleable precipice, overlooking a giddy abyss, at the bottom of which the Fium'Orbo wrestled for its course with an opposing army of fallen rocks. The path was so narrow and the height so terrifying that, at several places, our horses refused to move.

While we were in the defile the timber waggons arrived, and we watched them one after the other turn the elbow of the pass, where the angle is so sharp that the planks in turning actually overhang the abyss.

The story is told of a woman, who fell asleep reclining upon the timber, and being awakened by the sudden movement of the wood and the shouts of the carters as the corner was turned, found herself, as it were, suspended in mid-air, and died of fright on the spot.

To return to Ghisoni, the houses of the hamlet are grouped together in one spot at the bottom of the valley, unlike most other Corsican villages, which are generally scattered on the heights.

Another curious difference between Ghisoni and other places is in its burial customs. At Ghisoni the more well-to-do people bury their dead on their property, leaving a corner of land uncultivated for this purpose. The graves are marked by a wooden cross, but ever afterwards the place of sepulture is shunned by the survivors, who even take the greatest care to avoid mentioning the name of the deceased, as if they vowed the dead to eternal oblivion.

When any one is seriously ill, or believed to be in danger of death, the priest has the bell rung to summon the people to the chapel; and when all are assembled, and provided with lighted candles, the *viaticum* is conveyed in procession to the house of the sick, the people chanting funeral hymns as they go.

Whilst the priest is administering the last sacraments, they stand or kneel at the door, and recite litanies and the prayers for the dying. Then the priest, standing on the threshold, asks pardon on behalf of the dying for any offences he or she may have committed against those assembled, and at the same time forgives them for their trespasses against the sick person. The people bow the knee, and afterwards return to the church, singing the *Te Deum*.

This ceremony, imposing though it be, generally produces a disastrous effect on the sick, who, after so much solemnity in speeding their passage, naturally give themselves up for lost. Nor are they encouraged to live by seeing the members of their own family making ready for the funeral, ordering the coffin, and preparing the new grave-clothes. It is rarely, indeed, that the unfortunate sick person, worn out by physical weakness, can rally against the mental depression caused by such an extravagance of emotion.

When the deceased, as generally happens, is a member of the confraternity of penitents, his grave-clothes are all white, and he is followed to the grave by all the members of the confraternity likewise dressed in white, with their heads enveloped in a cowl.

It is impossible to picture a more sepulchral spectacle than a funeral procession of these masked penitents, as they pass like white phantoms, chanting a lugubrious *Miserere*, alike for their own sins and for those of the dead.

Evisa.

## CHAPTER V.

A Wild Gorge.—The Bandit and his Friend.—Niolo.—A Village of Giants.—A Blood-feud.—Woman in Corsica. — Along the West Coast. — Evisa.—The Spelunca.—The Forest of Aïtone.—A Greek Village.—The Pope and the Brigand.

M Y object in visiting Corsica was to study the remoter regions, where the people and the landscape have the charm of originality. Thus, my notice of the coast towns in these pages is necessarily brief and inadequate.

Bastia, for instance, whither I proceeded after leaving Ghisoni, is in reality no longer a Corsican town. Its inhabitants are polished and modern, lacking even the sturdy independence of manner which one meets at Ajaccio. The district round the town is charmingly pretty, but quite conventional. Calvi, *civitas semper fidelis*, is more picturesque, situated as it is on a rocky promontory fairly bristling with thorny cactus.

But after all, neither of these towns can be called Corsican, and one morning found me again in a carriage at Corte, on my way to Niolo, and the lost valleys beyond the grim defile, called the *Escala de Santa Regina*.

209                                    14

This gorge is even wilder, if less dangerous, than the Pass of Inzecca.

The cliffs rise to inconceivable heights, cleft into gorges and crevices, whose sides are sheer precipices. The hard, primitive rock, granite, dolomite, or porphyry, is dark or flame-coloured, and glitters like mica in the sun. The trees clinging to the sides seem to grasp the lips of the ledges, like the hands of a terrified mountaineer saving himself from falling. Massive boulders stand here and there like sentries, some proudly erect, others leaning over, as if fascinated by the deeps below. At the bottom of the gorge, along a bed whose whiteness contrasts strangely with the wild colour of the rocky walls, runs the Golo. The guardian stream of such a scene ought, one would think, to be a foaming, roaring torrent, or else, because at this time of year the springs were dry, a thin rivulet of dripping water. The stream was neither, but just a placid, almost currentless band of clear green water, sleeping on a stainless bed.

But 'ware such deceptive calmness! On certain days, or rather at certain hours, when the sky is dark and the peaks are swathed in mist, all the fissures of the mountains transform themselves into cataracts, and the rocks themselves crumble like melting snows. The stream becomes a monster, and its swollen, turgid waters hurtle down the glen with nameless clamour.

On New Year's day, 1888, eleven persons were seated at table in one of the houses of the tiny hamlet of Santa Regina, which had been built under the superintendence of the Board of Roads and Bridges. It was six o'clock in the evening. Rain had been falling for four-and-twenty hours, and the Golo was in spate. Suddenly a cyclone broke over the mountains. A huge landslide fell upon the house, and hurled it into the midst of the raging torrent, amid rolling boulders and waves of mud.

When the tempest subsided, a search was made for the victims. Six bodies were found, but the remaining five had disappeared.

I questioned an old woman, who was baking bread near the ruins of the house.

Tears came into her eyes.

" I was down there, on the other side of the road," said she, " and
I had not time to see. Everything was carried off in a whirlwind,
with a terrible roar. Ah! It was a judgment! They were bad
people and had bad books. God struck them, and their bodies will
never be found."

The carriage road is of quite recent construction, and before
it was built, the only means of reaching Niolo was by a goat-track,
which followed the line of the cliffs. At one place, the path consists
of eighty-four little zigzags, forming a sort of staircase to the
summits above, whence is derived the name Escala de Santa
Regina.

Like every other wild place in Corsica, the gorge has a brigand
story. It was here that the bandits Massoni and Arrighi were killed
by gendarmes. At daybreak the gendarmes surrounded a ravine
in which the brigands were concealed. A falling stone revealed
their presence, and the bandits fired a pistol, but without effect. The
gendarmes replied, and Massoni fell, mortally wounded. Feeling
that his end was near, he called the gendarme who had wounded him.

" Listen," said the brigand. "I pardon you my death ; you only
did your duty. Help me to do mine . . . place me in the sunlight,
lay a stone under my head, say the prayers for the dying . . . "

And he forthwith expired.

His companion, Arrighi, managed to hold out for three more
days, but in attempting to make his escape at midnight from the
cave in which he had taken refuge, was struck by two bullets,
though not before he had killed a brigadier and seriously wounded
a gendarme.

The Marshal Pasqualaggi followed the wounded brigand, and
summoned him to surrender.

The two men were acquainted, and even distantly connected.
The brigand, hiding behind the rocks in the darkness, called out
to the officer, " I don't want to surrender, yet I know I'm a lost
man. You were once my friend, and since I must be killed, I
would rather it were by your hand."

" As you like ! " said the officer, touched by this appeal.

" On one condition."

" Well ! "

" I have in my girdle one hundred and thirty-seven francs. You must take them. Go to the priest and ask him to say twenty masses for my soul ; pay him, and give the rest of the money to my family. You promise ? "

" I promise ! "

" Thanks ! Now, kill me ! "

" Yes ! But I don't see you ! "

" Wait, then. The moon will rise in an hour. When it does I will show myself."

Pasqualaggi, fearing a ruse, kept his eyes fixed on the bandit's hiding-place, but, worn out by the day's fatigue and the strain of keeping his attention fixed on one spot, gradually fell into a doze.

When the moon rose, the light disclosed Pasqualaggi standing on guard, with his carbine raised to his shoulder, but motionless as a statue.

A man lifted himself wearily from the rocks, and presently a voice asked,—

" Well, Pasqualaggi, aren't you ready ? "

" Here I am ! " exclaimed the officer, starting.

" Then fire ! "

The bullet sped on its mission, and the brigand fell dead.

The Escala de Santa Regina takes a long time to traverse ; but it grows less wild as one proceeds, the mountains decreasing in height and the precipices becoming less steep.

Night fell as we emerged on a difficult road, and, under the starry sky, soon saw stretching before us a wide strath embraced by undulating hills. It was the highland valley of Niolo, which lies like a saucer in the heart of the mountains. We lay that night at the village of Calacuccia, and early next day started on mule-back to visit Calasima, the highest village in Corsica.

The autumn sunlight was mellowed by a gauze-like mist, through which the mountain cascades shone like molten metal.

At Albertacce we mounted a steep track and reached the chaos of fallen rocks through which the path to Calasima threaded a maze-like way. The village itself clung, as it were, to the slope of a mountain, dominated by the lofty crests of Mount Cinto.

A picturesque mill stood by the side of a streamlet. It had been constructed at small cost, being little more than a heap of unmortared stones, a trough made of a hollowed tree trunk, and a wheel which turned as it listed. But the aridity of the walls was hidden by trailing ivy and festoons of clematis.

Our arrival was an event. The whole village turned out in a body to welcome us. No one ever visits this forgotten hamlet, lost in the midst of almost inaccessible summits; and the people seemed unable sufficiently to show their delight at seeing us. The noise was deafening, and my two

Woman spinning at Calasima.

companions and I had as much hand-shaking to perform as an American president.

The first transports over, and the women having returned to their distaffs and spindles, we walked down the street escorted by all the children and dogs in the place.

Men sitting by the doorways rose as we passed, and politely raised their caps. Their stature was surprising and their aspect full of energy; and all had fair hair and blue eyes.

Calasima was a village of giants, but of what race?

Much has been written and said concerning the origin of the

Corsicans, but no satisfactory decision has ever been reached. It has been alleged that they are of Italian origin. There is certainly a resemblance of language, but an examination of the character of Corsican physiognomy, and, above all, of manners and customs, soon disposes of the idea.

Except in language, there is little in common between Corsica and Italy, and there is, moreover, a traditional antipathy between the two races.

Ever since the Genoese occupation Italy has been the hereditary enemy of the Corsicans.

The epithet Lucchese (man of Lucca), applied to all Italians, whether from Rome, Florence, Lucca, or any other part of the peninsula, is an affront so serious that a true Corsican can never pardon it.

If a Corsican employs on his estate six labourers, of whom two are Italians, he will say, " I employ four men and two Lucchese." He will never say, " I employ six men, or six persons."

A girl who has had a misfortune, is comforted with the proverb :

> " *Alla fin di tanti guai*
> *Un Lucchese n' manca mai.*"

This saying, which applies also to ugly girls who cannot get a Corsican husband, may be rendered by, " Whatever you may lack, you'll never be at a loss for a Lucca-man ! "

In certain mountainous regions, like the Niolo, which were cut off from all communication with the outer world, the inhabitants are of a particular type, which is said to present every analogy to that of the ancient Goths.

When I saw at Calasima men over seven feet in height, obliged to stoop in order to enter their houses, I was simply stupefied. But they were fine objects to look at, as they walked down the street with proudly raised heads, wearing a heavy goat-skin cloak which I could hardly lift. I expected them to lift me up in their hands and examine me like a new Gulliver.

We entered a house where several men were playing cards. They

rose to their feet, and
nearly every man's head
touched the c e i l i n g.
The tallest man in Cala-
sima was absent, but I
saw him next day at
Calacuccia; he measured
seven feet four and a
half inches. One of the
card - players, however,
reached the respectable
height of seven feet two
inches. He, I learned,
in consequence of a *ven-
detta*, much to his credit
as a Corsican, had been
sentenced, and took to
the forest to escape the
law, but, as a matter of
fact, he spends most of
his time at home.

Ten gendarmes came
one day to arrest him,
but, as they rapped at
the door, he jumped out
of the window, rushed
in the midst of them,
knocked several of them
over, and, before they
recovered from their
surprise, escaped to the
mountain. Now he is
left in peace, being
much feared, as he com-

A Giant of Calasima.

bines Herculean strength with marvellous agility. The *vendetta* was

wiped out by the usual ceremony of making peace between the families at feud and consecrating friendship at the church of Calasima.

Wandering in the vicinity of the village, we were shown the burial-place of Massoni and two men of his band, on the slope of a mountain far from the cemetery.

Such a place was meet for the last resting-place of a brigand.

The bandit sleeps alone near the bare peaks, towards the lowering clouds, laid to rest in rough soil overgrown with brambles on the bank of a wild torrent, whose waters dash over blood-coloured porphyry rocks with a savage murmur, full of menace and eternal imprecation.

When we left Calasima, the name of which means in Corsican, " Near the summit," every one turned out to bid us farewell, and even when we reached the bottom of the hill, we could still hear voices far up the height calling " Good-bye."

We reached Calacuccia at twilight.

Several natives of the district came to spend the evening at the inn ; and listening to their conversation, I heard more stories of brigandage and *vendetta.*

The chief personage in the valley of the Niolo appeared to be a brigand named Capa, who enjoyed such general esteem that even the gendarmes did not interfere with him, as his capture would certainly entail bloody reprisals, which it was the interest of the authorities to avoid.

Brave and sober, Capa was very different from the majority of the men of his trade. When pressed by hunger, he would enter the first house he came to, and ask for a little bread and cheese and a glass of water ; for he never drank wine. He had no companion, and, like all brigands of mark, lived alone.

Another bandit once sought to enter into partnership with him.

" Do you fear hunger and thirst ? " asked Capa. " Do you drink wine ? "

" Certainly I do," said the other, proffering his gourd.

Capa waved the beverage away.

"Do you smoke?" he inquired.

"Yes, here's tobacco, and a flint and steel and tinder, at your service."

"Listen," said Capa, shaking his head. "I can't have a companion; for he who is with me must endure hunger and thirst, and avoid wine and tobacco. They are dangerous luxuries to a bandit. Our manner of living does not allow us to become the slaves of any habit. I sleep on the bare ground with a stone for pillow. I brave the hurricane and the snow, the freezing wind and the burning sun. I wander for days like a being accursed, through mournful solitudes, in peril of ambuscades, flying from my pursuers and stalking my enemies."

In the defile of Santa Regina, there is a plain cross by an abyss on the side of the road, marking the spot where Capa watched for weeks, with the patience of a Red Indian, for two of his enemies, till he shot them dead from an ambush in the rocks.

The most celebrated feud of the Niolo was that which formerly subsisted between the families of Leca and Tartarola. The dispute had already resulted in some twenty murders on one side and the other, when the following incident occurred:—

One evening, Leca was returning home with two relatives from an ambuscade, where they had been watching for some of their enemies. In order to reach their village, they had to pass through the hamlet inhabited by the Tartarola.

When but a short distance from the houses, Leca suddenly feared a trap and informed his companions. They did not share his fears, and continued to go forward; but Leca, feeling certain of the fate awaiting him, took a desperate resolution. Going boldly into the hamlet, he knocked at the door of Tartarola, the leader of his enemies; and even as the door opened, he heard the rattle of musketry in the distance.

"Who's there?" cried Tartarola.

"Leca, your enemy, who comes to ask hospitality for the night."

So saying, Leca passed his dagger, pistol, and gun through the door, to show his confidence in the loyalty of his adversary.

"Come in!" said Tartarola.

The hereditary enemy was then greeted as a guest. He refused to accept any food, and took a seat by the fire, where he and Tartarola watched through the night, chatting amicably on every subject except the one of their mutual enmity.

In the morning Tartarola, after warning his people to abstain from hostilities, accompanied Leca to the outskirts of the hamlet, and, as he pressed his hand in token of farewell, said, "Now we are again enemies as before; and when we meet again, guns or daggers must be our greeting."

Leca then returned home, to find that his fears had been too well founded, and that the shots which he had heard as he knocked at the door of Tartarola's house had been the death-warrants of his two companions.

Niolo was formerly notorious for its *vendette*, but nowadays such feuds are rare, though the people are still ready enough with their rifles.

The annual affair held at Casamaccioli on the 8th of September is always a scene of great disorder, and a strong force of *gendarmerie* has to be sent to maintain order and prevent the frequent battles between the inhabitants. This year there was an attempt to murder, but when the culprit was about to be arrested, thirty muskets were levelled at the officers of the law. The mayor then intervened, and, as the majesty of the law had to be vindicated, at least in appearance, ordered the arrest to be maintained, but at the same time promised to set the prisoner at liberty as soon as possible.

The people of the Niolo are almost entirely pastoral, and the shepherds, like those of the Coscione, go down from the mountains to winter in the plains, but do not take their wives and children, who pass the snow season in the villages weaving cloth and linen, and making clothes for the family.

The Corsican woman occupies a position of real inferiority. Her life may be summed up in three words—work, submission, and sacrifice. Her youth is brief, and her age premature; and she knows nothing of the intermediate stage, which in women of other

countries is usually the period of greatest activity and usefulness
and maybe of most genuine happiness.

Nevertheless she does not appear to rebel against these conditions. From her childhood she is inured to toil, which only ceases
with death. In Corsica the woman does not even sit at table, her

Corsican Woman and Girl.

part being simply to prepare the meal and wait on others. In
some households even two qualities of bread are baked, the better
kind for the man and the inferior quality for the remainder of the
family.

In the division of inheritances, the daughters invariably admit
the right of the sons to the larger share ; and public opinion would

be against the woman who claimed more, even if the father had devised his property to his children in equal parts.

But it must be admitted that, if the son gains more advantage, he never shrinks from accepting the duties and burdens thereby entailed upon him. He takes the place of the father, has his sisters educated, and gives them a dowry. He often, indeed, remains single in order better to be able to provide for the other members of the family.

But passive and submissive as the Corsican women are at ordinary times, they become perfect furies when there is a question of death or revenge.

As in other countries, moreover, love of women is the primary cause of many a blood-feud. For instance, when a girl has been compromised by any man's attentions she names the man to her parents, who at once order him to marry her. Should he refuse, or even get out of the way, war is declared, and the families of the young man and young woman enter upon a *vendetta*. The man may often be innocent of what is laid to his charge; but his oaths and protestations count for nothing, and he must sacrifice himself in order to divert still graver complications. Girls thus have it in their power to cause terrible mischief, and many a family history can offer examples of the awful consequences which have been entailed by their jealousy and unfounded allegations.

After a few days spent in exploring the valley of the Niolo, I left Calacuccia, and, passing a second time through the Escala de Santa Regina, returned by way of Corte, Vizzavone, and Bocognano to Ajaccio. Some days later, I started on a journey along the west coast of the island, accompanied by the faithful Antó.

The road from Ajaccio to Vico was somewhat monotonous at the outset, and in grey weather would have been even depressing. It is true that at first one had constant views of the shining cliffs of Monte Rosso, and that there was the perpetual freshness of sunlit verdure; but beyond Appietto, the road entered a gloomy district of monotonous hills, without trees and without rocks, lacking even grass and flowers. Here and there the sparse *makis* lay in stretches of desolate brake along the shore of the Gulf of Lava, but for the most part the land was naked ; long streaks of grey cinders lay on the mountain slopes, and the black soil looked carbonised. The forest had been burned away, leaving a veritable *tierra del fuego.* The little birds which formerly enlivened the verdant shades had departed, save a few trembling creatures which sought shelter in the few trees spared by the conflagration, where they were watched by the hawks and vultures, circling slowly above the desolate heights.

As if to increase the sombre aspect of the landscape, the sun became obscured by passing clouds, the sea grew the colour of lead, and the sadness of shadow fell athwart the land.

The road continually ascended, till at length we reached the ridge of San Bastiano, which seemed the dividing line of two different countries. Behind lay nakedness and gloom : in front lay light and verdure. The sky was clear, and the gulfs of Liscia and Sagone reflected the blue. The mountains were swathed with greenery, from which villages peeped out like rabbits in a warren, and the horizon was bounded by a rose-coloured promontory washed by blue waves, on the summit of which the Greek village of Cargesi glittered in the sun.

Immediately below lay the township of Calcatoggio, built on the flank of a mountain, which sloped down to a beach of pink sand, fringed by the silver of the crumbling wavelets.

I halted at a white inn by the wayside, and as I took my lunch feasted my eyes at the same time on a banquet of form and colour. The infinite space of the gulf stretched beneath the window, not repellent like northern seas, but warm and inviting under the mellow rays of the southern sun. The breeze that blew in from the west was sharp with sea-savours, yet balmy with the scent of aromatic grasses and the perfume of flowers. The colour-scheme was a harmony of pinks, lilacs, and pale aerial blues, shimmering in the distance with the sheen of satin or shot silk, and flashing with diamond-facets of iridescent light. Yet, even here there was a shadow.

"What's the matter with your arm, that you wear it in a sling?"
I asked of my hostess, as she waited upon me at table.

"Oh, nothing! Merely a sort of swelling which comes on at
intervals and goes away again."

"But there must be a reason for it!"

"It is a bruise," said she, blushing and looking discomposed.

"You are hiding something from me."

She then admitted that she had been shot in the arm, and that
the ball had never been extracted. She congratulated herself on
her escape; for the bullet had been intended to kill.

Thus everywhere in Corsica, one is confronted by the musket
and the dagger, and the *vendetta* sits like a skeleton at every feast.

From Calcatoggio we skirted the pleasing shore and crossed the
estuary of the Liamone, a sort of vast marshy pond, very malarious,
but affording good pasture on its shores.

Sagone, the next place of importance, is now a miserable hamlet,
but was once a large town, and the see of a bishop in the sixth
century.

The road then left the shore and wound up a valley through
the woods, below high cliffs, on the summit of which the westering
sun-rays lighted the houses of the village of Balogna.

Night had fallen when we reached the ridge of Saint Anthony,
and saw the lights of Vico glittering in the dark embrace of a
circle of severe-looking mountains, the most striking of which is a
huge rock, with an outline resembling a human figure, which is
called *la Sposata* (the betrothed).

From Vico onward the journey was a panorama of beauty, the
softness and verdure of which was dignified by the virile grandeur
of the bare slopes of the Inscinosa and the granite crags of Monte
San Angelo.

Through forests of chestnut, and thickets of ilex, passing quaint
villages hidden in remote valleys, we climbed ever upward towards
the pass of Levi, till we again reached the stony solitudes of the
highlands, where the only human being was some old, melancholy-
looking shepherd, guarding his goats, with his musket across his knees.

The summit of the ridge demanded a halt to contemplate the wonderful view of green forest and red rock which lay between us and the now distant sea. Then once more we hurried down through woods of oak and chestnut, catching strange glimpses of colour and light through the forest aisles, as we passed on our way down to Evisa.

Evisa is one of the most picturesque villages in Corsica, nestling in a chaos of red rocks. The Spelunca at Evisa is a sombre cañon; the descent into which, by the most breakneck path conceivable, occupies a good two hours. Evisa is about 2,660 feet above

Primitive Mill.

sea-level, while the bottom of the Spelunca is not more than 1,000 feet, if so much, above the sea. The depth of the ravine must therefore be over 1,600 feet. The precipices converge near the bottom, where a little bridge, built by the Genoese, spans a torrent, the bed of which is encumbered with blocks of granite fallen from the heights above. In winter, falls of rock are of frequent occurrence, and both sides of the ravine are seamed with the tracks left by the boulders, which destroy trees, pulverise stones, and sweep away everything in their path. Clinging to the slope of one of the highest cliffs is the village of Ota, overhung by a mass of rock which seems threatening to fall every instant.

But the good people of the place know that that particular rock can never fall, for is it not securely held by a net of goat-hair thread, the ends of which are held by saintly monks who dwell on top of the mountain expressly to retain them in place? Every night, while the village sleeps, women climb the peaks to take food to the good monks who watch over the safety of Ota, and give them oil with which to lubricate the threads in order to make them last longer.

In 1876, a young girl of Ota, known as the beautiful Fior di Spina, who was about to become a mother by the village school-master, shot her lover dead at the church door, as he was entering to solemnise his marriage with another girl. Fior di Spina was acquitted by the jury, and one of her companions composed a *vocero* of triumph which is still famous.

At the bottom of the Spelunca, I met a young man belonging to Evisa, who offered to be my companion and guide to the forests of Aïtone and Valdoniello. I willingly agreed, and on the morrow we drove to Aïtone, which was the finest forest in Corsica, before greed of gain felled much of the timber.

The trees are chiefly pines, and the woodland way was very silent. Now and then the breeze rustled mournfully in the swaying crests, or a ring-dove or wood-pigeon fluttered away in affright, but no birds sang at this late season of the year. The forest track is steep, and it took us over two good hours to reach the ridge of Vergio; though, truth to tell, we did not hurry, often leaving the path to look at a fall or a picturesque vista along the stream, and passing some time by a primitive mill, which stood among the rocks in the heart of the forest, in an open glade bathed in sunlight and girdled by the shadow of the woods.

In the Forest of Aïtone.

15

As we went higher, the forest changed in character. Rushing torrents crossed the pathway, the air freshened, and the pines gave way to beeches, firs, larches, and stunted birch trees. Autumn had laid its finger-mark on the foliage, and the sun shone warmly through red and gold leaves.

On the summit of the ridge of Vergio, a wooden cross marked where a man had died of cold only a few months before.

After a frugal lunch near a roadside spring, we penetrated a short distance into the adjacent forest of Valdoniello, and then returned to Evisa.

From there I proceeded to the far-famed rocks, known as the Calanches. The road, after crossing the Spelunca and passing the threatened village of Ota, enters a smiling country, well-wooded and well-watered, on the shores of the Gulf of Porto.

Beyond this are the Calanches.

For a mile and a half, the road is bordered on both sides by the wildest and most fantastic rocks imaginable. They are of an extraordinary colour, and gleam in the sun like burnished copper. I visited the place by moonlight, and never had I seen a stranger landscape. Torn, convulsed, weather-worn, precipitous, it was a nightmare of nature; while far off, at the foot of the unscaleable cliffs, stretched a calm expanse of silvered sea, strangely contrasting with the black stone monstrosities, which seemed like giants smitten with epilepsy. Yet, the sudden transition from the woods and waterfalls of the Porto road, to this wild discord of rock and sea, was eminently characteristic of Corsica, where tragic landscapes alternate with smiling scenes of streams and flowers, just as banditti and *vendette* interrupt the peaceful domesticities of life and love.

Thus, after leaving the Calanches, I again entered a fresh phase, both of scenery and human character. One day I shivered at the giddy abysses of Evisa, the next I wandered by moonlight amid the strange rocks of the Calanches, and, on the third day, I walked in a Grecian land, among orange and citron trees, on a headland overgrown with aromatic plants, in the midst of a people entirely differing from the Corsicans, both in their customs and in their type, which recalled the marble perfection achieved by classic sculptors.

I was in the village of Cargesi, inhabited by the descendants of a Greek colony, which emigrated from Greece in .the days of Turkish oppression, and, after wandering throughout the Mediterranean, received a grant of land in Corsica from the Ligurian Senate at Genoa. On the good news reaching Greece, two other vessels of refugees set sail for the new country. One of these was surprised by a Turkish fleet, and the emigrants were massacred, but the other ship safely reached Genoa.

After making an agreement with the Republic, the emigrants landed in Corsica, on March 14th, 1676, and settled at the spot chosen by the pioneers, as most resembling Greece in landscape and climate—a spreading promontory shaped like a peacock's tail, which received the name of *Paomia*.

The prosperity of the new colony was short-lived, however, for, after the departure of the Genoese, the Corsicans attacked the settlers, pillaged their farms, stole their flocks, and compelled them to take refuge at Ajaccio, where a chapel, called the *Madona del Carmine*, and afterwards known as the Greek chapel, was set aside for their special use.

Forty-three years later, the French established the refugees at Cargesi, where M. de Marbœuf, Governor of Corsica, built himself a castle. But in 1793 this was burned to the ground, and the Greeks were once more driven out of the settlement. Protected by several Corsican families, however, they gradually returned, and now dwell in peace. There have been frequent intermarriages between Greeks and Corsicans, but quite one-half of the population is still of pure Hellenic descent. Modern Greek is spoken by most families, and the religious services are conducted according to the ancient Greek rite.

The Corsicans settled at Cargesi, called *paysani* by the Greeks, mostly adopt the Greek usage ; but when they preponderate in the congregation, the village pope preaches, by courtesy, in Italian. The cemetery is common to the two rites.

The people of Cargesi are polite, quiet, and very industrious. They export corn and lemons, and are apparently prosperous.

Nevertheless, besides the taxes paid to the State, the inhabitants have to meet other secret imposts. Often, at night, there comes a knock at the door, and a man presents a letter written in pencil by a bandit, together with a list of various objects and provisions required, signed by the brigand.

This species of blackmail is levied not only at Cargesi, but in nearly all the villages of Corsica.

On the evening after my arrival, I received a visit from the pope, a young man of pleasing manners, who had studied for the priesthood at Rome. By way of helping to pass the evening pleasantly, he told me yet one more brigand story, as we walked together along the shore.

Some two years previously, he was spending the evening with a relative at Ota, when a countryman knocked at the door and said that, having heard that the pope was returning to Cargesi next day, he came to offer the priest a lift in his cart, as he was going in that direction on urgent private affairs.

As he would have otherwise been probably compelled to walk, and the road was long and tiring, the pope gratefully accepted the offer, and set out next day with his companion.

As they were slowly climbing a hill near the Calanches, they heard a curious noise in the bushes. The driver reined in his horse, and said to the pope in a grave voice,—

"That noise is produced by knocking two stones together. It is the signal generally used by the brigands when they wish to make known their presence and converse with any one. I'm sure there is a bandit in the brushwood yonder, who wants to speak to you. Don't be afraid, but alight, and no harm will befall you."

The pope trembled in every limb, but what could he do, save obey? He got down from the cart, and a man appeared in the thicket, and, pushing aside the branches, approached the two travellers. The stranger's appearance was not calculated to inspire confidence. His beard was unkempt, his hair dishevelled, and his face seamed

with lines of dissipation.   He held a gun in his hand, and the butt
of a pistol and the handle of a dagger protruded from his vest.

"Are you Cæsar Coty, the pope of Cargesi?" he asked the priest

The Pope of Cargesi.

"I knew you would pass on your way back, and I wanted to see you.
Don't be afraid of me; I am from Ota, and am a friend of your
father."

So saying, he effusively embraced the pope, and whispered in
his ear,—

An old Greek of Cargesi.

"I want to make my confession to you. I have many sins to avow, much restitution to make. Follow me into the wood!"

Then, to the driver of the cart, he cried sharply,—

"Drive on, do you hear! I want to be alone with the pope."

Bandit and priest then entered the wood.

The pope said, "Why don't you go to your own parish priest at Ota?" To which the brigand roughly replied, "What's that to do with you? Aren't you also a priest?"

The pope then seated himself on a stone. The bandit, laying on one side his gun, pistol, and dagger, knelt down among the brambles, and beat his breast.

"Seeing his penitence, I gave him absolution," said the pope to me.

When they parted, the brigand embraced his confessor several times, and thanked him warmly for the good deed he had done.

"I feel so relieved now, for I suffered terribly from remorse in the wild solitudes where I dwell alone," said he.

The bandit was named Pascuale. He was a native of Ota, and only three months later gendarmes surprised and "destroyed" him in a cave, in the middle of that same wood where he had confessed and had been shriven.

In Corsica, the word "destroy" is used when the killing of brigands is in question.

As the pope told me this story, we approached the village, and in the silence of the night heard distant voices singing old *lamenti*.

Sartène.

## CHAPTER VI.

Sartène.—Marriage Customs.—Good Friday Procession.—The *Catenaccio* and the Black Penitents.—A Romantic *Vendetta.*—The Tarantula.—Bonifacio.—The Straits.—The Lion of Roccapina.

White Penitents.

WE were already some distance along the road next morning, when the first sun-rays smote the pink promontory on which Cargesi is perched like a sea-bird's nest. I saw the white houses and the belfries of the two churches of different rites glittering in the distance, amid the deep purple of the fields, and the hedges of cochineal plant. The sound of church bells echoed across the plain : a few spirals of smoke from the household fires curled upward in the still air, and then, as we turned a corner, the picture disappeared.

Antó, breaking his usual silence, began to chant a plaintive

236

*lamento*, and the horses, conscious that they were returning homewards, broke into a brisk gallop.

We returned, by the same route as we had come, to Ajaccio, where
next day I took the steamer to Propriano. The night had been
stormy, and the mountains raised their snowy summits through a
flurry of torn cloud-wrack.

Ajaccio, enjoying its usual immunity from bad weather, slept in
light, the breeze scarcely rustling its palm trees, while the waters of
the harbour gently lapped the base of the lofty buildings on the
marge. But nearer the open sea the shores of the gulf were beaten
by angry waves. The horizon was an undulating line of white-
crested billows, and Cape Muro was ever and anon obscured by the
flying spindrift.

The passage took two hours, and the landing at Propriano was a
matter of some difficulty, the harbour being exposed to the full force
of westerly gales.

My clothes still damp with foam, and my face still tingling
with the lash of the wind, I took my place on the diligence for
Sartène.

The road winds considerably, crosses the Rizzanèse, and turns
to the right, when Sartène comes suddenly into view, situated on the
slope of a hill, beyond a rocky landslip, whence olive groves flow
down to the plain like livid cascades.

From a distance, the town resembles an immense fortress, its
rectangular and singularly tall houses, the dark windows of which
resemble loopholes, rising from among natural walls of bare, violet-
coloured granite.

On the left, as if to complete the stern picture, rises the bare
summit of the Incudine, and the scarped peaks of Asinao seem to
stab the clouds.

The mountain slope above the town gleams with white tombs,
several of which crown the head of the ridge as with a pale diadem.
The dead decidedly have a more joyful dwelling-place than the
living at Sartène, reposing as they do on sunny heights beneath
rustling olive trees in the warm soil which gives birth to a thousand

flowers. This austere land is dominated by sepulchres, which, seen from the sea, glitter like the sacred koubbas of Islamism.

Ancient ramparts, which formerly protected the town from the assaults of the Barbary corsairs, form a line of ruins along the rocks, and still show traces of turrets and battlements.

Sartène is in the heart of the *vendetta* country, the district commencing at the summit of San Pietro di Verde, embracing Zicavo, Sartène, and Porto Vecchio, and ending at the strange hills of Caña.

The Dolmen of Cauria.

It is in this part of the island that the Corsicans have most retained their old spirit of violence, and here that family feuds are still most frequent and most fierce.

In the neighbourhood are the famous dolmen and standing stones of Cauria, called by the Corsicans *Stazzone del Diavolo* and *Stantare*. As in the Balearic Isles and Sardinia, these constructions form a peg on which archæologists hang the wildest and most conflicting theories; but when all is said and done, their origin remains wrapped in mystery. Even the earliest writers do not agree as to the aboriginal inhabitants of Corsica. Pausanias speaks of the Libyans as the first settlers, while Seneca, who lived in exile on the island, attributes to the people the manners and customs of the Iberians. Herodotus mentions a Phocian immigration, and Diodorus Siculus states that the soil was first tilled by Etruscans. But, no doubt, the strange memorials are the more impressive for the mystery surrounding their origin ; and in contemplating them, imagination has free scope, without being fettered by " ill-conditioned facts."

Wandering by the stream which kept company with the road from Sartène to Cauria, I came upon several shepherds who had come down from the Coscione to winter in the low country. There they stood, solemn and motionless, watching their flocks with a meditative eye from a slab of rock ; just as sad and just as dreamy on these low hills by the sea, as I had seen them on the heights near the clouds.

But presently my conception of their impassiveness was rudely broken by a cavalcade which swept by like a whirlwind across the rough ground, followed by a second group of horsemen climbing the hill more leisurely.

It was a shepherd's wedding.

The bride, dressed in white and wearing a wreath of orange blossom, was mounted on a white mare, escorted by armed cavaliers, who from time to time fired a volley of joy. The other horsemen who had first passed went to the fields to pick flowers, and raced back to the bride, the first to reach her offering the young woman a flower, and then kissing her and paying her a compliment in verse.

When the bridal party crosses a river or stream, the bride soaks in the water one of the cakes (*canistroni*) prepared specially for feast-days, and launches on the current an olive branch or a flower, symbol of abundance, peace, and happiness for the shores washed by the flowing water.

Sometimes she dismounts and kneels by the stream, and, taking water in her hands, raises them above her head and lets the liquid fall drop by drop, at the same time murmuring a prayer that this water, like the lustral water of the ancients, may render her pure and spotless.

When the invocation is concluded, all the water ought to have left the hand ; evil omens being thus averted. The party then rise from their knees, remount their horses, and pursue their journey, singing *lamenti*.

On reaching the nuptial abode, the bride is met on the threshold by her mother-in-law, who presents her with a spindle and a key, at the same time sprinkling her with handfuls of rice and corn, tokens of abundance.

A volley of musketry is then fired, amid cheers, to mark the *bonaventura*, the fortunate welcome, and the wife is led into her new home.

The wedding feast lasts till evening, and, at intervals, country dances are performed to the music of rustic pipes. Each relative and guest clinks glasses with the newly-married couple, and compliments them in improvised verse.

Sometimes the bridal procession, on arriving near the house, encounters a barrier (*travata*), which the bride cannot surmount alone without exposing herself to evil omens, but one of the cavaliers of her escort always assists her to pass.

The ceremony of betrothal (*abraccio*) generally takes place in winter.

One evening, the nearest relatives of the girl go to fetch the young man and bring him to their house. The young people kiss each other and sit down side by side, while the members of the two families share a repast of cake and wine, as they arrange the conditions of the marriage contract.

The young man seldom returns home that night. . . . It is an admitted custom, for the *abraccio* binds the betrothed to each other, and the subsequent civil contract and religious ceremony merely ratify the engagement contracted in the two families. The actual marriage, in fact, takes place much later, and it is nothing unusual for the bride at that time either to have just had or to be about to have her first child.

If the man dies before marriage, the children of the voluntary union are treated as fully legitimate, and are entitled to their due share of the inheritance, while the girl wears mourning and is regarded as a widow.

When the betrothed pair do not belong to the same village, the bride goes on horseback to her husband's home, escorted by often as many as forty or fifty cavaliers. When the cavalcade nears the village, the young men hurry ahead at the top of their speed, and the first to reach the house fetches an olive branch, a bouquet, and a white veil, prepared beforehand by the husband's family, and hastens back with them to the bride, who then enters the village at a gallop, holding the branch in her hand. As they pass down the street, all the windows are thrown open, and rice, wheat, and flowers are showered on the couple. These are the *grazié* or good wishes, symbolical of abundance and prosperity.

The customs vary a little, of course, in different villages. Thus, at Ghisonacce, the bride goes to church provided with a collection of pocket-handkerchiefs, more or less embroidered according to her means, and distributes them among her friends, each and all of whom come out to kiss her, as she passes their house.

As soon as the bride's foot touches the ground before her husband's house, a young girl presents her with a bouquet; and when she has entered and is seated, a little boy is placed on her knees, generally a brother or cousin of the bridegroom. This is done in the hope that the young wife's first child will be a boy. Another quaint custom, now seldom observed, however, is that of washing the bride's face with wine, as soon as she enters the house.

The guests are supposed to keep the bride and bridegroom company on the three evenings before the wedding, and to accompany them to church on the three Sundays following the marriage-day.

In poor families, the bride's dowry consists of a distaff and spindles, and a *capitala* or pad with which to carry burdens on her head. After the wedding the family of the *sposata* and the nearest relatives contribute bread, ham, sausages, and *canistroni* (the national cakes) towards the larder of the new household.

So much I learned of Corsican marriage customs while riding back

16

to Sartène from the dolmen of Cauria; and when we reached the convent of SS. Cosmas and Damian near the town, the upper windows of the tall buildings were all aflame with the last sunset rays.

The evenings at Sartène are dull and melancholy. The great square, called the *Porta*, surrounded on three sides by mausoleum-like houses, borders on a deep valley, which at night seems an unfathomable abyss. The narrow alleys of the old town, sombre enough by day, are gloomy defiles of black masonry at night. Moreover, the streets are not always safe, and it is nothing unusual to meet with characters who, to say the least, are suspicious. A friend of my own, passing through a street one night, heard the rattle of a musket. "Who's there?" he cried. "Go your way! It doesn't concern you!" was the answer. On another occasion, he saw a man disguised as a woman with a *faldetta* on his head, and armed to the teeth. Only a month before my arrival he was stopped, as he was returning home, by two men, who, after scrutinising his face by the vague moonlight, said, "You can go on! You are not the person we are looking for!"

Brigands often visit the cafés of an evening, usually in disguise; and one may see a group of gendarmes at one table, while a bandit is treating his friends at the next.

I myself saw a well-known criminal, who had committed two murders, walking down the public street chatting with a gendarme; though it is fair to add that the man had been acquitted of these particular charges, on the ground that he had acted under provocation.

One of the most familiar objects on the *Porta* was a poor, emaciated creature, who had had both ankle-bones broken by a shot intended for another man.

The great, dull square, surrounded by tall, forbidding-looking houses, on which the gateway leading to the old quarter opens like the orifice of a cave, has been, and still is, occasionally the stage for dramatic scenes. It was for a long time the battle-ground of the two opposing factions of the town, and its grey stones have echoed to the rattle of musketry and the cries of the wounded. Nowadays the most striking spectacle to be seen at Sartène is the Good Friday procession. At dusk on that day every house is lighted up, and for once in the year, at all events, the obscurest corners of the town are illuminated. The road from the valley is crowded with country folk from the adjacent villages and shepherds from the hills.

Suddenly the great doors of the parish church are thrown open, and the Confraternity of the Holy Sacrament emerges. The penitents wear a white tunic descending to their heels, their head is covered by a cowl of the same hue, and over their shoulders is a short red cloak with a Host embroidered in gold on the breast. They advance slowly in two long lines, carrying candles in their hands, and in the midst of

Penitents and Monks.

them walks the *catenaccio*, representing the Christ as the bearer of the sins of the world. He wears a long black cape, his head is hidden beneath a sable cowl pierced with two eye-holes, and his feet are bare, while his right leg drags a large iron chain, and his shoulders are bowed by the weight of an immense cross. The *catenaccio* is a penitent, who thus expiates some crime or grave sin, and the part, with the countenance of the Prior of the Penitents, is often taken by a brigand.

Behind the *catenaccio* follow the Black Penitents, carrying a bier supporting the figure of Christ, which has been removed from the great cross. The limbs of the figure are jointed, and fall into natural attitudes. This, joined with the livid colour of the flesh, the bleeding wounds, and the thorny crown from which the blood seems to trickle drop by drop, produces a realism of effect almost cruel.

The solemn procession proceeds through the tortuous streets to the oratory of San Bastiano, where an image of the Virgin Mary, draped with crape, is seen weeping by the tomb of Christ. The only light comes from a few candles, in whose dim radiance the ghastly figure of the dead, the immense arms of the cross, and the black-robed penitents appear like so many phantoms. Sometimes the moon is just rising over the mountains, and lends her pale light to the strange spectacle. After a brief pause the *cortège* returns to the church, followed by the parish clergy chanting the *Miserere*, and the entire adult population, bare-headed and often sobbing, while the rear is brought up by the old women and children.

On reaching the church overlooking Place Porta, from which it is separated by a terrace, the clergy come to a halt, and a friar standing on the wall of the terrace, holding the figure of the Christ in his arms, preaches the Passion to the silent and kneeling crowd.

However sensuous or open to criticism it may be, the scene is wonderfully impressive. The articulated figure of the Christ leans its head on the friar's shoulder, and its arms and legs change their attitudes with the movements of the preacher. Profound silence prevails, and the stillness of the night is only broken by the impassioned voice of the friar, whose face is irradiated by the wild gleam of torches. When the sermon is over, the preacher raises the two hands of the life-size figure, and makes with them the sign of the Cross over the people, who thus seem to be blessed by the effigy itself.

The friar is always a member of the Franciscan community of SS. Cosmas and Damian near the town. This community consists of a superior and some twenty friars, who live entirely on the alms of the townsfolk, never accepting money, but subsisting solely on the fruits of the earth. In return for the charity of the townspeople,.

the good friars themselves give alms to the poor, visit the sick and the dying, follow funerals, and even help in the manual labour of poor households. The view from the convent is superb, stretching from the Coscione and the peaks of Asinao to the distant valley which shelters the village of Carbini. It was in this village that, at the end of the fourteenth century, arose the strange socialistic sect of the Giovannali, so called because it recognised only the Gospel of St. John. The members had an absolute community of goods, land, money, and even wives. They used to assemble at night in the churches, and after service extinguish the lights and hold monstrous orgies. They were excommunicated by Pope Innocent VI., and, after bitter persecution, were finally massacred by the Corsicans.

Carbini was subsequently repopulated by families from Sartène. In modern days the village has been the scene of a remarkable *vendetta* story, the end of which has not even yet been seen.

Napoleon Nicolaï, of Carbini, eloped with Catherine Lafranchi ; and the latter's parents refused to consent to their marriage, the Nicolaï being simple farmers, while the Lafranchi passed at Porto Vecchio for wealthy landowners. After staying at Bastia, the lovers returned to Porto Vecchio to make a final appeal to the parents to allow the marriage ; but the family proved obdurate, drove away the young man and shut up the girl, whom they are said to have beaten and maltreated. Not long afterwards, moreover, a son of the house, in order to avenge the honour of his sister, killed Nicolaï. The shot, which was fired point-blank, set fire to the clothes of the victim, whose body was so charred as to be almost unrecognisable. Nicolaï's young brother, on hearing of the murder, came to Porto Vecchio, soaked his handkerchief in the wound, and took an oath of revenge, which he soon afterwards fulfilled. After killing his brother's murderer, he took to the *makis*, where he led a wandering existence for two years. Although a proscribed man, the police authorities were not hostile to him, his youth, the circumstances of the murder, and the force of Corsican tradition all being in his favour. The public prosecutor of Sartène made every effort to take him into custody, in order that he might serve a short sentence and then be free to resume his ordinary life.

But the Lafranchi pursued the young man with unappeasable ferocity, joining the *gendarmerie* in tracking him down, and hesitating at no stratagem in the hope of destroying him. At length they learned that one of Nicolaï's intimate friends was to be married, and there was every reason to suppose that Nicolaï himself, with the generous imprudence of youth, would not fail to attend the wedding.

The surmise proved correct, and on the night of the wedding the nuptial festivites were rudely interrupted by a loud knocking at the door. An attempt was made to gain time by parleying with the gendarmes, but the brigadier, Delbos, insisted upon entering.

The house was entirely surrounded, and resistance was useless. Nicolaï adopted the desperate expedient of donning the robes of the bride and going to the door on the arm of the bridegroom, who affected anxiety to go out, in order to leave the room free to the gendarmes. But the ruse failed, and Nicolaï then sought to escape by a back window. But as he climbed over the sill, his boots betrayed him. Two shots were fired, and he fell dead, still attired in the bride's wedding dress.

Such was the sad end of this young man, who had received a good education, and only owed his fate to his compliance with the fatal laws of honour of his race.

During his wanderings in the forest, he composed several *lamenti*. The following is a stanza in which he expressed his sorrow and regret :—

| "DISGRAZIATO. | "OUTLAWED. |
|---|---|
| "*Sono io, per li foreste* | "Wandering through the forest, |
| *Tutto l' inverno* | All the winter |
| *Esposto a gli tempeste,* | Exposed to the storm, |
| *Sempre erranto e pellegrino;* | Ever a stranger and pilgrim ; |
| *Dite-mi che vita è questa,* | Tell me what life is this, |
| *Una pietra per cuscino* | With a stone for pillow |
| *La notte sotto alla testa?*" | Beneath my head by night?" |

I met the poor young man's father at Bonifacio. He had left Carbini, and lived, a prey to gnawing grief, in a house the windows of which were always darkened, brooding over how to avenge the violent death of his two sons.

Nicolaï was a sympathetic figure, but the same cannot be said of the majority of the outlaws or brigands, of whom, when I was in Corsica, no fewer than six hundred infested the forests. It is high time that the romance with which the bandit is invested should be got rid of. As a matter of fact, four years passed in the *makis* suffice to make a man a dangerous assassin. It becomes with them no longer a question of gratifying private revenge, but of cowardly assassination. They must gratify their passions at any cost. From some they demand their money, from others their honour. Knowing themselves to be objects of terror, their pride becomes unbounded. Every vestige of human feeling fades away, and the bandit becomes a creature of brutality, viciousness, and cunning. Rocchini, for instance, was a feelingless brute ; and the Corsicans, who have a great knack of bestowing appropriate nicknames, called him the *animale*.

In order not to waste a day on a monotonous road which I already knew, I left Sartène in the middle of the night. At a short distance from the town I was shown a wooden cross by the wayside, marking where Rocchini and another brigand had fired at two gendarmes, merely to practise their skill. One of the poor fellows was killed, and the other only escaped owing to his horse jibbing at the report of the gun.

As we drove on across the desolate country towards the sea, I fell into a kind of doze, in which I was horribly haunted by my recollection of an insect I had seen at Cargesi, the only venomous creature in Corsica. It is called the *malmignato* or *ragno rosso*, and is a tarantula, a sort of cross between a spider and an ant. Its body is black, with red spots on the belly, and its head is hard and bony. When a person is stung by the beast, he is seized with convulsive tremblings, his temperature falls, and a cold sweat breaks out all over his body. This is bad enough, but some of the remedies in vogue among the country folk are perhaps worse. The favourite mode is to place the sufferer in a hot oven, after first making him intoxicated with spirits. The shepherds of Sartène burn the afflicted place with blazing tow, others plaster it over with potter's earth. At Zicavo the experiment had been tried of plunging the sufferer in boiling water, but this empirical remedy had only resulted in the death of the patient. Personally, I should have preferred the old method of having the evil exorcised, by persons skilled in the art of charming away all malefic influences.

Thinking thus I fell more deeply under the enchantment of sleep, until I imagined I had myself been stung and was baking in the heat of an oven, which had given me an attack of intermittent fever. I was awakened from my nightmare by the rays of the rising sun striking me full in the eyes, and looking out of the window, I saw ahead a steep hill ending in a chalk cliff surmounted by a cross.

"Yonder is the hermitage of the Trinity!" said my travelling companion, rubbing his eyes.

The character of the scenery had completely changed. The stern mountains and sombre ravines were things of the past. We had just crossed a sterile region dominated by a lofty rock, the *Uomo de Cagna*, which seemed the motionless guardian of these solitudes, and were now in the southernmost extremity of Corsica, where nothing was visible save chalky cliffs and arid plains, swept clean by the sea wind, with only a few stunted and burnt-up olives to take the place of the glorious chestnuts and oaks of the interior.

The sun was up when we clambered on foot to the hermitage of the Trinity, a white building surrounded by rocks and olive trees. The prior was slowly pacing up and down by the white wall, conning his book of hours. He is prior by courtesy, for he lives alone with but one monk, who acts as begging friar, with the aid of a small donkey. The latter, though he may have taken no vows, is an important member of the community, inasmuch as it is his task to carry the offerings of the faithful.

Looking from the terrace of the convent, the eye follows the winding of striated cliffs till it reaches the strange outline of Bonifacio, whose towers and bastions crown the naked rocks of the promontory, beyond which stretch the wavy lines of the Straits of Bonifacio, and, further away, the north coast of Sardinia, whose white villages

The Begging Friar

and jagged summits carry the sight onward and upward to the sky-line.

After spending several pleasant hours at the hermitage, entertained by the grave courtesy of the Italian prior, and the unconscious humour of his almoner and the donkey, we drove on along the dusty road to Bonifacio.

Large black crosses stood by the wayside, but they merely marked religious stations, and not the scenes of murders; for in this part of the country *vendette* are unknown.

The fields were divided by rough stone walls, built with infinite patience and labour to shelter the vegetation from the violence of the wind, which blows almost persistently across the arid peninsula. Sun, wind, dust, and a bleached, clean-swept soil, where the only plants are a few tufts of pallid wormwood—such is the landward approach to the rock of Bonifacio.

We reached the town by a long slope hewn out of the rock, alongside the harbour, which is a deep, narrow lagoon bordered by ancient ramparts.

The extraordinary situation of the town, perhaps the most curious in Europe, is best appreciated from seaward, whence one perceives the massive natural foundations on which it is built,—a range of lofty, stratified cliffs, the base of which is gnawed away by the sea, and pierced at intervals by deep caverns, one of which runs far beneath the town. The line of buildings above is crowned by the famous *Torione*, a massive tower erected in the year 840, which was for a long period the town's only defence against the Barbary corsairs. The rocky rampart, falling sheer to the sea, is crossed by a narrow stairway, the "stairway of the King of Aragon." Alfonso V. was besieging the town. The Aragonese artillery had already destroyed the chief defences and set many of the houses on fire by bombs; yet the besieged, small in number and weakened by hunger, still defended themselves with energy, and repulsed the assailants, when Alfonso had this stairway hewn out of the rock, without his workmen being perceived from Bonifacio. When it was completed, he tried to carry the place by assault. The principal attack was made on the other side of the town, where women, children, priests, and monks all took part in the defence, hurling stones and boiling oil and pitch over the ramparts, and fighting hand to hand with the Aragonese who reached the parapet. At the height of the conflict, a woman named Margaret Bobia suddenly perceived the invaders swarming into the town in the rear, by means of the staircase, of which the brave defenders had not even known the existence. A rush was made to this new point of attack, and after a fierce tussle the Aragonese were repulsed and large numbers hurled over the ramparts into the sea.

On the second day after my arrival, I had an experience of one of the gales which are so frequent on this coast. The wind seemed to shake the very cliffs, and the town was full of the noise of flapping shutters and creaking roofs. The sea thundered along the rocks, and the straits were a boiling cauldron of foam and spindrift. Perched on a giddy corner, overhanging the water at a height of some two hundred feet, I passed the entire morning watching the waves breaking one over the other in their mad rush landwards, while the whole promontory seemed to quiver like the bows of a vessel meeting the shock of the billows. Following with my eye the rough road of the *campo romanello*, I saw looming through the mist the dark outline of the island of Lavezzi, the scene of the wreck of the frigate *Sémillante*, a catastrophe which has been rendered classic by Alphonse Daudet, in one of the most charming of the sketches whimsically entitled "Letters from my Mill." Nearly a thousand bodies are said to have been thrown up on the coast after this terrible wreck, among them being the body of the captain in full uniform.

The people of Bonifacio speak an old Genoese dialect, and bear no resemblance to the other inhabitants of Corsica, by whom they are to a certain extent looked down upon, their neighbours of the district of Sartène especially speaking of them with a contempt and dislike only second to the hatred entertained for the Corsicans' old enemies, the Genoese. Undeterred by this, however, the good folk of Bonifacio are industrious and full of initiative, though prudent

Bonifacio.

to a degree. The men, mounted
on donkeys, go off in the morning to work in the fields, and
return in the evening on their
tiny mounts, which are almost
hidden by their burden of vegetables, trusses of hay, and little
barrels of water, filled at the
spring by the gate of the town.
It is amusing to watch the
return of the workers, as the
motley procession climbs the
steep slope leading to the ancient
fortified gateway of the upper
town.

The portcullis
of this gate is made
of wood from the
wreckage of the
*Sémillante.*

There is a
legend that, after
Bonifacio had been
sacked by the Sara-
cens, some passers-
by perceived an
ox and an ass
reverently kneel-
ing before a spring
called the *Corcone.*
The news of this
unusual spectacle

Ancient Gateway.

spread through the town, and the clergy came down to
see the animals, who still remained in the same worshipping attitude. The usually placid spring was boiling like a geyser, and

in the midst a small piece of wood was gyrating on the surface. The fragment was recognised by the clergy as a relic of the True Cross. Ever since that time, when storms rage in the straits and vessels are in peril, the clergy carry the relic to the top of the cliffs and solemnly bless the waves with it, that He who said, " Peace, be still !" may again calm the tumultuous waters.

The Bonifacians are very superstitious, and to the usual beliefs and customs of the Corsican mountaineers add several of their own. Mothers never allow their children to sleep with their feet pointing to the door, as it is thus that corpses are carried out of the house. When a member of a family is sick or absent, his place at table is laid as usual, but never occupied ; and that side of the table is even placed against the wall, in order that no one may sit down there by inadvertence.

When noon strikes, sailors on a land journey pick up four little stones, which they throw, one in front, another to left, another to right, and the fourth behind them, thus making the sign of the cross, and averting evil chances. The will-o'-the-wisps or jack-o'-lanterns which sometimes play on the rock of Lavezzi, where the drowned sailors of the *Sémillante* are buried, are regarded with the greatest terror by old sailors, so much so as to render them quite ill.

The tillers of the soil, on their side, are quite as superstitious, and when their fruit trees begin to wither, call in the Capuchin monks to come and avert the evil by blessing the trees.

Bonifacio has sheltered two great men in its time—Charles V. and Napoleon. Bonaparte remained in garrison here for five months. The old people show a ruined house with an unrailed staircase, up which Napoleon escaped when attacked one evening by "roughs," as he was coming up from the port.

In the same street as this house is a small chapel dedicated to Saint Roch, and held in great veneration by sailors. It was here that the last victim died of the plague, which decimated Bonifacio in 1598.

Several churches show that Bonifacio was once an important city, and still contain relics of its bygone wealth. The porch of

Santa Maria Maggiore is overshadowed by an immense *loggia*, where the notables of the town used to assemble to discuss public affairs. The mutilated belfry of this church is very elegant, and some of its ornamentation is highly artistic.

The church of St. Dominic is also interesting, and contains two immense reliquaries, representing, the one the martyrdom of Saint Bartholomew, and the other St. Mary Magdalene. Their weight is considerable, and on the occasion of religious processions, each

The Lion of Roccapina.

requires twelve men to carry it. To be one óf the bearers is an eagerly sought honour, to obtain which even money is paid, but the coveted honour is a burdensome toil, and during the procession not a few of the perspiring bearers are heard to swear and mutter such oaths as " *Sangue di san Bourtoumia!* "

But my stay in Bonifacio soon came to an end, and for the last time I passed along the dusty road past the hermitage of the

17

Trinity, on my way to Ajaccio to embark on the steamer for Sardinia.

Looking across the sea, I saw, beyond the projecting reefs of the *Monacci*, a long cape surmounted by an ancient watch-tower, and terminating in the rock known as the Lion of Roccapina, a stony monster, pensively watching the sea and the distant coast of Sardinia.

# Part III.
# SARDINIA.

Roman Bridge at Porto Torres.

## CHAPTER I.

First Impressions.—Porto Torres and Roman Remains.—San Gavino.—Sassari.—A Town of Contrasts.—The *Zappatori.*—Carnival Time.—The Battle of the Standard.—Old Monasteries.—Sennori.

A Sardinian of "Logudoro."

SARDINIA, rarely visited even by its Italian masters, and almost unknown to the rest of Europe, had always haunted my imagination as a kind of accursed land, blighted by malaria, and peopled by morose beings, half savage and wholly brigand. My knowledge of the classics brought to mind the not very reassuring words of Cicero to his brother, " *Cura, mi frater, ut valeas et quamvis sit*

261

*hiems Sardiniam istam esse cogites,"* and again this line of the poet,—

*" Sed tristis cælo ac multa vitiata palude."*

The Romans, I was aware, had used Sardinia as a Van Diemen's Land for convicts sentenced to transportation, knowing that their graves were dug there in advance. " You will find Sardinia even at Tivoli," said the poet, when he wished to say, " Whatever you may do, you must die ! " " Sardinia will either cause you fear or pity," said a Corsican friend. " But," he added, " even if you should be saddened at first, do not be cast down, for you will find much to charm and surprise you.".

It was in this spirit of sadness, tempered by expectation, that, after a stormy night passage from Ajaccio, I watched the cold sky slowly warming to a rosy dawn, against which stood a range of mountains. Over the starboard bow stretched the long rocky belt forming the Island of Asinara, and far astern the hills of Corsica hid their snowy summits in radiant cloud-fleeces. Straight ahead was Sardinia, called by the Pelasgians by the Greek name of *Ichnusa*, because of the resemblance of its outline to the shape of a sandal.

The steamer forged slowly on, and Porto Torres, the first Sardinian town and the port of Sassari, hove in sight. Its appearance is not inviting. The harbour resembles a stagnant pond, and the low houses on either side of the long main street are squalid and swarming with pallid children, like a back alley in London slums. Yet lordly memories dwell in the deserted buildings beyond and in the ruined monuments of the diverse races which once inhabited the town. The Spaniards, at the height of their glory, built yonder embrasured turrets, reflected in the waters of the harbour. The Romans constructed those ruins, appearing through a trellis-work of cactus, as a Temple of Fortune, and the crumbling walls hard by are those of the *Palazzo del re barbaro*, an old basilica, restored by the Emperor Philip the Arabian in A.D. 247.

The rising ground above the town is crowned by the church of San Gavino, dating from the eleventh century, and restored in the thirteenth by a seigneur of Logudoro. Beyond the houses and ruins,

a landscape of ample, severe outlines undulates back to the inland
horizon,—a pallid, sad-looking country under a torn sky of dead
white clouds, with deep-blue spaces in between.

Porto Torres, which only now seems beginning to awake from
the long slumber which fell upon it at the close of the Middle Ages,
was in its day a great city, and, under its Roman name of *Turris*

Sardinians of Porto Torres.

*Libyssonis*, capital of Northern Sardinia.  Its ancient splendour is
proved by the mutilated statues and marble divinities still found
embedded in the marshy soil, and the precious mosaics, columns and
capitals, elaborate weapons, coins, and medals still struck by the
ploughshares and spades of the farmers.  There is, moreover, still
visible evidence of greatness, in the ruins of the palace and aqueducts,
and the massive seven-arched Roman bridge crossing the ancient
*flumen Turritanum*.

The French vice-consul at Sassari accompanied me on my pilgrimage to these ruins of past greatness, along the grass-grown vestiges of the Roman way, where we encountered Sardinian horsemen of strange aspect, wearing the national *capotu* on their heads, while their long, raven hair and untrimmed beards contrasted oddly with the classic regularity of their profiles. The consul, who regarded such passers-by with the indifference born of custom, was surprised at my taking the trouble to stop and look at the people.

The Roman bridge crosses the mouth of the river. Its buttresses, formed of blocks of porphyry, sink into the stagnant water, which lies still and dark amid tall grasses, with-

Porch of San Gavino.

out sound or ripple, reflecting the massive arches, like a black, burnished mirror. But for all its apparent stillness, the water is for ever actively distilling poison, and Porto Torres is notorious as one of the most malarious towns in Sardinia.

The basilica of San Gavino, now merely the parish church of

the town, was at the end of the fifteenth century the cathedral of a powerful archbishopric. As early as the eighth century its walls witnessed solemn services of thanksgiving, celebrated by the magnates of Torres for victories gained over the Saracens, whose bodies and armour were heaped up on the steps before the porch The interior of the basilica is divided into three naves, or, more properly speaking, a central nave and two side aisles, separated by marble, granite, and porphyry columns in different styles. These pillars, several of which came from the Roman Temple of Fortune, uphold the juniper-wood beams supporting the open roof. One of these beams is always more or less humid—a phenomenon regarded as miraculous by the simple country folk. The crypt contains the bones of three martyrs, San Proto, San Giannario, and San Gavino who is the patron saint of Northern Sardinia.

His feast day, celebrated on the eve of Whit-Sunday, is a time of rejoicing, during which Porto Torres assumes an unwontedly animated aspect, and is invaded by troops of country people in gala costume from all parts of the district of Logudoro. Many of the pilgrims come with the object of making the round of each column in the basilica on their knees, kissing the pillars devoutly, and concluding with prayers before the equestrian statue of the saint. The legend runs that San Gavino raised one of the columns from the bottom of the sea, and, placing it upright on his saddle-bow, carried it into the church.

Before leaving Porto Torres the pilgrims, taking their wives behind them, ride their horses breast-deep into 'the sea; for the waters of the gulf, formerly sanctified by the martyrs who were thrown into them, possess great virtue and render the horses immune from all maladies!

The proprietary rights of the basilica are vested in the town of Sassari, on condition that the municipality visits Porto Torres each year on the feast of San Gavino, and holds a corporate banquet, at which the one indispensable dish is—a rib of veal! The members of the town council in their robes of office, preceded by mace-bearers, are formally received by the canon in residence at

Porto Torres, who, standing on a platform, gravely presents the
keys of the church to the *Sindaco*. The latter, after taking them
in his hand to notify his proprietorship, gives them back to the
canon and begs him to watch over the charge confided to him by
the town of Sassari.

Another strange custom, which was still practised a few years
ago, was for pilgrims from Sassari to visit the crypt of San Gavino,
and there give themselves the discipline till the blood flowed, chanting
the *Miserere* the while.

From Porto Torres to Sassari takes three-quarters of an hour
in the train. The line crosses a vast uncultivated waste, where the
only objects to break the monotony are a ruined *nuraghe* or a broken
arch of the old Roman aqueduct. At intervals one catches sight
of a solitary shepherd, watching herds of black goats browsing on
the thorny bushes covering the thin soil ; but not a tree, big or little,
gladdens the eye with its verdure or enlivens the solitude with its
waving shadow. All this confirmed the gloomy anticipations I had
formed of Sardinian town and country life, and I was inclined
to regret that I had come to the island, when the scenery began
to change. First came cochineal plants and fig trees, on the low
ground ; then, wooded heights and cultivated fields ; and finally, the
town. The brief autumn day was just closing, and the last sunset
rays reddened the roofs of the houses, from which the smoke of
evening fires was rising in vertical blue columns : the wind was
lulled, and a crescent moon hung over the town like a pale
diadem.

Sassari, the chief town of the island next to Cagliari, is built
on the slope of a hill, looking towards the sea, surrounded by forest.
The courtesy of its people is proverbial. They are distinguished
both by customs and dialect from the remainder of the island, and
speak, indeed, with a certain contempt of the other inhabitants.
The latter are Sardinians, that is, barbarians ; but *they* are
*Sassaresi.*

The town itself, apart from the main streets and public squares,
is a maze of tiny streets, so narrow that one often has to stand in

a doorway to permit of the passage of some Sardinian horseman, cloaked in black, with his hand on his hip, his gun across the saddle bow, his long pipe in his mouth, and his wife riding on a pillion behind him.

The shops in these narrow ways are dark and low-pitched, and through the half-opened doors one generally perceives in the darkness the dim lamps burning before a pale *Madonna*. The men and women who pass and repass in the sombre passages, seem as unsubstantial as shadows. Some of the fronts of these buildings, however, contrast strongly with the dark interiors. A red flag floating over the doorway, inscribed in black letters with the word *Vino*, indicates a wine shop, and in nearly every case the character of the goods sold in the establishment is told by the sign over the door—a piece of coal, a tomato, a candle, a dried fig, macaroni, a loaf, an apple, or a flagon of oil or wine, often both in the same bottle, suspended by a chain from the lintel. The chief article on sale appears to be a splendid kind of waxy-looking apple, called *melappio*, heaps of which lie on nearly every threshold, filling the whole street with their sweet smell.

Sassari is above all a town of contrasts.

With its chief buildings, palaces, institutions, and fine shops, the place looks as modern as a brand-new suburb of London, yet the majority of the people still conform to the customs of their ancestors, and preserve a savage self-assertiveness of demeanour, as if in their hearts, like the Goths in ancient Rome, they secretly despised the conveniences and luxury of civilisation. The sumptuous wares of Paris, lavishly displayed behind plate-glass fronts, are passed by with scarcely a glance of curiosity by proud beggars clad in little but rags. A tattered garment is considered an adornment, almost an affectation and an advertisement of the dignity of impecuniosity.

The air of activity and industry in the streets is very striking. Every one seems in a hurry about his or her own business, and the cafés, of which there are but few, are little frequented.

On the evening of the day after my arrival, when the darkening

sky cast upon the earth the strange blue twilight, peculiar to the
white cities of the south at nightfall, I went for a ramble in the
poorer quarters of the town. The narrow streets seemed all alive
with flying sparks from the charcoal-braziers, which it is the custom
of the housewives to kindle at nightfall in the open air, before preparing the evening meal. Some of the women were leaning over the
red glow and blowing with all the force of their lungs, others
were fanning the charcoal with round straw mats, and the
lazy ones were letting the wind act as bellows. The strange
performance is repeated every night, as the houses in general have
no chimneys.

The churches of Sassari are very numerous, but for the most part
uninteresting. The façade of the cathedral is striking, but over-
decorated. In bright sunlight, however, the peculiar yellow tinge of
the stone produces wonderful effects, and the lofty cornices and
profuse sculpture gleam almost like burnished metal.

As usual, my errant footsteps led me to one of the pompous but
lugubrious ceremonies which, in all these Mediterranean islands,
invest death with the horror attached to it by the Catholic Church,
when she speaks of it as one of the " four last things to be remembered." Entering the cathedral one evening, I found the nave
dark and full of mystery. A black carpet embroidered with yellow
lay on the flags in front of the choir. The design on the carpet
was a representation of Death in the form of a crowned skeleton
sitting on a throne, with a sceptre in one hand and a scythe in
the other, while at his feet were heaped a tiara, a mitre, a bishop's
crosier, a helmet with waving plumes, some half-opened books,
and a bird. Immense candelabra stood at the four corners of this
strange tapestry. On one side stood a priest holding a thurible
in one hand, while the other was over his heart. Opposite him
was an old server bearing a silver cross, the stem of which rested on
the ground. On the third side were three priests in black capes,
bordered with yellow, the midmost one of whom was chanting
the service for the dead. When the prayers were over, the officiating
priest blessed the black tapestry with holy water, while another priest

censed it. The candles were then extinguished and the carpet was rolled up and removed.

Coming out of the dark cathedral into the open air almost blinded my eyes, although the hour was late and daylight was failing. There was just a glimpse of pale blue through a ragged, cloudy sky, and a rich crimson light fluted the high cornices of the building.

It was the hour when the *zappatori*, day field-labourers, return to the town. Here they came, singly or in groups, some mounted, some on foot, carrying their wallets, and each leading in a leash the little dog which guards their provisions while they are at work.

They leave the town just after the sun is up and return before sunset, in order to avoid the miasma which rises chiefly before sunrise and immediately after sundown. The length of the working day is thus necessarily regulated

Zappatori.

by considerations of health, but it is an arrangement at which the proprietors grumble considerably, more especially as the men show no anxiety to make up for the hours wasted in going to and returning from labour, but, on the contrary, display a remarkable ingenuity in still further curtailing the actual period of work, by a whole series of short intervals for refreshments, and adopt every expedient to do as little as possible.

But the masters dare not quarrel with them. The *zappatori* form a powerful guild, or, to be more modern, "union," which has to be reckoned with at Sassari, where for over a century there has been a sort of labour exchange. The men assemble on some public place, generally at the entrance of the town, as in Palestine in the time of Christ, and wait there to be hired. The engagement is generally for a week, and since the year 1848 the wages have always to be paid in advance.

The *zappatori* form one of the ancient guilds known as *gremii*, which have existed at Sassari since the Middle Ages. These guilds play a prominent part in public processions, particularly in that of the *candellieri*, the most popular of all.

In order to take part in this ceremony, which is in fulfilment of a vow made during the plague which raged in the town in 1582, the representatives of the guilds attire themselves as fantastically as possible, and carry immense candlesticks decked with many-coloured ribbons. The statue of the Virgin, carried in this procession, represents her as dead and lying on a bed.

Throughout Sardinia the inhabitants of the towns give themselves up to merrymaking with the careless enthusiasm of children. At Sassari during carnival time the entire population is masked, and assembles in the public squares to dance and play all sorts of high jinks. On Shrove-Monday, young girls in costume perambulate the town with baskets of violets, which they distribute among the people as they pass.

A curious observance to be noted is that, during the carnival, every one, from the richest to the poorest, wears gloves. Some of the people are marvellous mimics. They will imitate the prefect or a city magistrate to the life, copying his clothes and gestures, and making up their faces to resemble his very features. Whence arise endless quips and cranks and delicious merriment.

On Shrove-Tuesday the figure of King Carnival is carried through the town, and burnt in the evening on the *Piazza Castello*, the chief square of Sassari, to the sound of music. The people then dance the national *douro-douro*, by the light of Venetian lamps. During the last three days of carnival, the municipality is compelled to engage men to sweep up the litter of *confetti* and other missiles in the streets.

Yet, during all this excitement and abandonment to sheer merry-making, there is never an angry word nor a quarrel, not even a single case of drunkenness. In fact, I never once met a drunken man during the whole time of my stay in Sardinia.

The religious ceremonies, apart from the *candellieri* processions mentioned above, are very curious at Sassari. They all preserve a certain element of grimness, traceable no doubt to Spanish traditions.

During the last three days of Holy Week, the procession of the Passion takes place. This somewhat resembles the Corsican processions. The figure of Christ, after the taking down from the cross, is carried in a white sheet by penitents, followed by men dressed like Jews and wearing cardboard masks painted to resemble the traditional Jewish physiognomy. These carry the instruments of the Passion, while others, by some strange freak of anachronism or ignorance, bear, on a salver, a decapitated head. Finally comes the Virgin in tears, clad in mourning, a handkerchief in her hand and seven swords protruding from her heart.

The sepulchres, or Altars of Repose, on which the Host is kept from Maunday Thursday till Good Friday morning, are ornamented with a number of small vases, containing wheat. This is sown a fortnight previously, and, if it germinates without delay, is considered a fortunate augury for the next harvest.

In 1848 religious processions were forbidden, but the cholera visitation of 1855 was regarded as a judgment inflicted on the city for its abandonment of these pious practices, and they were forthwith restored.

A certain canon called Scavo, once called down upon himself the curses of all the guilds in Sassari (and heaven knows they are numerous enough!) for ordering the churches to be closed at sunset, night processions by torchlight being a diversion of which the people are passionately fond.

Nevertheless, the canon acted from excellent motives, as the processions have, on more than one occasion, given rise to scandal and even tumults, chiefly owing to the jealousies subsisting between the various guilds, notably between that of the tailors and that of the cordwainers.

One night, on the feast of St. Crispin, the cordwainers were marching in full array to the chapel of their patron, while the tailors were already in church, praying before the statue of St. Anthony, represented with his traditional pig. This animal was also portrayed on the white silk banner of the guild, which had been placed in a corner of the church. While the tailors were devoutly murmuring litanies, a young shoemaker, seeing the banner, amused himself by drawing two immense horns on the head of the pig. After the prayers, the banner was displayed before the statue of St. Anthony to be blessed, and the awful profanation became plain to see. The tailors' guild rose as one man, and rushed upon the cordwainers with loud shouts and imprecations. Knives and daggers were drawn, and before order could be restored many were wounded on either side.

One of the principal religious festivals of Sassari is the feast day of San Gavino, whose relics are preserved in the crypt of the basilica of Porto Torres, while his statue decorates the cathedral. This statue, which is about three feet high, is of massive silver. In 1793, the French troops landed on the northern coast of Sardinia, and the terrified inhabitants flocked to Sassari to invoke the protection of San Gavino. They explained to him their position and trouble, and implored him to save them from their enemies. In order to secure the saint on their side, they represented to him that he himself would suffer from the invasion. "O San Gavino," said they, "observe that, more for thee than for ourselves, it is necessary that the enemy do not conquer our country. Remember, O Saint! that thou art of precious metal, and these French robbers of churches will make of thy sacred person two bushels of small

coin.   Reflect, O Gavino! that thou wilt be transformed into
innumerable *pesos de cincu* " (Sardinian pieces of five *soldi*).

Whether because the saint deprecated being converted into coin

Water-carrier at Sassari.

or for some other reason, the French retired, and the island was
saved,—a result naturally attributed to the influence of Gavino.

The days passed quickly at Sassari, although it was the depth
of the winter season, and the rains were persistent and threatened
to continue for another month.

18

Nevertheless, whenever the sun did break through the clouds, it was as if the country suddenly threw off mourning for the attire of a bride.  In these bright intervals, I managed to visit most of what is worth seeing in and around Sassari.

The much-vaunted *Fontana del Rosello*, on the east side of the town, is a marble fountain in the tasteless style of the seventeenth century, with four statues at the corners representing the four seasons. An abundant flow of water is vomited from the mouths of several masks, and the fountain is ornamented with the arms of the town of Sassari and of Aragon, and surmounted by an equestrian statue of San Gavino, in warrior's costume.  One side of the erection bears the inscription, " *Feliciter regnante potentissimo Hispaniarum et Sardini rege Philippo III.,*" *etc.*

More interesting than the fountain were the scenes among the water-carriers and their small donkeys, who convey the water to the town in small barrels.  They were the smallest and most submissive donkeys I had ever seen.  They must have been strong too, poor beasts, to carry three barrels of water and the driver seated atop, up the steep road to the town.

The neighbourhood of Sassari is rich in old monasteries, now chiefly occupied by modern, " active " orders, whose obliterated life in the silence and chill peace of the lofty monastic corridors is one of sublime devotion.  Among those I visited, was one formerly occupied by Capuchins, but which now shelters the sisters of St. Vincent of Paul, who have converted the building into a home for foundlings.

Poverty, and even distress, seemed to exhale from the old walls and float in the twilight of the dim corridors.  The colours of the sparse flowers in the garden gained in brilliancy, from the contrast which they afforded to the severe-looking building, under a cloudy sky, on a land sobered by autumn.

But the children rescued by the holy women lead a life of useful industry.  The very young children are left to play about to their hearts' content, but the older girls weave for the convent, and the boys are taught trades which generally enable them to earn their own livelihood after leaving the institution.

The Rosello Fountain at Sassari.

The sisters of St. Vincent of Paul conduct several important charitable institutions in Sardinia, having houses at Alghero, Ozieri, Oristano, Iglesias, and Cagliari, but all serve their probation at the mother-house in Paris.

Owing to this fact, French is better known in Sardinia than in any other Italian province.

Another monastery which I visited was that of *San Pietro in Silchi*, a massy pile of buildings buried in olive groves, and occupied by Franciscans and sisters of charity, the latter of whom have a home for old people. The nuns' garden, which is magnificent, is tended entirely by the pensioners, who thus recompense to some extent the care lavished on them by the good sisters.

At the Franciscan friary we were received by the superior in an immense sacristy, hung with weird-looking pictures of saints in archaic attitudes, made dimly visible by the light from the high windows. The church was damp and dark, and our footsteps re-echoed lugubriously on the tombstones forming the flags, while the friars appeared mere ghosts in the gloom.

As the twilight fell and we drove homeward along the road, gleaming mysteriously white through the trees, I was haunted by the memory of this church, as of something vague and distant like a dream. The other buildings of Sassari, however, are far from possessing this charm of vagueness. The prefecture is vast, and its apartments are sumptuously furnished, but in the most execrable taste, at once pretentious and ugly.

There is an interesting collection of pictures at the town-hall, and a library of 37,000 volumes at the university, besides the beginnings of a museum of antiquities, but, otherwise, nature is far more attractive than art at Sassari.

Unfortunately, nature had hitherto been marred by almost incessant rain ; but at length came a Sunday morning when my sleeping-room was inundated by a flow of southern sunlight, and I eagerly fell in with a proposal of my friend Mariani that we should visit Sennori ; though what Sennori was, whether mountain, forest, gorge, or town, I had not the remotest idea. But had it been the

great Panjandrum himself, I should have gone with equal delight, so
vivified were my spirits by the great flood of sunshine, bathing field,
forest, and building in one impartial radiance.

We drove northward along a lofty road, with views of the distant
sea, dipping at intervals into rich valleys, where the palms shimmered
in the breeze and the red roses were a foil to the golden oranges.
Now we would plunge into the shade of a grove of olives, whose
leaves, still glistening with moisture, showered down a rain of tepid,
silvery tears as we passed.   White houses shone in an embowerment
of verdure, and damp masses hung like velvet from the old walls of
an occasional ruin.   From the valley we climbed gradually to the
sloping side of a lofty hill, and suddenly saw, far to the northward,
an entrancing vision of the snowy peaks of Corsica, which seemed to
float like clouds in the blue.   We tried to distinguish the different
mountains, but with indifferent success, so altered did the outlines
appear from those we had learned to know in Corsica.   So we
contented ourselves with sheer enjoyment of the beauty of the
prospect, many a pure delight being marred by man's crude instinct
for classification and analysis.

From this distance, the island appeared a jewel of opal and
mother-of-pearl set in a sea of amethyst ; so why have reduced it to
matter-of-fact rock, earth, and water ?

As we admired, the sound of a bell broke on our ears, and turning
a corner, we came suddenly upon Sennori, an ideal village, rising in
tiers among the trees, to culminate in a picturesque spire.

Leaving the carriage at the entrance to the village, we climbed
the steep, deserted streets to the church, where every one was now
hearing mass.   The men stood in groups before the door, most of
them wearing the ancient, national dress, which harmonised so well
with their characteristic faces.   They politely made way for us as we
entered the building, which was crowded, chiefly with women, who, in
spite of their gay costumes, knelt bravely on the bare stone flags of
the floor.

When service was over, the widows were the first to come out,
with their immense pleated skirts turned up over their head, the

In Gala Costume.

Head-dress of Sennori Women.

sombreness of their striking dress enhancing the pallor of their faces. Behind the widows came a joyous bevy of young women and maidens, who quite brightened the old stone steps leading down to the platform on which the church was built. The mingled white, red, and blue of their dresses, their golden corsets, their chased necklaces and studs, the white linen head-dress, not unlike the hoods of sisters of charity, and their demure faces, wreathed in little smiles of surprise at the appearance of strangers, composed a pleasing picture of youth and colour, which vanished all too soon, like the memory of a time that has been and is not.

I was made welcome at the house of a friend, and was struck by the simplicity and bareness of the village-interiors, which, both at Sennori and elsewhere, are strangely disproportionate to the richness of the dresses.

Dress, it appears, is one of the chief pre-occupations of the Sardinian girls. Immediately after their first Communion, they set about preparing their wedding dresses, which are so elaborate that they occupy several years in the making. If a girl dies, she is buried in the dress which she has got ready for her marriage.

At Sennori, this dress consists of a short vest of crimson velvet, with sleeves slashed in the mediæval fashion, so as to display the white chemise underneath. These sleeves are ornamented at the wrist by a row of gold or silver filigree buttons, only one of which is fastened. The open bosom of the vest displays a gold-embroidered corset, laced in front with red. The skirt is made of coarse black cloth, woven in the country and pleated by the women themselves. At the bottom of the skirt there is a broad band of white silk embroidered with flowers of various colours. The apron is of blue silk with a black fringe. The head-dress is a sort of wimple of fine linen, not unlike the style common in France under Charles VI.

On ordinary occasions the velvet vest is replaced by a brown vest, the slashed sleeves of which are made of two large bands, one red and the other blue. During the week, the women often veil the lower part of the face with a silk handkerchief, reminding one of a Turkish yashmak, but worn in order to protect the mouth and prevent the inhalation of the miasma from the marshes. Bare feet are the rule ;

Basket-making.

but when shoes are worn, they are elegant little slippers, and not fashionable Parisian monstrosities.

Having seen the women of Sennori on a Sunday, I wondered what these finely attired princesses did on a week-day, and took advantage of the next fine day to gratify my curiosity.

I saw again the tortuous streets, the old houses and the poor church, and in the streets my princesses, mostly barefoot, but still dressed in the same bright colours. Some were sitting in the sunlight before the doors weaving large flat baskets of reeds, which is a habitual occupation of the women of the country, while others were working alone in whitewashed rooms, dimly lighted by a grated window. Occasionally, several wove their reeds together, in bare spacious rooms, where half-naked children basked or crawled on the sun-warmed floor. My proud princesses and grave maidens of the previous Sunday were transformed into industrious toilers, laughing and chattering, and occasionally singing some ancient stave, such as—

| | |
|---|---|
| " *Convertidas sunt in iras* | " Changed to rage |
| *Sas amorosas fiammas,*" *etc.* | Is the flame of his love," etc. |

Everywhere at Sennori I received a cordial welcome; but this was nothing surprising, for the Sardinian is very hospitable. "*Sa domo est minore, su core est manu*" ("His house is small, but his heart is big"), as the Sardinian proverb hath it.

A foreign engineer, weary with a long ride through mountains and forests, and weak from hunger, once stopped at the first house he came to, and asked to buy some bread. "We don't sell bread," was the only reply. Further on, he applied at another house, and received the self-same answer. The coincidence made him reflect. "Well!" said he, "if you don't sell bread, perhaps you will give me some? I'm hungry." Whereupon he was made eagerly welcome, and given ample to satisfy his appetite.

Seeing a good-looking girl in one of the houses, I begged her to sit for her portrait. She obstinately refused at first, notwithstanding the wish of her mother, but suddenly changing her mind, sullenly

On the Threshold.

crossed her arms and
sat in front of the
door, saying, " There !
take my portrait, if
it pleases you so
much."

When I had
finished, she had not
even the curiosity to
look at my sketch,
and re-entered the
house. I followed her
and offered her some
money to recom-
pense her for her
trouble, but she
blushed and shrugged
her shoulders, without
even deigning to re-
fuse my present.

At the lower end
of the village, in a
valley threaded by a
little stream, I found
an orange orchard.
The fruit was just
ripening, and the in-
tense green of the
foliage was starred
with innumerable
golden spheres.

" What is the
meaning of those
horns fastened to the branches ?" I asked of a Sardinian who was
passing.

"It is to ward off evil influences, which would render the trees sterile, that we hang rams' horns to the branches, as you see!"

The shadows slowly lengthened, the lights in the woodland died away, and soon only the lofty church of Sennori showed a trembling ray suspended from the vault of heaven above the obscure village, like the light of a sanctuary lamp. Even this was presently obscured by the twilight, and night fell. As I drove back to Sassari along the dark, silent road, looking over the sea, which reflected the pale radiance of a waning moon, I seemed to hear an interior voice murmuring the fragment of Sardinian poetry—

> " *Convertidas sunt in iras*
> *Sas amorosas fiammas. . . ."*

Not only passionate love, but everything else changes. The smiles of to-day are succeeded by the tears of to-morrow, and even while the sun gleams on the foliage, clouds are massing in the offing.

Among the Limbara Mountains.

## CHAPTER II.

Sorso.—A Classical Picture.—Fevers.—An Allegory on the Road.—Osilo.—The Manor of Malespina.—A Sardinian *Vendetta.*—The Tragic Story of Giovanni.

NOVEMBER, chill and dark in Northern Europe, is wayward and morose in Sardinia, where torrential rains and sudden gales alternate with days of calm and spring-like airs.

On such a day of sunlight, succeeding a night of storm, I took leave of the excellent *Albergo Azuni*, where I had stayed at Sassari, and started for Sorso.

After a long spell of bad weather, nature was smiling like a convalescent child. The azure of the sky was of singular trans-lucency, and the few fleecy clouds, slowly floating north-eastward, seemed immeasurably detached from the deep, receding sky. A faint mist shimmered over the lowlands, but the air on the heights was pure and bright, and laden with the suavity of a thousand aromatic plants.

In fine weather, the neighbourhood of Sassari, with its valleys shaded by orange groves, and the white or pink country houses shining like azalea blossoms in the tawny woods, seems to merit the name bestowed on the northern portion of Sardinia—the *logudoro* or country of gold.

Sorso is the next village to Sennori, but the inhabitants appear of a different race. Here, the women affect white or pink for their dress, and their faces are often partially veiled like those of the Moorish women in North Africa. They glide noiselessly through the streets in their strange costume, which is absolutely devoid of ornament, but, from its simplicity, both of form and colour, has the

Old Man of Sorso.

quality of giving the women an appearance of stature and grace, often more than their own.

The men have a wild aspect, very like that of the Corsican mountaineers; nor is this surprising when we know that the north coast of Sardinia was for long a place of refuge for the oppressed

19

people of the sister isle. Certain villages of the Gallura, the northern-most province, are peopled by the descendants of bandits from the other side of the Straits of Bonifacio.

I saw two typical old men seated on a stone bench outside a house—sombre, cowled veterans, etched in mezzotint against the white wall. One of them was pleased to sit to me for his portrait, and proved one of the best fellows in the world, having nothing in common with a malefactor except his aspect ; but all the same, 1 should not have relished meeting such a figure at nightfall at the corner of a wood.

At Sorso, as elsewhere, I was treated with wide hospitality, and my friend, Signor Catta, a member of the district council, even introduced me to his wife, which, following southern and eastern precedent, is not the custom of the country. Owing to this lack of introduction, it sometimes befalls a stranger to mistake the mistress of the house for one of the servants, and vice versâ. My Sorso hostess was too distinguished-looking, however, for such an error to be possible, and we conversed cordially and with passable comprehension, in Catalan, the dialect most resembling Sardinian.

The public fountain, which Sorso owes to the Spaniards, is a white stone erection, pleasantly embowered in dense foliage, situated at the lower end of a steeply sloping avenue, terminating in a flight of broad steps. To see the women drawing water, or waiting by this fountain with their amphora poised on their heads, is to see a classic picture, such as might come from the brush of Mr. Poynter. Their long, severe garments with flowing folds, and the pure harmony between the pure colour and texture of the fabric and the white stone fountain and green foliage, make up a composition quite Hellenic in its effective simplicity.

At the end of the avenue opposite to the fountain rises the cathedral, a pseudo-Moorish building, the cupolas of which soar above the trees like a lofty mosque.

Beyond the village are the ruins of the manor-house of the Mores family, progenitors of the Dukes of Asinara and Vallombrosa. The house was sacked by the Sardinian peasants in 1793. In the door-

way of a house opposite this sombre relic of departed grandeur, I
saw a young woman wearing a sort of turban, and with her breast
covered with ornaments. She resembled the Jewesses one meets
in the Kasbah of Algiers, and her dress harmonised with her Oriental
type of face. But the face was pitiable to see, it was so ravaged and
wasted by fever. Sorso is especially malarious on account of the
exhalations from the *stagno di Platamona*, between the village and
the sea. Fever not only strikes adults, but even children, and it is
painful to observe the poor little things, lying pallid and moaning in
the arms of their mothers.

The sun grew slightly obscured as the day wore on, and the light
became of a strange, lurid, orange hue, which made distant objects
gleam like fused metal. In the shadow of the woods, women
were gathering olives,—vague figures in half-tint, like those in an
impression by Corot. Men were returning from work, their tools,
and often a bundle of faggots besides, on their shoulders.

" *Bona sera !* " said each one in passing ; and looking seaward, we
saw, against the bank of clouds, into which the sun had fallen, the
signal of night blinking from the lighthouse of Porto Torres.

South-west of Sorso, and nearly equidistant from that town and
Sassari, is Osilo, one of the most important country towns in
Sardinia, with a population exceeding five thousand. Built on a
lofty hill, it is free from malaria, but is exposed both to the great
heats of summer and the rain-storms of winter.

The way through the olive woods on the road from Sassari to
Osilo is made interesting by many quaint encounters, forming
almost a mediæval allegory of life.

Now passes a priest on horseback, his breviary in hand, his gun
across his saddle-bow, his housekeeper riding pillion behind him—
now a cluster of dark, cowled horsemen, riding like the wind and
disappearing in a cloud of dust.

Hither, more leisurely, come two lovers on the same mount,
conversing in whispers scarce distinguishable from the rustling of the
leaves, which brush their heads as they pass. Her arms are tightly
locked round him, with the excuse of thus maintaining a firmer seat.

Her head is bent forward so that her lips are at his ear ; he half looks over his shoulder to answer. The neglected nag which bears them, ambles leisurely along at his own sweet will—sweeter to him than all the lovers' whispers—and, not infrequently, stops to crop the grass in a shady spot by the road, where the man and girl are hidden for a moment behind the friendly foliage-screen.

So they pass, and with them the woods and greenery of the foothills. The heat grows more intense, and the road reaches a volcanic tableland, where a large solitary pine dominates the naked landscape.

Over against us, frowned upon by the dark turrets of a ruined castle, Osilo glitters in the sun on the summit of a wild, bare mountain, the slopes of which appear to have cracked into fissures from the heat.

The road before ascending, dips down to the pastures where the herds stand silent and panting in the noonday. Round and about are hills of crenellated rock, like fortresses, divided by shallow valleys of brown woodland. The track skirts an arid ravine, the rocky walls of which are honeycombed with prehistoric cave dwellings.

The isolated house at the foot of Mount Osilo is a *cantoniera*, a primitive inn or refuge, where belated travellers may pass the night on the bare floor,—poor accommodation enough, but often not to be despised in the mountain solitudes of Sardinia.

As we ascended the mountain, the air freshened, but the whole landscape glared with heat. Suddenly, near the summit, the sterile ground appeared to have given birth to beds of brilliant flowers. The arid volcanic slope was flecked with groups of laughing girls, whose red petticoats, white linen head-dresses, and gold-embroidered corsets glittered in the sun. They were the washerwomen of Osilo, making the most of the rivulets filtering through the depressions in the soil or carefully husbanded in shallow, artificial basins. After weeks of rain and storm, these women were taking advantage of the fine day to get through their work while the supply of water lasted.

Leaving the laughing company behind, I plunged into a labyrinth of narrow streets, and asked my way to the castle. Two men

Washing Linen at Osilo.

offered to guide me to the ruins, which are some two thousand feet above sea-level, and command a splendid view of the surrounding country.

On the very crest of the mountain rise two broken towers, built of blocks of black basalt stained by orange-coloured lichen. The walls of the courtyard are crumbling, and the wind whistles between the disjointed stones. Far away to the northward, beyond the streak of sea and the cliffs of Bonifacio, rise the mountains of Corsica, snow-capped, rocky, and streaked with dark lines, which are forests. At one's feet lies Sardinia, a rude contrast to the splendour of the more distant isle ; for this region of Anglona is bare and sad, and all the highlands of Gallura have that wildness of aspect which suggests remoteness and even estrangement from humanity.

My two Sardinian guides were sitting on their haunches on the ground. The light of the setting sun gave a sort of ruddy varnish to their rough, brown faces : the wind fluttered their unkempt beards and tangled hair. The noises of Osilo rose with singular distinctness in the evening stillness, but of the town itself only the tiled roofs were visible, with here and there the dark furrow of a narrow street. The sea-horizon faded into immensity of distance ; a pale band of foreshore marked the winding, but bare and cliffless coast-line of Sardinia ; the bare summits of the Limbara mountains were purple ash-colour in the last of the light ; a few villages gleamed here and there like foam flakes, and a haze of blue smoke rising from the forest marked the site of Sassari.

The two ebon-hued towers protected me from the wind, and by my side were my savage-looking guides.

The elder spoke.

" This manor-house," said he, " of which you see the keep calcined by the sun, burned by the lightning, and flayed by the winds, was the house of the Malespina. Later on, it belonged to Alfonso of Aragon, and to the Doria family. After being several times besieged, the castle was at length carried by assault, and laid waste to such good purpose that the place was forgotten, and stone by stone its proud walls began to crumble away. At the beginning of this century, the Serra and Fadda families of Osilo were at feud, and one of them took refuge in this castle, and sustained a long siege, in which even the women cut and thrust with the best of the warriors, a terrible instance of the fury of the *vendettas*, which have resulted in the shedding of so much Sardinian blood.

"When a family enters upon a *vendetta*, they begin by cutting off the ears or tail, often both, of one or several of their enemy's horses. This is the first warning—an injury cruelly resented, because the horse is the animal best beloved of the Sardinians.

"The second warning is similar, and consists in ham-stringing the enemy's cattle.

"For the third and last token, three shots are fired at one of the windows of the house.

"War is then declared. Each murder, no matter who may be either victim or assailant, leads to terrible dramas, exceeding in violence and horror even the most tragic of Corsican *vendettas*. In certain Sardinian villages, the relatives smear their faces with the blood of the murdered man, and take oath never to wash their faces or trim their beards, and to wear the same clothes and same linen, until their vengeance is fulfilled.

"A *vendetta* which made a great noise in the country was that of Giovanni Cano, a native of Ozieri, a village over yonder in the mountains"—and my guide pointed to the east. "Giovanni was studying at Sassari University when his father died. His mother had already succumbed in giving birth to her only daughter, Adelita, who had henceforward to depend upon the support of her brother. Giovanni, leaving the university, returned home to Ozieri, and was busy arranging matters connected with his inheritance, when certain disquieting rumours came to his ears regarding the nature of his sister's relations with one of his friends, named Luigi, a young Lombard doctor. Although ascribing these reports to malice, Giovanni thought fit to warn his friend. 'I beg you to go away,' said he, 'and do not injure Adelita's reputation.'

"Luigi left accordingly, but returned to Adelita every time her

Young Woman of Osilo.

brother was absent from Ozieri. One evening Giovanni returned unexpectedly, and surprising the lovers together, only spared Luigi's life on condition that he quitted the district. He himself then left, and established himself with his sister in his grandfather's house, at Oschiri. Some time later he went to Sassari on a visit, but, before leaving, charged his head shepherd Antonio to watch well over Adelita, and, above all, to see that she was not visited by the young doctor. At Sassari, however, Giovanni fell ill, and when he was recovering, Antonio sent him news that frequent visits had been paid to the house during his absence by Luigi.

"Notwithstanding his weakness, he at once set off on horseback for Oschiri, where he arrived the same night. Antonio met him on the road, and they watched together till morning. At the first streak of dawn, Luigi came out of the house. Giovanni rushed upon him, but not wishing to kill his former friend, dragged him by the collar to the brink of a precipice. 'There,' said Giovanni afterwards, 'we could fight man to man, till one of us fell into the abyss ; and Antonio would act as second in our duel.'

"But the struggle was not over, when Luigi suddenly fired his pistol and took to flight. He had not gone far, before two shots followed in quick succession. The one from Giovanni's pistol missed ; the other, from Antonio's gun, did not miss. Luigi fell dead, and poor Adelita, who had been a spectator of the combat, rushed out of the house, and threw herself on the body of her lover.

"The sound of the firing was heard by two mounted carabineers, who were passing near at the time, and they hurried to the scene. On perceiving the dead body of Luigi, they covered Giovanni and Antonio with their rifles, and called upon them, in the king's name, to surrender. For reply Antonio fired, and wounded one of the men. The other promptly retorted with a shot which stretched the shepherd dead on the ground. Scarcely had he fallen before Giovanni had avenged his death, and the carabineer, with a bullet in his heart, fell back lifeless across the flanks of his horse, which, mad with terror, bolted across country with its lifeless rider hanging inert over its back. Adelita, bathed in her lover's blood, had fainted, and Giovanni,

seizing her in his arms, carried her into the house, and, mounting
a horse, fled to the forests of the Limbara, an outcast and a marked
man.   After a period of miserable wandering in the wilds, he was
seized with home-hunger, and was anxious to learn how fared his
sister, whom he still loved.   One evening found him at twilight near
Oschiri.   An old man whom he did not know was creeping along
the road.   To this man he addressed himself, and, with feigned
indifference, spoke of Giovanni.   The old man sighed.

"'See,' said he, 'that is his house yonder; but there is no light,
because no one lives there now.   Giovanni has a great and noble
heart, yet he has been sentenced to death, and his sister died of
grief a few days ago.'

"Having thus spoken, the old man slowly wended his way to
the village.   But Giovanni, fired by despair, remounted his horse,
rode like a maniac across the fields and plains, and coming to the
brink of a precipice, leaped over into the chasm.   Some shepherds
who saw him pass, his face of an ashen pallor, his hair streaming
in the wind, his spurs dug rowel-deep in the sides of his affrighted
steed, took him for a phantom.

"Wonderful to relate, however, he escaped with his life, and
only his horse was dashed to pieces.   The bandit Gian Domenico
Porqueddu, happening to pass the spot, found Giovanni lying senseless at the bottom of the precipice, and, after bandaging his wounds,
brought him to a cave, where he nursed him back to health.

"Gian, who had been a bandit for twenty-five years, became
very much attached to the young man, with whose misfortunes he
was well acquainted.   He was moreover always ready to befriend
outcasts like himself, who led a wandering life in Gallura, Anglona,
and on the mountains of Acuto.

"In Sardinia, however, as in Corsica, the clergy with the aid of
the civil and military authorities sometimes succeed in concluding
peace between the hostile families, who otherwise would be at feud
till the end of the world.   Giovanni, worn out by the rude life of
a bandit in the forest solitudes, and weary of hunger, exposure, and
the constant necessity of being on the alert, was one of those who

signed the peace compact of Tempio, concluded by the intervention of Bishop Varesini. But his misfortunes were not over. Armed with the safe conduct given to every man who came to give evidence, he found himself one day seated at the same table as the carabineer, who had been wounded by Antonio in the brisk combat in which he, Giovanni, had killed the carabineer's comrade.

"On seeing the murderer of his mate, the carabineer felt hate in his heart. He swore to be revenged, and tracked his man with such remorseless assiduity that Giovanni had once more to fly and seek shelter in the mountains of Limbara. But, coming one day to Macomer to sell some game, the carabineer, who was lying in wait, fired on him. The shot missed its aim, but Giovanni, driven to desperation, fired in his turn, and with deadly effect.

"After this fresh murder, his life grew still harder and more miserable. He worked in the mines of Sulcis, became a day labourer, and even a shepherd, without ever finding rest.

"Always in danger of pursuit, he crossed the island to the district of Nurra, furnished with letters of recommendation to a family named Marras, who lived at a farm known as *la Poneda*. Nearly dead of fatigue, he stopped to rest late one evening on the margin of a spring, at the same moment that a young girl of marvellous beauty came there to draw water. As fearless and kindly as she was lovely, the girl chatted pleasantly with the wild-looking man, and proved to be none other than the daughter of Signor Marras, the master of *la Poneda*. She led Giovanni to her father, and, in a very short time, the outcast found that he had fallen in love, with all the fierceness of his proud, tempestuous nature. But even in this, he was crossed by his cruel destiny. Mimmia, for that was the girl's name, was already betrothed, and the wedding day was even already at hand. Giovanni, maddened by this fresh disappointment, took again to his wandering life, dragging heavy, careless feet along the sorrowful way which his life seemed fated to follow. He defied Destiny to wound him again, and Destiny, taking up the gage, wounded him still more cruelly; for Mimmia was suddenly attacked by cholera, and died in a few hours, in the heyday of her youth and beauty. That was the last blow. Giovanni returned to Oschiri to pray and weep at the grave of his sister Adelita, and it was there that, covered with the mud of the cemetery, his face bathed in tears, his feet torn by the thorns of the forest, he was arrested one evening by the carabineers. He made no resistance and, being sentenced to death, met his end with serenity and even with joy."

The old guide rose from his seat, and I saw that while I had been absorbed in listening to his story night had fallen. I followed him down the narrow pathway and returned to the inn, if I can give such a hospitable name to the dirty lodging, in which a miserable repast awaited me under the name of dinner.

Next morning I wandered through the town, where every street echoed the noise of primitive trades.

Osilo is renowned for its cloth, called *orbace*, which is woven at home by the women. As in Chaucer's day, "the spinsters and the knitters in the sun did use to chaunt," so here the matrons were sitting in front of their doors, spinning or winding the wool, or making dye in large copper cauldrons, filled with madder, gathered in the vicinity of the town.

The men were mostly at work in the fields or woods, but the old people sat basking in the sun along the walls.

The people of Osilo have scarcely changed their manner of existence for centuries. They continue to live on the flesh and milk of their goats and sheep, whose hair and wool are woven by the women. They grow corn, and grind it into flour in primitive querns according to their requirements. They make wine from their own grapes and oil from their own olives. They have no industry, no commerce, and no ambition. But the tranquillity of their lives is reflected in the serenity of their faces, and, having no wants which nature does not satisfy, their lot is perhaps more enviable than that of many a more civilised community.

The City of Alghero.

## CHAPTER III.

The Spanish City of Alghero.—The "Snail's Staircase."—Tempio and the Limbara Mountains.—Torralba and the *Nuraghi.*—Across Sardinia.—Oristano.—The City of Tharros.—A Sardinian Judith.—Cagliari.—The Pertinacious Porters.

IN Corsica I had found a Genoese city and a Greek village, and in the Balearic group, Iviza, an island peopled by Arabs. I was now to visit in Sardinia a Spanish, or more correctly a Catalan, town. The Mediterranean islands are full of such ethnographical surprises, but nowhere have the distinguishing characteristics of a people been so preserved, in spite of an alien soil and the lapse of centuries, as they have been at Alghero, the Spanish town of Sardinia.

Alghero is on the coast, twenty-one miles south-west of Sassari, with which it is connected by a narrow-gauge railway. The line at first followed the course of a valley, dotted with ruined *nuraghi*, but soon entered a sterile region, where the stony soil was only broken by stunted arbutus and lentisk trees, interspersed with dwarf-palms. Here and there pools of stagnant water reflected a cloudy sky, and, on the left, a sad-looking village straggled up a bony-looking hill. It was Olmedo ; and a nun, who was in the same carriage as I, covered

303

her rubicund face with her white veil and shivered at the sight, whispering to me that there were many bad characters at Olmedo. They had murdered their parish priest, and, generally speaking, preferred knives to any other form of argument.

Two carabineers alighted at the station, and the good sister observed, "See, there must be another murder. The police know the way to Olmedo only too well!"

Leaving the ill-reputed place behind, we steamed on towards the sea, and, as we approached Alghero, I could almost fancy myself back in Spain. Here were the same picturesque little houses, with the plumes of the palm tree peering up above the white walls, the same reed huts, the Spanish wheels for raising water, the verandahs, fields, and gardens of the Peninsula. But the country was evidently poverty-stricken, and the misery, which is general throughout Sardinia, was even more pronounced here than elsewhere.

Nevertheless, the appearance of Alghero is captivating. Charles V., who landed here on his way to Africa in 1541, is said to have exclaimed on beholding the town, " *Bonita, per ma fé, y bien asestada !* " ("Charming, by my faith, and well situated !").

The epithets were well deserved, and time passed very pleasantly in exploring the town, with its queer little harbour, its cathedral built by the Genoese family Doria who founded the city, and its theatre, built with the revenues of the canons who abound in the town, and may often be seen, so it is said, witnessing the performance of *La Traviata*, with penitent faces.

The window of the room in the *Casa Albis*, occupied by Charles V. during his visit, is walled up, so that it may not be profaned by any lesser mortal, and the palace, for many centuries, had rights of sanctuary.

Walking through the streets, I seemed to have left Sardinia and to have returned to Catalonia. Here were the same faces, the same houses, the same dialect, the same accent. I met the same *manolas*, with their jet black hair and dainty ringlets on their foreheads, a bunch of red carnations fastened to their breast, and eyes that shot " love's arrows at every glance "; and, with the girls, the same toothless

Ancient Aragonese Tower.

old duennas as I had seen at Barcelona or Cadiz. The men who passed had the proverbially haughty air of the Spanish *caballero*, and rested one hand on their hip, as if ready to grasp the pommel of the sword, to exact swift indemnity for real or fancied insult.

I spoke to these people in their own language, Catalan, and I was understood by, and myself understood, every one.

The children gathered round me, and followed me about everywhere. They were as talkative, and, let me add, as noisy and impudent, as in Catalonia. Some of them were gnawing the root or bulb of the dwarf-palm, in which they seemed to take an epicurean enjoyment.

These roots, which are called *margaillons*, are much prized as articles of food, both at Alghero and at Sorso, and I had seen them exposed for sale in the market at the latter place. The bulb of the dwarf-palm attains a size in these regions unknown even in Africa. It is said that the Moors set great store by its nourishing qualities, and first introduced the Sardinians to its use.

In order to get rid of the children, I made the tour of the city by the circular road, and at length found myself alone on the rocky coast. The sky was aglow with the dying day, and the waves moaned as they broke in foam on the fringe of reefs. The quaint outline of the old Spanish town, with its frowning ramparts, belfries and domes, the bastions of its citadel, and white houses, loomed dimly through the pale twilight. But the rhythmic beat of the waves and the flutter of some passing sea-bird's wing were the only sounds. The town grew yet darker, till the buildings became merged into one confused black mass, with only the sharp-pointed belfries standing out distinctly against a sky-belt of crimson, striated with the violet coils of smoke rising from the chimneys. The clamour of the sea appeared to grow in volume as the light waned, and human cries seemed to mingle with the heavy thudding of the surf, the voices perchance of the victims put to the sword by Don Pietro II., *Il Ceremonioso*, as he was called, though in truth he showed little of the quality which earned the epithet, when he captured Alghero from the Genoese and spared neither man, woman, nor child.

Of that massacre not one survived, and the city was repopulated by Spaniards brought from Catalonia, who wakened the sounds of the guitar and danced the joyous fandango on the very soil saturated with so much Italian blood.

The Spanish colony thus planted in the island was naturally at constant war with the Sardinians, and on the festival day of the town, it was customary to celebrate the memory of a great victory gained over a Sardinian lieutenant of the Viscount of Narbonne, by burning a straw mannikin dressed in Sardinian uniform, to the singing of scurrilous verses abusing the enemy. For a long time, Sassari and Alghero were at open war, and even now it cannot be said that the traditional hatred is extinguished.

Alghero is noted for the caverns, known as the Grottoes of Neptune, at the foot of a lofty cliff, some distance from the town ; but to visit these requires exceptionally favourable conditions, and many visitors have made the attempt in vain. The entrance is very low, the top of the arch being little above the level of the water, and if the sea rises while the visitor is inside, it is dangerous and sometimes fatal to attempt to escape. To explore the grottoes at all involves a regular expedition, with a supply of food and candles, and a flat-bottomed boat with which to cross the pools inside the cavern. The caves still contain some fine stalactites, notwithstanding the vandalism of the captain of a Sardinian frigate, who blew down the natural columns in the outer cave with cannon, in order to decorate his villa at Nice. A similar charge of philistinism is brought against a captain in the British Navy.

The branch railway to Alghero joins the main line at Caniga, the next station to Sassari ; but the road from the latter is more direct, and introduces the traveller to the picturesque *Scala di Giocca*, meaning in Sardinian, the "Snail's Staircase." Emerging from the shadows of the thick forest around Sassari, one comes suddenly and without any transition to the verge of a deep gorge, at the bottom of which a foaming stream turns the wheel of a primitive mill, and disappears in a grove of willows. The road winds capriciously down to the lowest point, and reascends the opposite cliff. The traveller would willingly linger by the stream among the weeping willows, but he is scared away from the quiet spot by the warning presence of the eucalyptus; for wherever this tree flourishes fevers flourish also, and from the beginning of summer to the end of autumn, he who lingered in such a spot would be promptly punished for his temerity.

The gorge has been the scene of many bandit adventures, and

The Valley of Ossi.

particularly of the exploits of a certain brigand of Osilo, a man of excellent reputation and perfect honesty, so say the Sardinians, but outlawed for having deliberately stabbed a priest who had compromised his wife. He was sentenced to the galleys and transported to Genoa, but succeeded in escaping, and returned to Sardinia, where his arrival was soon made known throughout the district of Osilo by the murder of at least twenty persons, all of them witnesses who had given evidence against him at his trial. His reputation increased with the terror which he inspired. From very fear, the peasants acted as his spies; and for over twenty years he succeeded in evading justice, though frequently visiting Sassari, and being met with at church and even at the theatre. Ultimately he was betrayed by a woman whom he loved, and sold his life dearly, fighting to the last.

Beyond the *Scala di Giocca* the road crosses a rocky wilderness, from which it rapidly descends to the charming valley, from the bottom of which the light, graceful spire of Ossi points to the sky.

Ossi is a village of considerable size, and here, as at Osilo, the gorgeously dressed women may be seen seated before their doorways, weaving the cloth which, with that made in the neighbouring village of Tissi, is considered the finest in Sardinia. Both villages are near the main railway line from Sassari to Chilivani, the junction for Tempio and the north.

The scenery from the railway is, however, not cheering. I left Sassari early one morning, just as a pale dawn was breaking in a low, cloudy sky. Everything green was shining wet, and the soil was soaked. In the cold light of daybreak the country appeared livid. The waters of the swollen streams glided along noiselessly like oil.

Gradually ascending from the valleys, we came to volcanic slopes, where churches built of black lava brooded over equally sombre villages. Finally we reached the great tableland of the interior, a country of wide, sweeping lines, and vast, sad horizons, bounded only by the grave, hazy masses of the distant mountains. The sole living objects breaking the monotony of this treeless and uncultivated plain were the herds, which grazed at immense distances from each other, under the care of grim-looking shepherds, wearing the ancient *mastrucca.*

The train stopped at the village of Ploaghe, built at the foot of an extinct volcanic crater. The costume of the *contadine* (peasants) of this village is of great picturesqueness, especially the head-dress, which is a blue woollen square, embroidered behind with a large yellow cross.

The next halt of importance was at Chilivani, where I changed trains for Tempio, and as I had an hour to wait, visited the refreshment room, the only one on the line. The bill of fare did not offer much choice, however, comprising merely the two dishes *minestra* (vermicelli soup) and *arrosto di vitello* (roast veal), which are as invariable in Sardinia as corned beef and boiled mutton used to be on a certain line of Highland steamers. Chilivani railway station is notorious as the scene of one of the midnight assassinations not uncommon in Sardinia, of which more anon.

After a wearisome journey across uninteresting country, I reached Tempio at nightfall.

Tempio is the most populous town in Gallura. Its lofty houses, built of regular blocks of granite, mortared with clay, would resemble fortresses, except for the immense wooden balconies projecting from each storey, and casting queerly foreshortened shadows on the pavement below. The women spend far more of the day working and gossiping on these balconies than they do in their rooms, so that the otherwise solemn street is kept perpetually merry with the chatter of female voices.

Contadina of Ploaghe.

The roads are paved with large flagstones, on which the horses' hoofs make a hollow clatter, as if there were dungeons beneath. The men who pass are invariably clad in black, and generally wear hoods, giving them a sad, monastic aspect, agreeably relieved by the young girls who, here as elsewhere, pass and repass with their amphora on their heads. Altogether, however, the prevailing sentiment at Tempio is one of melancholy, notwithstanding the beauty of the sky, which is almost always clear.

Not far from the city rises the granite chain of the Limbara mountains, the highest peak of which, the Giugantinu, has an altitude of 5,906 feet. It is a rocky mass of characteristic appearance. The side opposite Tempio faces northwards, and only gets the sun at its setting ; hence the climate is comparatively cold. The town itself is nearly 2,000 feet above sea-level, and the air is healthy and bracing. The vicinity is dotted with shepherds' huts (*stazzi*), built of rough stones below, while the upper part of the walls is constructed of wattles. Several hundred families dwell here, banded together in a sort of federation called *cussorgie*, living a primitive, pastoral life, varied only by occasional hunting expeditions.

Except for the sight of the changing lights and shadows on the mountains, there is not much to detain the traveller at Tempio ; and, on the second day after my arrival, I again entered the toy-train, which runs up the mountain railway from Monti, and by noon found myself back at Chilivani, whence I continued my journey southwards towards Cagliari.

On either side the view embraced only the same stony mountains and arid defiles. Thirteen miles beyond Chilivani we passed Torralba, a village infinitely sad of aspect, built of black or red volcanic stone, with an ancient church, formerly episcopal, containing mediæval sculptures. Torralba is in the heart of the country of the *nuraghi*, those mysterious cyclopean monuments peculiar to Sardinia, the origin of which is such a riddle to archæologists.

The interior of these constructions, which are in the form of a truncated cone, is divided into two, and, in rare instances, three chambers superposed. The lower room is the loftier, and is often sixteen feet across by twenty-two feet in height. Entrance is obtained by a doorway, so low that it is necessary to lie flat on the ground in order to creep through. A spiral staircase, constructed in the thickness of the walls, and entered from the narrow passage between the outer door and the lowermost chamber, gives access to the upper room and the platform above, though this in most

Nuraghe of Torralba.

instances is now destroyed. In each chamber are two or three niches, each capable of holding a man standing erect ; and, at the entrance, which can be closed from inside by a large rock, there is an excavation in the passage, which served, no doubt, as a refuge for the man guarding the building from attack. The interior is quite dark, and visitors require to carry candles. The *nuraghi* generally occur in groups, varying in number from three or four to two hundred. The most general number is three or five, contained in a double or sometimes triple circle of walls. But whether found singly or in groups, the monuments are always disposed on strategic lines, which enabled them to communicate with each other by signals. They are built generally on eminences, and almost invariably in rocky soil, far from land suitable for agriculture. Near the *nuraghi* are found the so-called Giants' Graves (*Tumbas de los Gigantes*), oblong piles of stones, often over thirty feet in length. The height of the *nuraghi* varies from thirty to sixty feet, and their diameter from thirty-five to one hundred.

The two *nuraghi* at Torralba, those of Sant' Antino and Oes, are two of the best preserved in the island. In some places the prehistoric dwellings serve as human habitations, and one sees at the door wild faces, which seem to suit the rough lodgment that shelters them.

Seven miles beyond Torralba, the railway turns eastward to Bornova and curves round the sides of an extinct volcano. The ground is as discoloured and stained as if it were the site of a chemical laboratory. Here black as coal, there apparently covered with verdigris, elsewhere as if blood-stained, it has a wild, not to say tragic aspect, with which the walls, built of a singular pale green stone, seem curiously out of keeping.

This passed, the empire of stone resumes its sway. There is one brief, cultivated valley, and then again under a low, grey sky, the immense tableland of rock and volcanic *débris*, where a few twisted and stunted oaks rattle their branches on the margin of stagnant ponds and marshes, of the same leaden hue as the clouds.

A few cows with velvety hides graze here and there; in the distance, the mountains stretch in long undulating lines; in the foreground, a stream glides noiselessly between bare, treeless, and even flowerless banks. Far away, the snowy peak of the Gennargentu dominates the immensity of land and sky.

At the southern extremity of the plateau is the small town of Macomer, built on basaltic rocks on the slope of the mountains of the Catena del Marghine, at a height of 1,890 feet above the sea. It is

an antiquated-looking town, with low houses built of lava *débris*, and
in such a rocky, bare situation that scarce a tree can find space to
grow. The landscape is the perfection of desolation, and the eye
roams over desert tablelands and bare plains, dotted with ruined
*nuraghi* and giants' tombs, from the midst of which rise the arid
mount Santo Padre and the melancholy Lussurghi, while the horizon
is bounded by the lofty chain in which the giant of Sardinia, the
Gennargentu, towers heavenward, its majestic front often silvered
with snow, and nearly always crowned with clouds. The winds
whistle over Macomer at all seasons of the year, and in spring the
dreaded mistral blows for weeks together. When the spring storms
are spent, the sun beats upon the sterile rocks; and the heated
marshes, ponds, and streams of the plain exhale poisonous malaria,
while in autumn the town is whipped with icy rains or blotted out
by fogs. "Our climate is not unhealthy," say the people, "but care
must be taken to avoid catching cold."

Nevertheless, deaths from pneumonia and rheumatic fever are
common, due to the effect of the rapid changes of temperature upon
constitutions already weakened by miasmatic poison.

The train creeps on across the desolate country. The plain is
flecked with innumerable pools, on the margin of which grow a few
rickety cochineal plants or faded asphodels. Everywhere are the same
ruined *nuraghi*, half buried in rank grass, and the same miserable
volcanic villages surmounted by the cupola of the church. Far off,
near the peak of Lussurghi, which stands out against a pale glow of
saffron, as if a new, unexpected dawn were about to brighten the grey
day, the sky is streaked with long slanting lines, marking where a
shower is passing before or behind us.

At Abbasanta, fifteen miles from Macomer, some men were
taking leave of each other at the station, and, as the custom is in
Sardinia, kissed each other on the lips. A handsome church somewhat brightens the scene here, but half a mile further the line passes
close by two *nuraghi*. One is of black lava encrusted with orange
lichen; the other is in ruins. Obscene-looking crows circle slowly
over the fallen stones.

This part of Sardinia has always a funereal appearance, whether crossed in sunlight or on a grey day, by moonlight or by starlight. The soil seems burnt, and is streaked with crude colours, purple, livid, and black. Not a tree is visible, only sad horizons, restless birds of prey, arid *kopjies*, and blood-red lava.

Yet the hills and basaltic rocks hide an oasis, where the village of Milis nestles at the foot of Monte Ferru, in the midst of orange gardens said to contain over 300,000 trees, some of which are seven centuries old.

The best way to reach Milis is from Oristano, a town by the sea, on the verge of the great plain which we have just crossed.

The most prominent figure in the history of Oristano, which is full of stirring episodes, is a woman, the celebrated Eleanora d'Arborea, whose statue adorns the piazza in front of the cathedral. She was not only a military tactician and patriot, who subdued the Aragonese, but also a great legislator, and her code of laws is quoted to this day as a model of good sense and wisdom. One of its clauses could only have been devised by a woman. Whoever took away the character of a married woman was rendered liable to a fine of twenty-five pounds; but if the accused was *unable* to prove the truth of the alleged slander, the fine was reduced to fifteen pounds. Thus subtly was a woman's honour protected by an appeal to the self-interest of her traducer, and perjury made a less heinous offence than truth-telling. Civilisation may have advanced, but the human intellect remains the same, and no modern legislation contains a more ingenious clause than this Sardinian statute of the fourteenth century.

Nowadays, the old walls and strong fortress of Oristano are in ruins, and the population does not exceed seven thousand. Desolate marshes surround the town on all sides, and transform it practically into a fever hospital. The doctors say that no stranger has ever taken up his abode there and survived.

The suburbs, which consist of long monotonous streets of low houses of poverty-stricken aspect, built of clay bricks dried in the sun, are chiefly inhabited by potters. Oristano is the chief centre of the Sardinian pottery industry, and manufactures an immense quantity of jars of elegant antique shape, Greek or Roman. The colour of the ware is often superb, a special kind of varnish being used to secure a brilliancy equalling that of bronze or burnished copper.

At some distance from Oristano is the ancient ruined city of Tharros, the inhabitants of which worshipped the divinities of Egypt. The origin and history of Tharros are mysterious, and the only historian who makes mention of the place is Anthony of Tharros, a prisoner in Palestine, who thus apostrophises the town of his birth :—

"O great misfortune! Tharros, my poor native town! Thou art the third city which hath been repeatedly destroyed. O most beautiful and wealthy city, founded by the famous Tarrha, wife of Inova, who reigned over the Phœnician and Egyptian peoples!"

The town was destroyed by the Saracens in A.D. 1000. Immense numbers of antiquities have been found on the site, including two thousand scarabæi, mostly Egyptian, mounted in gold. These discoveries caused great excitement in the country, and the earth was dug and turned over by the people throughout the district, so that every peasant's house became a perfect museum of antiquities, filled with urns, glass and earthen vases, sepulchral lamps, plates, carved figures, idols, amulets, scarabæi, and weapons of all kinds.

From Oristano southwards, the vegetation assumes an African character. The black volcanic rocks and lava are left behind, and in their stead are groves of olive trees with palms and cacti.

Towards Cagliari and Iglesías, and across the *Campidano*, the sky is barred with black clouds, and the sun gleams for an instant on tawny-hued mountains, to be obscured the next moment by a storm, which, nevertheless, does not last long. Various stations are passed in the train, and as the rain ceases, we draw up at Sanluri, a large village sleeping in the shadow of an old domed church, and a massive fortress, where in 1345 a treaty of peace was signed between the Aragonese and the delegates of Arborea. The place is also the scene of a victory gained over the Spaniards by the Princess Eleanora, and of the defeat after a bloody battle, in 1409, of the Viscount of Narbonne, nephew of Eleanora, and

Brancaleone Doria, her husband, by a son of the Aragonese king Don Martin of Sicily.

The annals of Sardinian patriotism record the self-sacrifice of a singular Judith, the *bella di Sanluri*, who swore to compass the death of the king, Don Martin. As she had a horror of bloodshed, however, it was with the darts of Cupid that she sought to rid the country of the oppressor, and she succeeded to such good purpose, that Don Martin died in her arms.

In the environs of Sanluri, there is a large pond, now generally dried up. In former days, the Procurator Fiscal used to compel the peasants of neighbouring villages to drive down their horses and cattle to break up the crust of salt deposited by evaporation at the end of summer, so as to prevent the formation of a saline deposit, by which the poor people might have profited, to the prejudice of the salt monopoly.

After long stops at various stations, we saw the lights of Cagliari gleaming through the dusk, and soon entered the station. As the porters came out with the passengers' luggage, a perfect army of loafers threw themselves on our trunks, and we literally were compelled to resort to kicks and fisticuffs to defend ourselves and our belongings. Choosing the least rowdy-looking of these ruffians, I told him to take my things to the *Ristorante della Scala di Ferro*, which had been recommended to me as the best hotel in the city. There was no omnibus, and there were no carriages, not even hand-barrows. The porter deftly rolled his handkerchief into a sort of rope, fastened my bag to one end and my umbrella and miscellaneous articles to the other, slung this over his left shoulder, hoisted my box on his right, and trudged off along the wet, muddy streets. Other men followed him, and under pretext of helping him, rid him little by little of my bag, my umbrella, and box, leaving him finally with only a parasol.

We climbed a number of steep, narrow streets, which seemed as if they were never coming to an end, and entering a gateway, ascended the narrow steps of the *Scala di Ferro*. All the rooms were full!

We retraced our steps in the dark to the *Albergo dei Quattro Mori*, where I was fortunate enough to find shelter in a vast and lofty room. Then followed a dispute with the porters, who demanded neither more nor less than fifteen lire. After much fierce outcry and even threats on their part, I dismissed my gentlemen with a third of that sum, vowing to myself in future always to strike a bargain beforehand with Sir Porter. Unhappily it is not only with porters that one has to arrange prices beforehand in Sardinia, but with hotel-keepers, muleteers, and coachmen, with every one in fact who is employed in what the Germans expressively call the "stranger-trade."

Woman of Quartu.

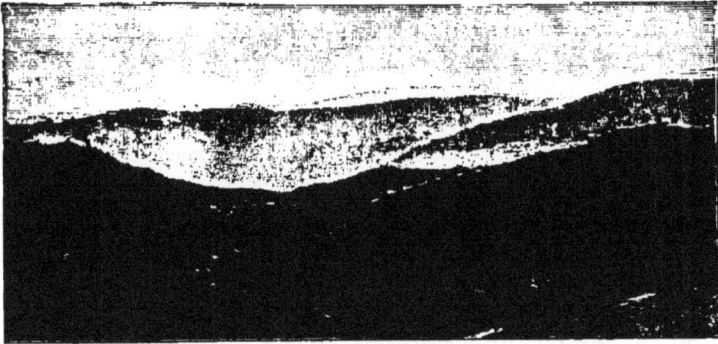

Slopes of the Gennargentu.

## CHAPTER IV.

Cagliari.—The Vanity of Achievement.—The Gate of the Elephant.—The Roman Amphitheatre.—Divination and Sorcery.—The Cathedral.—Some Monuments and their Moral.—The Castle of Ugolin.—In the Campidano.—An Arcadian Festival.—Religious Services and Processions.—The Migrations of a Saint.— The Philosophic Donkey.—Peasants' Dresses.—Tunny-fishing.

CAGLIARI, the ancient Caralis, is built in the form of an amphi-theatre on the slope of an isolated hill. Its curious streets, with their lengthy balconies of forged iron obtained from the Spaniards, its domed houses, its antique towers and old ramparts, its belfries, and the high quarter on a platform of volcanic rock, all make it a city well worth a visit. From a distance it resembles an Eastern town, and imagination might compare it to a gigantic bird taking flight towards Tunis. It is surrounded by extensive salt-lagoons, and faces the spacious Gulf of Angels, *degli Angeli*, now better known as the Gulf of Cagliari.

The origin of the town dates from remote antiquity. The Carthaginians extended it, and it was for long in the occupation of the Romans. It was invaded by the Vandals, fell into the power of the Goths, and at a later period was sacked and put to fire and sword by the Saracens. Pisans, Genoese, Aragonese, and Spaniards in turn contributed to it their arts, laws, and customs. All these

320

divers peoples have left their impress, not only on the buildings, but also on the beliefs and customs and even the dress of the people.

The narrow Via de Barcelona, for instance, almost overshadowed by its artistic wrought-iron balconies, is almost as Spanish as a street in the town after which it is named. A singular effect is produced by the multitude of ropes fastened transversely across the street and used for drying linen; the white and coloured cloths floating in the wind giving the impression of festival decorations.

I had a letter of recommendation to the Rev. Father Fondacci, Superior of the Dominican Priory, and late one evening I climbed the steep streets to the monastery. The entrance porch gave access to a cloister. The corridor, which was deserted and dimly lighted, was bordered by lofty wrought-iron railings, through which I saw a vague glitter of ornaments on the altars of side-chapels. At the far end of the cloister, under the very arch of the vault, my attention was arrested by a large picture, representing a dead knight clad in armour, with his hands crossed on his breast. Above him was an immense genealogical tree, the leaves of which consisted of miniatures of people of all ranks and professions, bishops, priests, rough warriors, grave students, pensive nuns, and young women with pale, transparent faces. The effect of this picture in the uncertain light of the ancient cloister was very singular, and suggested a whole train of thought of the vanity of human life. Generation had succeeded generation, and each had produced people of importance in their day—women famed for their beauty, warriors who had won glory by their courage, students and ecclesiastics noted for learning or for piety; yet what remained of them now, save these pale miniatures on a forgotten picture in an obscure monastery? Methought the good friars were well advised if they intended the picture as a reminder of the paltriness of this life. No religious emblem could have pointed the moral so well.

When I left the priory, the streets of the quarter of Villanova, in which it is situated, were deserted, and in contrast with the psalmody to which I had just been listening in the monastic church, I heard the distant tinkle of guitars.

On the next day I again visited the priory, and saw the father
superior. A gale had been blowing all night, and the wind, which
was still high, shook the white habit of the Dominican, and his brown
mantle, which he vainly sought to keep in place, floated in large folds
round his face. With the priest for Virgil, I then set out to visit the
town. Passing through the old Pisan quarter, with its lofty houses
and long vistas of narrow streets, we emerged by one of the gates,
opening on the square in which stands the famous Towers of the
Elephant, *Torre dell' Elefante*, erected by the Pisans in 1307. The
two square towers are perhaps the most prominent objects in Cagliari,
and quite dominate this lofty quarter of the city. The towers, which
are exceedingly well-preserved, probably owe their name to the figure
of an elephant carved on one of the projections of the building.
The interior was long used as a prison for those condemned to death.
While I was gazing at the dark, yawning gateway under the
edifice, some Sardinians, strangers to Cagliari, suddenly emerged
from the shadows, and as the sunlight fell on their strong faces and
velvet doublets, I almost imagined myself transported back to the
Middle Ages.

The most interesting monument in Cagliari is undoubtedly the
Roman Amphitheatre, which occupies the middle of a ravine, and
was capable, it is said, of containing twenty thousand spectators.
Certainly its dimensions appear very large, but as a matter of fact
the ruin cannot compare in size with the similar remains in Italy or
even Southern France, which is proof of the subordinate importance of
Sardinia at that epoch. The vomitories and rows of seats are mostly
hewn out of the solid rock, the tiers on one side rising to the level of
the summit of the hill, while on the other side, where the ground is
flatter, the amphitheatre was completed by masonry. The vaults
beneath the arena still contain iron rings, to which wild beasts were
fastened ; and an immense cistern in the vicinity, dating from the
period, leads some to the belief that the representations occasionally
included the naval fights which were so popular a feature of the
Roman games.

In the evening I returned with the reverend father to the priory,

Gate of the Elephant.

where, sitting in the immense sacristy at twilight, we talked of the people and their beliefs and customs. He was a Corsican, and being thoroughly acquainted with all the legends and superstitions of his native island, was better able to appreciate those of Sardinia.

He considered the Sardinians quite as superstitious as the Corsicans, and said they were still addicted to all kinds of witchcraft.

Roman Amphitheatre.

Some, in fact, made scorcery a trade, with no other object than that of abusing the innocence and credulity of the poor.

"I knew two men," said the reverend father, "who had advanced several hundred lire to a reputed witch, and, by her advice, performed all sorts of ridiculous rites to secure the success of a venture in which they were engaged. The witch had given them charms, which they always wore, but were on no account ever to open, for fear of breaking the spell and bringing great misfortunes on themselves. One of these amulets came into my possession, and I had the curiosity to open it. What do you think it contained? A few blades of grass and pieces of palm leaf. It is nothing unusual for us, priests and monks, to be asked for *uno scritticellu*, that is to say a fetish paper bearing some mystical words, or a picture to bring good luck.

"The Sardinians are much given to cabalistic practices. A man, with whom I was well acquainted, passed for a great divinator, and was specially famed for discovering the site of buried treasure. One day, three men came to consult him regarding a field which they knew contained a treasure, though they were ignorant of the exact spot where it was buried. The divinator gave his services for payment of a large sum in advance, and accompanied the treasure-hunters to the place indicated. There he described some cabalistic curves on the ground, murmured some unintelligible words, and thought profoundly. 'Yes!' said he at length in a grave voice, 'the treasure is there, but it cannot yet be taken.' 'Why?' asked the men. The sorcerer sadly averted his head without answering, but as the men insisted on a reply, finally said, 'Well, since you are so bent upon having the truth, know that the treasure cannot be removed unless one of you, it doesn't matter which, die before the Angelus.' Thereupon the three Sardinians took to flight, in terror, and—all three are still living.

"The Sardinians believe firmly in dreams. One day I was sent for by an old woman from a neighbouring village. I went, and she told me that her husband had dreamed that he had seen a treasure in a certain field. On awaking, he told his wife, and both were convinced that their fortune was made. The man, without loss of time, went to the place he had seen in his dream, and there, sure enough, he beheld the treasure and even touched it with his hands. It was a massive ingot of gold, but so sunk in the earth as to require a pick-axe to extricate it. He hurried home joyfully to fetch the implement, but lo! when he came back to the field the ingot was gone, and he could not even rediscover the spot where he had seen it. He returned sorrowfully to his wife, and the poor woman immediately sent for me to give her some object which would enable them to find the treasure, of the existence of which they were firmly persuaded ; for had not the man actually handled it ? The woman could not be made to understand that her husband, full of his dream, had been the victim of a hallucination.

"The lower classes of Cagliari have absolute confidence in the priests, especially in the monks, whom they believe capable by the mere exercise of their will, not of removing mountains perhaps, but of the more difficult achievement of conferring or

Pisan Gateway.

taking away wealth and happiness. They are so miserably poor, that their constant idea is to discover a treasure. They are the prey of superstitions without number. They believe in the *jettatura*, the *streghe*, and omens of all sorts. Even their religion is superstition. Often, after mass, mothers bring children who are cutting their teeth to the priest, that he may place his fingers on the gums to soothe the pain. When they have a headache, they pray to the saints—and if they are not cured, they blame the saints, saying, 'They are deaf, or they don't listen, and yet I have made many *novenas.*'"

The day after my visit to the amphitheatre I devoted again to the old Pisan quarter, and inspected the cathedral which is dedicated to Saint Cecilia. This edifice was erected by the Spaniards, on the site of the old Pisan church which threatened to fall. Two side-doors still remain of the older building, and show that it must have been much finer than its successor. One of them contains fragments of still more ancient masonry, and the architrave is made of a Roman sarcophagus. The façade, of comparatively modern date, is composed entirely of marble, and is of great richness, but the general effect is heavy. The same criticism applies to the interior, where red Sicilian marble has been far too lavishly employed. At the same time, the high altar, with its marble reredos, a fine crucifix, and four candlesticks of wrought silver, is certainly very beautiful, and the silver tabernacle ten feet high is a noble object, not so much because of the precious metal of which it is composed, as for its artistic qualities.

The marble crypt contains three chapels, in one of which, dedicated to *Saint Lucifer*, who is much revered in Sardinia, is a monument to the queen of Louis XVIII., who died in London in 1810. Her remains were brought to the island, and interred in this mausoleum, which was restored by her brother, Charles Felix, king of Piedmont and Sardinia, by whose orders, no doubt, was carved the figure of a weeping angel, which surmounts the tomb.

What a contrast there was between this place of sepulture and the monuments in the *Campo Santo*, which I visited with the Dominican on the same day!

The monuments in the cemetery were of extraordinary elaborateness. White symbolical statues gleamed among the black cypresses, and immense bouquets of flowers, wreaths, and crowns, brought to the graves on All Souls' Day, still scented the air. There was nothing funereal or solemn in the whole graveyard, which spoke far more of the pride of life than of the humility of death. It seemed as if the survivors, in honouring their dead, were influenced rather by the ambition of display and vanity of wealth or rank than by the simple wish to show respect to the last resting-places of their loved ones. The statues were formal and in the worst taste. One was that of a young woman, dressed with great care, leaning forwards with clasped hands to meet a dead man, represented by a bust, rising from the tombs. The inscriptions, which were revoltingly bombastic, were in golden or red letters on panels of white marble.

The most humble and most solitary of village " God's acres " were more congenial, I thought, than this superficial display.

I left Cagliari early one morning to visit the castle of Acquafredda. It was still dark as we sped along the margin of the lagoons of Decimomannu, where I changed into the branch train that goes to Iglesias. The sunrise was reddening the ruins of the castle, as I alighted at the station of Siliqua, for the village of that name, which is situated in an extensive plain dotted here and there with dark carob trees.

The inhabitants of Siliqua are practical socialists. They possess in common a vast orchard, in which each family enjoys the produce of a certain number of trees, and scrupulously respects those belonging to other families. This community entails neither disputes nor conflicts, and these peaceable villagers in an out-of-the-way corner of the world seem to have realised, simply and without disturbance, the theories which elsewhere have caused the waste of such oceans of ink and often of rivers of blood. They are swayed by no sordid ambition, and never dream of living in idleness at the cost of others : their wants are few, and having their own rights, they respect the rights of others, and dwell in industrious peace.

The walls of the old castle, which I had come to visit, crown an

isolated porphyry rock, some thousand feet high, rising in the middle
of the plain, on the margin of the slow waters of the Bixerri. The
ascent is rough and even dangerous in places, but the view over the
Campidano is magnificent.

Standing alone on the arid summit, I thought of the emaciated
form of the unfortunate Ugolin, once the master of this strong castle
and of the fair valley at my feet. I realised the pages of Dante's
*Inferno*, in which Ugolin is described as gnawing the nape of the
neck of his executioner, the archbishop Ruggieri, and after wiping his
lips on the hair of the archbishop's head, saying to his visitor, " Dost
thou wish me to recount a desperate grief, the mere memory of which
oppresses my heart, before I even speak of it ? "

I seemed to see the dungeon and hear the pitiful cry of one of his
children,—

| " *'Padre mio, che non m' aiuti?'* | "'Thou dost not help me, my father?' |
| *Quivi mori."* | Whereupon he died." |

And for three days afterwards, the bereaved father called despairingly
upon his children, *poi che fu morti*, when they were dead. If the
immortal pages of Dante can make one shudder when one peruses
them, as it were, in cold blood, how much greater is the effect when
one reads them in the very ruins of the castle of one of the characters
whom he mentions, sitting alone on a bare summit where only dead
things recall those which have lived !

Nature herself seemed to heighten the realism of the scene. At
early morning, the sun had bathed the Campidano with light, the
distant buildings of Cagliari had glittered like glass on a shining
shore, and the mountains had been softened by a translucent azure
haze. Now, the sky was being swept by livid clouds : a rising wind
whistled through the ruins, and the plain was darkened by shadows.

Count Alberto Ferrero della Marmora, in his exhaustive work
on Sardinia, describes a lugubrious encounter which befell him at
Domusnovas, a hamlet lying to the left of Siliqua. Coming to the
village in a storm, he rode under an archway which he took to be the
entrance, when his face was suddenly swept by something dank and

clammy, like wet sea-weed, and, raising his eyes, he saw a human head with long hair, placed on a transverse beam. At the same moment a flash of lightning illuminated the dead face with its sunken cheeks, sunken eyes, and open mouth. In fact the archway was a gallows-tree, and the head was that of a woman, executed a month before, and, according to the old custom, nailed to the arm of the instrument as a warning to other evil-doers.

After these depressing souvenirs, it was quite cheering to find that the clouds had been dispersed by the wind, and to see the Campidano once more smiling in the sunlight. As I went along the road, more-over, I was favoured with one of the most charming pictures of rustic gaiety I had ever seen. On an immense car, drawn by oxen with wide-spreading horns, was a group of men and women, the latter in flame-coloured robes bordered with gold, the former in purple velvet doublets and wearing the Phrygian cap. One of the women was playing a tambourine, accompanied by a player on the *launedda*, a flageolet with three reeds, the *tibiæ impares* of the ancients.

The car halted, and, with the exception of the musicians, men and women, masters and servants without distinction, alighted on the sward and danced a graceful round dance, known as the *ballo tondo*. The performers kept strict time to the somewhat serious measure, which, I was told, is very difficult to learn.

After dancing for some minutes, the party reascended the car, which slowly proceeded, the sounds of the tambourine becoming fainter as it receded; and presently I could only distinguish the sharp notes of the flageolet. When a considerable distance off, the vehicle again stopped, and the occupiers once more alighted to foot it for a few moments on the turf, as if their joy could not be contained and required to find expression at intervals by means of the dance.

Such pleasant parties are often to be encountered in the Campi-dano, the occupants of the car often being townsfolk proceeding to, or returning from, some rustic festivity. The vehicles are provided with mattresses, provisions, and kitchen utensils. In the warm nights of spring and summer, the travellers sleep and prepare their meals in the open air. The entire household down to the smallest children

take part in these outings, and often entire days are passed singing,
dancing, reciting verses, and resting under the shade of the trees.
To see these simple merry-makings is to imagine oneself in Arcady
in the Golden Age.

I returned to Siliqua as the sun was setting behind the mountains
of Sulcis, and it was night when I reached the city.

Cagliari has several convents and a few monasteries ; but for the
most part their days of prosperity are over, and many are deserted
or entirely abandoned.

The Emperor Charles V. conferred the title of "Royal" on the
Dominican Priory, where I visited Father Fondacci, and gave it
numerous privileges. Three of its friars have at different times been
called to occupy archiepiscopal sees.

The church of the Dominicans is nowadays the most frequented
in the city, and the festival of St. Blasius, whose relics are preserved
in the edifice, is one of the most popular holidays of Cagliari. For
forty-eight hours there is a constant procession of the faithful to kiss
the relic ; and as they place their offering in the collection-plate, the
priest gives to each a handful of small, round biscuits called *bisto-
quellus*, basketfuls of which stand ready by the side of the minister.
These blessed biscuits are carefully preserved as charms against
misfortune.

The same church is also used for the *novena* before Christmas,
which the Sardinians call the *novena de la speranza* (novena of hope),
during which there is not only a sermon and benediction every
afternoon, but high mass followed by morning benediction an hour
before sunrise each day. The people of Cagliari, who are otherwise
habitually late risers, even in summer, take care not to miss these
services, and the church is always full by daybreak ; the common
people side by side with the wealthy middle class and the aristocracy.
On Christmas Eve, great is the throng to hear the midnight mass, the
nave, the sacristy, and even the cloisters being crowded as early as
ten o'clock. Shortly before midnight a deacon ascends the pulpit,
and chants the genealogy of our Saviour from the Gospel of Matthew,
and when the hour strikes the mass begins. As the priest intones

the *Gloria in excelsis*, a curtain concealing the "crib" is drawn aside, and the Holy Infant appears above the altar, lying in the manger between the Blessed Virgin and Saint Joseph. At the same moment an angel, guided by a wire, descends from the roof of the church at the end opposite the high altar, and stops above the "crib." The figure carries a scroll, on which is written, " The Angel of the shepherds of Bethlehem. *Gloria in excelsis Deo.*"

The excitement caused among the congregation by this dramatic representation is indescribable, even finding vent in loud cries and shouts of joy.

Most of the religious ceremonies in vogue at Cagliari were instituted by the Spaniards, and up to quite recently certain services were conducted in Spanish. The societies and confraternities are innumerable. The oldest and most celebrated is that of the Rosary, dating from the year 1334, the date of the foundation of the Dominican Priory. This confraternity possesses the flag under which, in 1571, the four hundred Sardinian soldiers, who took part in the battle of Lepanto, fought on board the flagship, *Don John of Austria*. Historians even say that it was the Sardinians who killed the Turkish commander, Ali Pacha, and thus greatly contributed to the defeat of the infidels.

The churches of Cagliari number about fifty, without including the oratories and chapels. Several of them are well worth a visit, especially that of San Francisco, which is a fine example of Gothic architecture, and that of San Efisio, in the walls of which are imbedded some of the cannon-balls and other projectiles fired by the French in 1793. The repulse of this expedition, in fact, was attributed by the common people to the intervention of the saint, and increased the veneration in which his memory has been held ever since the great plague which desolated Sardinia in 1656.

Dating from that epoch, it has been the custom every year to carry the statue of San Efisio in solemn procession to Cape Pula, where a chapel has been built in his honour, and near which he is traditionally believed to have been decapitated by order of Diocletian, whose general he was. The statue, which is painted in vivid colours, represents the saint wearing a cuirass, and a helmet decked with ostrich plumes. A Spanish mantle covers the shoulders. One hand is placed on his heart, and the other holds the martyr's palm.

On the 1st of May in each year, the statue is fixed in a kind of crystal chair, decked with streamers, and placed on a blue and gilt car, drawn by black oxen, specially bred and fattened for the occasion. Their horns are ornamented with oranges, tufts of bright-

Car of San Efisio.

coloured wool, tiny mirrors, necklaces, and bells, while a large bell is suspended round their necks.

The procession is the great event of the year, and is attended by people from all parts of Sardinia, the number of persons following being estimated at twenty thousand.

It is related that the inhabitants of Pula were much aggrieved at seeing the relics of the saint fall into the hands of the people of Cagliari, and after much persevering agitation, at length were granted the privilege of being permitted to take charge of the remains of the saint for three days in each year. This was the origin of the famous procession, but the greatest precautions were taken on either side to watch the relics during the transit, the people of Cagliari suspecting that the Pula folk might substitute some casual skeleton for the sacred bones, while those of Pula imagined that the Cagliarese might try to palm off on them a common body for the genuine article.

San Efisio is not the only Sardinian saint whose remains undergo an annual translation. In the Middle Ages the relics of San Antioco were preserved at Sulcis; but as that town, from its position on the seaboard, was exposed to piratical incursions, the treasure was removed to Iglesias for safety, and merely conveyed in procession every year to Sulcis, where it remained for one day, and was then taken back to Iglesias.

Unhappily it was Iglesias which was eventually sacked by the Saracens, and the terrified inhabitants abandoned the saint to the votaries of Mahomed. When, later on, a search was made for the relics, they could not be found, whereupon some piously fraudulent individuals collected a few bones from a heap of skeletons and bore them back in triumph to Sulcis, where for a long time they were venerated as the genuine relics of the holy man. Such at least is one of the stories told by the sceptical.

Another religious " lion " is to be found at Cagliari in the church of St. Augustine, behind the high altar of which the body of the Bishop of Hippo reposed for two centuries, after being brought from Africa by St. Fulgentius. At the end of that period the Saracens captured the body in one of their periodical descents on Sardinia, and sold it for a high price to Luitbrand, king of the Lombards, who wished to place it in a shrine at Pavia. The Sardinians, furious at being deprived of the relic, attacked both the Saracens and Lombards, but were defeated, and only succeeded in recovering the doctor's vestments, which they have religiously preserved ever since.

The houses of the poorer classes in the suburbs of Cagliari are only one-storey buildings, generally containing but a single room, receiving both air and light by means of the door. Thus the passer-by can see the whole domestic life of the family at one glance. I was much struck by the invariable cleanliness of these interiors. Nearly every house has its mill—a primitive apparatus, turned by a miniature donkey, with its eyes blindfolded and a muzzle on its mouth, to prevent the greedy creature snatching an occasional brimmer of flour for its own consumption.

An old author states that Pittacus of Mitylene used to pass the time by turning his own mill, and that he found the exercise very conducive to thought. This being so, the Sardinian donkeys must be great philosophers, for they turn the mill for fully seventeen hours out of the twenty-four.

One Sunday afternoon, I visited Quartu, one of the most important villages in the neighbourhood of Cagliari. It is separated from the city by the lagoon of Molentargiu, which is about four miles across. The hamlet, the roads of which are paved, in consequence of the mud which accumulates in winter, offers nothing remarkable in itself; but the costume of the women is superb. The people were dancing in the public square when I visited the village; and I was amazed at the richness and originality of their attire, the bright colours of the brocades, the wealth of embroidery and lace, and the jewels flashing on the breasts of the women. I had the good fortune to meet a wedding party passing down the street to the music of *launeddas*, and could not but admire the radiant costume of the bride.

Walking on along the road, I passed others villages—Quartuccio, where dancing was also in progress; Selargius, surrounded by gardens; Pauli-Pirri; and finally Pirri, the hamlet nearest to Cagliari, from which it is little more than a mile distant. Here I saw another wedding, the bride's costume being similar to that of Quartu, while the bridegroom's dress was even more remarkable.

Seeing all this brilliancy of attire, one could not but think of the reverse of the picture, and of the constant fever which decimates these poor *contadini*. The whole region is poisoned by the emanations from the lagoons, and the most showy costumes often cover

Bride and Bridegroom of Pirri.

emaciated, broken-down
figures, and only serve to
enhance the sickly pallor
of malaria-furrowed faces.

Half an hour's distance
from Cagliari, in another
direction, is the monastery
of Santa Maria di Buonaria,
which, together with an
adjacent castle, was built
in the year 1323 by King
Alfonso of Aragon, who
gave them to the Mer-
cedaires, monks who en-
joyed the double privilege
of wearing the escutcheon
of Aragon round their
necks and assisting at
public ceremonies with
swords by their sides.

The castle is now in
ruins, and only the church
of the monastery is standing. From the roof of the
nave hangs a miraculous
ivory carving of a small
ship, once brought to the
place by an unknown
pilgrim. This vessel
is said to act as a
weathercock, its bows
always pointing in the
direction of the wind
that may be blowing
in the gulf.

A Panattara.

On my return from my visit to Buonaria, I met at the entrance
to the city a man wearing a singular dress, totally different from any
that I had yet seen in Sardinia. He was a native of Iglesias, where
the Spanish character seems to be preserved in the dress as well
as in the faces of the people.

Behind the mountains of Sulcis, where the town of Iglesias is
situated, are the famous tunny fisheries, which are at their height
in the month of May, when the *mattanza* takes place. The fish
are driven into a narrow space called by the fishermen the "death-
chamber," and are attacked on all sides with harpoons. The
scene is said to be very remarkable, the tunny making the most
desperate efforts to escape, lashing the water with their tails until
it becomes a mass of foam crimsoned with the blood from their
wounds. Formerly as many as thirty thousand fish a year were
captured in these "drives," but, nowadays, the number has greatly
fallen off.

One of the charms of Cagliari is the distinctive character of each
separate quarter of the town, giving one the impression of a number
of separate cities, each with its own characteristics and separate
population.

The maritime quarter, with its low houses and terraced roofs,
is quite different from Stampace, the commercial quarter; and
Villanova, which is a Spanish town, bears no resemblance to Saint
Avendrace.

But all have this in common, that wherever one roams, one
encounters at every turn the costumes, traditions, and customs of
former times.

The *panattare*, a name formerly restricted to women-bakers, but
now applied to all working-class women, dress in red on feast days.
A large silk mantilla embroidered with brocade covers their head and
shoulders, their skirt is of white lace, and their neck and bosom
glitter with jewels.

The *rigattieri*, or men of the people, generally sellers of vegetables, the *pescatori*, fishermen, and *carretieri*, carters, are all addicted
to bright colours in their dress, generally wearing a sort of scarlet

tunic, *corpetto*, with large buttons on the sleeves, woollen or leather gaiters, and a tall red cap. The fishermen also wear scarlet trousers, and a scarf of many colours fastened round their waists.

The small square at the gates of the high town is a magnificent view-point, and the sunsets to be seen from here are often superb.

The *Monte Santo* and the hills of Iglesias fade into a purple haze which obscures all confusing detail, while the level rays transform some solitary crest into a veritable beacon, or falling on the lagoons, make the water resemble molten metal. Then, quite gradually, the light dies away; the sea becomes grey and cold; the lagoons sleep darkly in the long shadows, and the lamps of the town and harbour below, or of the vessels at anchor in the bay, seem like reflections of the stars, coming out overhead.

A Rigattiere.

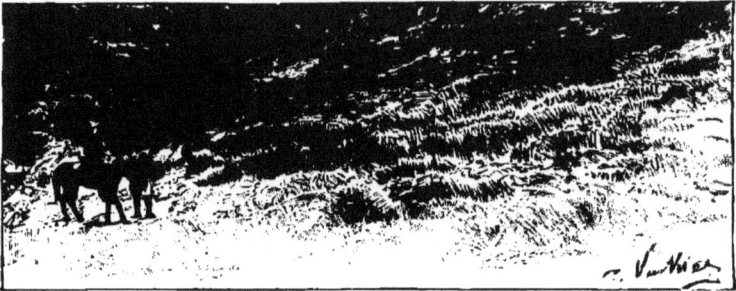

At the Foot of the Gennargentu.

## CHAPTER V.

La Barbagia.—The Plain of Sarcidano.—Belvi.—An Artist's Dream.—The *Douro-Douro.*—Sardinian Music.—The *Grassazione.*—Raids and Raiders.—A Heroic Girl.—The Major's Adventure.—Up the Gennargentu.—Snow and Mist.—Sardinian Women.—Evening at Aritzo.

H OWEVER much the traveller may see of that part of Sardinia accessible by train and steamer, of its desert tablelands, strange monuments, village-crowned heights, or malaria-infested plains, the real Sardinia, that which preserves the characters, manners, and dress of the nebulous days of its early history, escapes his ken. For this, as in the Balearic Isles and in Corsica, he must adventure into the wild recesses of the mountains, but, if he do so, his temerity will be well rewarded.

The Latin Islands have known many successive invasions and immigrations, and have been subjected to the influence of many diverse peoples, whether in conquest by the sword or in the arts of peace. More than that, they must undoubtedly have been a gathering place for the many races dwelling on the borders of the inland sea, even before the historic epoch. Hence, in Sardinia itself, we have met with Spaniards, Corsicans, Italians, Moors, and Sardinians, whose blood is a commingling of five races. But the influx of foreign elements has always been confined to the coasts and plains and low-lying valleys, and, except for a few casual splashes, as it were, primitive Sardinia has been unaffected by the successive waves of immigration, and the mountaineers of the remote districts are the same to-day as they were in the earliest ages.

The granite outcrop in the centre of the island, a region of alternate forest and stony summits, of mountain pastures and deep

Aritzo.

ravines threaded by impetuous torrents, is the home or a little-known race of strong and hardy people, who have retained, almost intact for ages, their original dress and primitive manners.

The two chief races are the *Iliesi* and the *Barbaracini*, and the district which they inhabit has for many ages borne the name of *Barbagia*, the country of the barbarians.

A double origin is traditionally ascribed to these people. The older section were Trojans, who, after the fall of Troy, wandered about the Mediterranean, and finally settled in Sardinia, where they occupied a part of Barbagia, to which they gave the name of Iliesi.

The *Barbaracini*, as the name implies, are of more savage descent. When Genseric, king of the Vandals, after laying waste Northern Africa, invaded Sardinia, where he shed torrents of blood, he brought with him a horde of Numidians, upon whom he bestowed the district of the Gennargentu, thinking that this wild region of inaccessible mountains, dangerous passes, and impenetrable forests well suited a race of marauding savages.

The event proved the correctness of the idea, and if Genseric wished to leave behind him a perpetual reminder of his invasion, he certainly attained his object, for the descendants of these Numidians were for years a scourge to the whole island, carrying terror and desolation wherever they went. Their constant raids and acts of pillage at length forced the more peaceable inhabitants to combine in making an attempt to put down the freebooters, and after a prolonged and varied guerilla warfare, the Barbaracini, finding themselves prevented from living on other people, were compelled by sheer necessity to turn from rapine to more peaceful industries. The spear became the shepherd's crook, and the sword was exchanged for the spade and mattock. Finally, in the year 594, peace was concluded between them and the rest of the Sardinians. Under the terms of this treaty the barbarians consented to renounce their idolatry and receive baptism ; but they still clung to their pagan customs, and retained, in the bleak mountain fastnesses of this remote island, the superstitious traditions and gorgeous dress brought by their Numidian forefathers from the burning soil of Africa.

The women of Barbagia have a reputation for unchastity, to which Dante alludes in the " Divine Comedy,"—

> " Che la Barbagia de Sardinia assai
> Nelle femine sue è più pudica
> Che la Barbagia dov' io la lasciai."

Even now, the women of this mountain region of Sardinia display a certain looseness in their attire, which is, to say the least, unconventional. Their breasts are barely hidden by a chemise of flimsy texture ; and it is little probable that they have altered the dress worn by the women of antiquity, since the men are still clad in the *mastrucca* which they wore in the days of Cicero. The *mastrucca* is the national garment. It is formed of four goat skins sewn together, leaving two openings for the arms, and is sleeveless. A mountaineer, wearing these long-haired skins, through which protrude his scarcely less hairy, muscular arms, with his legs encased in brown gaiters, and his shaggy locks covered by a red Phrygian cap, might well pass for one of the barbarians of former days.

The centre and crown of the Barbagia country is the snowy summit of the Gennargentu, the ascent of which is one of the most interesting excursions to be made in Sardinia.

Availing myself of the narrow-gauge mountain railway, which connects Cagliari with Aritzo and Nuoro, I started early one morning on my visit to this remote district and its chief mountain, the Silvern Gate, as its name signifies. On leaving the city the line runs for some distance along the border of the lagoons, the still waters of which

The Mastrucca.

reflected the pale sky of dawn, and stretched sad and silent to an apparent infinity of distance. Here and there a flock of rose-coloured ibis slept on the marge, and the monotonous shore-line was pleasantly diversified by an occasional coppice of palm trees. Looking back, as the train rounded a curve, I saw Cagliari, more than ever like an Eastern city, with its white cupolas, belfries, and turrets, reddened by the first rays of sunrise.

As the line rises towards the interior, the character of the country gradually changes, and the marshlands give place to bare, mono-tonous undulations, which in turn yield to steep, stony hills, where the train climbs sharp gradients and rounds unexpected curves.

From time to time, I noticed from the windows processions of men and women marching gravely behind immense cattle with exaggerated horns, recalling forcibly the archaic figures of men and animals, which one sees in early Italian pictures on a background of gold.

Gradually the prospect widens, and on the heights we once more meet the skin-clad shepherds, who seem to lead so contemplative a life, leaning on their crooks and gazing constantly on the infinity of sea and sky.

Wind-driven trees find a scanty lodgment on the rocky slopes, and on some of the lower heights rise ruined chapels with broken belfries, through the gaps in which one sees the sky beyond.

Sardinian Shepherd.

Near Fontanamela, seventy miles from Cagliari, the line skirts a series of wild, wooded gorges, the hills overlooking which are covered with forests of beech and chestnut. The sun gleams occasionally through the clouds ; and twice from the lower slopes of the Gennargentu, which we are now climbing, we see the whole country through which we have passed, stretching in undulation upon undulation to the vague line of the distant sea.

Grey and white clouds, fragments of spent storms, float in the luminous atmosphere and cast broad bands of moving shadows, which give the country the appearance of an ocean of monstrous waves. We cross the vast shelving plain of Sarcidano, formerly covered with forests of oak, but now for the most part an arid waste. At the western end, the plateau ends in a vertical precipice three hundred feet high, at the foot of which the village of Laconi is built in the form of an amphitheatre, on the banks of the torrent which descends from the heights above.

Laconi is a great centre for sportsmen. Deer and wild boar abound on the Sarcidano plateau, and *mouflons*, driven down by the snow from the Gennargentu, are occasionally to be met with in winter and early spring. The hunts are organised on a large scale, and a special train is generally requisitioned to bring the hunters, with their beaters and hounds, from the city. After leaving Laconi, the train buries itself in a dense forest, to emerge on the edge of a precipitous and tortuous valley, the windings of which are followed by the line as far the station of Belvi, where I alighted.

Great was my surprise, as I crossed the platform, to be addressed in French by one of the station men. The poor fellow, it appeared, was a French boy who had been deserted in Sardinia some years previously by his father, and after a futile search for more remunerative work, had ended by obtaining employment at this poverty-stricken station of Belvi.

Belvi is the station for Aritzo, a mountain village at the foot of the Fontana Congiada, and the most convenient starting-point for the wild district of the Barbagia. Belvi itself is an Alpine village much like those in the French cantons of Switzerland, and the houses with their projecting balconies resemble the model Swiss *châlets*, familiar to us from childhood. A steep path leads from Belvi to Aritzo, which is situated nearly 3,000 feet above the sea. As I walked up, I caught my first glimpse of the primitive people of the mountains. Women dressed in red skirts, with a slight chemise barely veiling their ample bosoms, were working in the fields, and men passed us attired, some in blue velvet doublets, and others, to mark the contrast, in sheepskin vests with the skin outermost.

The first view of Aritzo, as I ascended from the railway was very charming. The village seemed to be clinging to the mountain side in a lofty gorge ; and its Pisan belfry, and red, yellow, and ebony houses, with their old, carved-wood balconies, harmonised well with the mellow tints of the surrounding forest, the autumnal colouring of which took a new lustre in the light of the spring-like sun shining overhead.

Aritzo is an artist's dream realised. Most of the houses are built of a slaty schist, which glitters like silver in the sunlight, and, in the shadow, is a deep, lustrous purple. The roofs are of red tiles, and project over quaint, wooden balconies, hanging like swallows' nests beneath the eaves, and, for the twitter of birds, we hear the pleasant chatter of young mothers and the cooing of their babies. Tumble-down stairways, shored up with irregularly placed beams, form as it were hanging verandahs, simple but charmingly

Street in Belvi.

picturesque, especially when they enframe some handsome face of
sweet expression, or form the setting for a brilliant figure attired
in scarlet with puffed mediæval sleeves, and a slanting ray, falling
through a fissure in the woodwork, bars the velvet corsage with gold.

Balcony at Aritzo.

The time to see the dresses of the village is as the people come
out from high mass on Sunday or holiday. You will find women
dressed literally in purple and fine linen, and in shimmering brocades,

brilliant with the brilliancy of the Oriental, and quaint with the quaintness of the mediæval. They descend the steps, with mother-of-pearl and silver rosaries in their hands, and pass slowly into the diaphanous shadow of the narrow streets, followed by the widows, clad in black.

On the Sunday afternoon, you may, an it so pleases you, go down to Belvi, to the dancing on the *plaza*. For my part, I passed the time listening to four singers. The Sardinian rhythm, for it is not melody, is the most extraordinary music in the world, and, once heard, can never be forgotten.

It does not sound like the human voice. It is rather a harmonious murmur, which grows, dies away, and again swells to full volume. Sometimes one note dominates, sonorous and pure ; then the bass takes the upper part. Occasionally the voices are in unison, while across the low accompaniment one voice seems to shake the phrases of a recitative. This strange rhythm, which is very difficult to understand, can only be compared to the music with which the Arabs accompany their sacred chants.

At the sound of this singular music, the young men and women of the village assembled together and gathered in a large circle round the performers. The girls, holding each other by the hand, then formed themselves into one group, while the young men did likewise ; after which, the two parties formed a sort of chain, and quietly moved in a ring, turning, advancing, and drawing back to the cadence of the singers' voices. It was the favourite Sardinian dance, known as the *douro-douro*. The music was grave and sweet, and grave also was the movement of the dancers, which was rather an undulation than a dance.

The richness of the dresses, the character or beauty of the faces, the last rays of the setting sun falling in stained-glass tints upon the autumnal hues of the forest, the distant valleys veiled with evening mist, and the setting of the picturesque village, with its narrow streets, and the woodwork of the houses, all combined to give the spectacle the character of some fair, or *kermesse*, such as were common in the Middle Ages.

A Widow.

Returning from Belvi, I reascended to Aritzo by a charming
mountain path. I paced slowly through the village street in the
twilight, wondering how best to utilise the hour, without returning to

the inn. Presently I struck a path bathed in shadow, alongside a
murmuring stream, which buried itself in a thicket of bare trees.
Here I met some women returning from the spring, with their
pitchers on their heads. They walked one behind the other, and the
crisp dead leaves on the pathway rustled beneath their tread.

In an adjacent clearing, I came upon a ruined chapel. The roof
had fallen in, and only some carved woodwork indicated the site of
the altar, which was bare and empty, without even a crucifix. The
ground was littered with the rubbish of the crumbling walls and the
dust of the dry-rot in the rafters. The last glimmer of twilight
vaguely lighted the interior, and I fell into a reverie, standing alone
in the wood, before these ruins which looked so sad and solemn in the
oncoming darkness. Suddenly I shuddered, as a sound fell on my
ear. Something was moving in the *débris*, close at hand. I looked
and saw what seemed a bundle of living rags ! A man was prostrate
on the ground, his rosary in his hand, murmuring God knows what
orisons of despair. A blood-red gleam from the west suddenly smote
the stones of the building, and the man rose slowly to his knees and
stretched out his arms towards the naked altar ; but the light faded
as quickly as it came, leaving the ruin the darker for the evanescent
radiance.

I shivered and turned homewards, finding my way back to the
village through the chill darkness by the uncertain starlight.

At dinner with mine host that evening, my feet turned comfortably to the *brasero*, and the traditional macaroni smoking on the
table before us, I related what I had seen in the ruined chapel.

" That man," said the innkeeper, " is making a novena. For nine
days in succession, he will go and grovel in the ruins of that venerated sanctuary to expiate some fault. That is the way of it, in our
country. At one time or another the men will take arms by night,
as they did at Belvi, and a hundred of them will make a descent upon
some hamlet. After firing their guns to intimidate the suddenly
awakened villagers, who barricade themselves in their cottages, the
raiders attack the house of the parish priest or some notable, torture
him by holding his feet to a heated stove, possibly strangle him, and

finally set fire to the house. Then, after all this, they come and grovel at the foot of the altar to make amends. The parish priest of Belvi died last year, in consequence of a raid of this sort. He lingered in agony for several months, a prey to terrible hallucinations and delirium, always still seeing and hearing his murderers."

As mine host was speaking, I thought of the romantic village and its white rectory nestling amid the trees, where the birds sang all day long, and seemed to see again the handsome faces and striking dresses of the dancers and hear the strange rhythm of the singers.

"Then," said I, to the inn-keeper, "do you really believe that those pleasant-looking young men, whom I saw dancing, would be a party to such deeds of violence?"

"It's very possible, even probable. In any case, it is rare that a *grassazione*—which is the name given to these nocturnal raids—takes place without the people of the village of Fonni being mixed up in it."

Group at Aritzo.

The inhabitants of Fonni, it appears, are mostly shepherds. They come down to the *Campidano** about the month of May to pasture their flocks, and strike up relations with the servants of some rich family. These domestics, seduced by the promise of a share in the booty, treacherously admit the robbers, tell them what precautions to adopt, and which is the easiest road to follow; and also apprise them when their masters have received a large sum of money.

* The *Campidani* are the vast cultivated plains in the south and south-east of Sardinia.

*Grassazione* are rare in summer, owing to the shortness of the nights, which do not allow of the robbers having time to get home before dawn. Moreover, the poverty which is the most general incentive to crime, does not press so hardly on the people in the fine weather.

But whether robbery or vengeance be the motive, the raids are always planned and carried out with as much care and energy as a military expedition.

The chiefs in command, for there are generally several, are not known to each other, but each brings his own men, on whom he can rely.

At the appointed time the men assemble, their faces smeared with soot or concealed by a black cowl ; and the chiefs hold a council of war on the Moellone, near Tetti, and the cairn built by La Marmora for surveying purposes.

At midnight or at one in the morning, the marauders set forth, preceded by torch-bearers to light the way ; and, provided that nothing happens to alarm the chiefs or make them retreat, the raiders fall with all the fury of an attacking party upon the village, giving vent to savage cries. " *Niscinuo besseda !* " (" Let no one come out !") they shout, and fire again and again, aiming chiefly at the windows, which they riddle with shot.

While some shout and fire their guns, others, with hatchets, levers, and pikes, attack the door of the house which is the object of assault. Desperate cries are raised of " *Adjutorio! adjutorio !* " (" Help ! help !"). The door-panels fly in splinters, the people are killed or are spared, as the case may be ; but in any event the house is ransacked from cellar to garret, and everything of value is taken.

When the head of the family refuses to point out where his wealth is hidden, or pleads poverty, the *grassatori*, who do not stand upon ceremony, and are not easy to convince, light a stove and "smoke" his feet. If he persists in his obstinacy, they make him sit on the stove lid.

The gendarmes are not always able to cope with the miscreants ; and the carabineers of Busachi and San Vero Milis have been known to be blockaded in their barracks, while the *grassatori* were engaged in "making money," as they say.

The raids are not always easily carried out, however, and the brigands sometimes meet with desperate resistance. Quite recently, at a place called Lei, a poor village on a height above the river Tirso, the *grassatori* surrounded the house of the parish priest, while the gendarmes were absent on a route-march. Two gendarmes had stayed behind, however ; one a brave man, named Picardi, the other little more than a boy.

The brigands tried at first to get Picardi out of the way by inviting him to a carousal at some distance from the village, but with such insistence, that the gendarme suspected a ruse, and, under plea of fatigue, did not leave the barracks. Remaining in his clothes, he watched all the evening, and towards midnight heard a distant fusillade. Taking off his uniform trousers and wearing only his drawers, which at night bore some resemblance to the trousers of the countrymen, he put on his tunic inside out, girded his cartridge box round his waist, took his gun, and sallied out bareheaded, followed by his young comrade, who had imitated the disguise of his senior. They crept along beneath the houses, guided by the men's shouts and the sound of the firing, and reached the presbytery, to find that it was being besieged by forty *grassatori*.

The priest, hatchet in hand, was bravely defending himself behind his half-broken door. Picardi, in his disguise, ran among the crowd, and fired point-blank with a charge of shot, while his comrade, standing at a little distance, picked off individual men.

Some of the brigands fell, and a panic seized the others. They thought they were betrayed and began to disperse, whereupon Picardi shouted in stentorian tones, " Forward, my men ! Here they are ! Present ! Fire ! "

" Curse them ! here are the *carabinieri !* " yelled the brigands, taking to flight with all speed.

Thus was prevented this particular *grassazione*, which was even more dastardly than usual, being an attempt on the part of the villagers against their own priest, who had the reputation of being rich.

Generally speaking, the *grass.itori* come from a distance, and they take cunning care so to arrange their movements as to be able to prove an *alibi*, if they should happen to be brought to justice. When any of them fall in action, their comrades immediately chop off their heads, so that the bodies shall not be identified. The division of the spoil does not take place immediately after the raid ; the money is entrusted to a *bugone*, receiver. of stolen goods, or buried in the ground, and the chiefs only distribute each man's share some time later, when the robbery is beginning to be forgotten. *Grassazione* are of only too common occurrence in Sardinia, and the law seems powerless to prevent them.

Only a month or two before my arrival, the station of Chilivani, on the main line of railway, was attacked by fifty men, and the employés, after defending themselves for an hour, and exhausting their ammunition, were compelled to seek safety in flight.

I must say that I did not suspect this blot upon the country. As an artist, I was greatly attracted by the' character and beauty of the people's faces, the originality, richness, and variety of their costumes, and their perfect politeness ; but I thought that the fever was quite sufficient scourge for the island, without brigandage being added.

There is no end to the stories of these *grassazione*. At eleven o'clock one night a band of twenty brigands entered the township of Arroli, shouting "*Avanti Garibaldi !*" and fired several volleys at the house of one Ghiani, a notary, while four of the miscreants at the same time attacked the door with hatchets. The panels were just giving way when the notary's daughter, a young girl in her 'teens, seized a revolver, and fired all six chambers at the robbers from a window. Several were wounded, and they took to flight ; but the poor girl did not benefit by her heroism, for that same night she lost her reason, from sheer terror.

Occasionally the raids are marked by terrible carnage.

On the night of November 6th, 1892, the inhabitants of Sorradile were awakened by the sound of firing, accompanied by loud shouts and cries of "*Fuoco ! avanti ! morte !*" ("Fire ! forward ! death !").

A wailing voice rose amid the uproar, crying desperately "*Aiuto !
aiuto !*" ("Help! help!").

It appeared that after blockading the post of the *carabinieri*,
a large band of *grassatori* had carried by assault the house of the
parish priest, Bachisio Angelo Mariello. They had broken in the
door and rushed into the house like wild beasts. The cries for help
were those of their victim. Meanwhile five men of the village, aroused
by the sound of firing, hastily seized their arms, and, attacking the
sentinels of the *grassatori*, put them to flight. They then hurried to
the priest's house, but on the very threshold one carabineer and the
mayor of the village fell to the ground with bullets through their
breasts. "*Coraggio, Sorradile !*" ("Courage, Sorradile!") were the
mayor's last words.

The priest already lay stretched dead among the fragments of his
broken furniture. But the death of all three men was avenged, and
the streets of Sorradile and the fields of the vicinity ran red with the
blood of their murderers.

M. Georges Chapelle, a well-known Sardinian sportsman, told me
that, while on a hunting expedition with a friend, he received
hospitality for the night at a house in one of the mountain villages.
In the middle of the night they were awakened by the sound of
firing, and, being both well acquainted with Sardinia, guessed at
once what had happened. They dressed hurriedly, and, seizing their
guns, were making for the door to go out to the defence of the house
attacked, when their host came up and begged them not to court
certain death. Seeing that the hunters were disinclined to listen to
him, he called his wife and children, who went on their knees and
implored their guests to stay where they were. "You don't seem to
understand," said the host, "that they will kill you, and that your
death will do no good. On the contrary, the *grassatori* will be
infuriated, and to-morrow or the day after will come and attack my
house, and murder my wife and children." With this he commenced
tearing his hair and crying, "Ah! Accursed be the day on which we
received you under our roof! Accursed the hospitality which we
have shown you!"

M. Chapelle and his friend shed tears of rage, on hearing the piteous cries for help raised by the victims of the brigands ; but the children screamed, and the wife in tears clung to their clothes.  For two hours they continued to hear cries of distress from the village, and begged and prayed to be allowed to go to the rescue, but to no purpose. They were unable to escape from the clutches of their host's family.

An amusing adventure is told of Count Spada, commander of the *carabinieri* in the province of Sassari.  He confidently boasted that he would soon free the country from *grassazione*, and caused it to be announced that, if any brigands would surrender voluntarily, he would restore them to liberty, after inflicting a brief punishment as a matter of form.  Some of the malefactors, believing in this assurance, gave themselves up, whereupon they were mercilessly sentenced to long terms of hard labour.

One evening at table at a mountain inn, the major boasted of the security which, thanks to his energy, prevailed in the district.

"No more *grassazione*," said he, rubbing his hands.  "We are safer on these mountains than on the public square of Sassari.  How times have changed!"

Later in the evening—the date was May 4th, 1886—he entered the mail coach to return to Macomer, accompanied by a notable of Nuoro, and the syndic of Bolotana.  The conversation continued, and the major looked complacently at the mountains, the wild ridges of which could be faintly discerned against the sky.

"You see," said he, "the night is as black as my hat, and we are in the heart of the mountains, in utter solitude.  Yet there is nothing to fear, gentlemen.  We are quite safe."

Hardly were the words out of his mouth, when a hailstorm of bullets shivered the glass of the carriage windows.  The horses rolled over on the road, the driver was wounded, and the travellers only escaped death by a miracle.

The brigands at once surrounded the carriage, and, aiming their guns at the major and his two companions, ordered them to alight. The bandits wore the dress of the village of Orgosolo with sandals of wild boar hide, and their faces and hands were blackened.  The chief gave his orders in Italian, mingled with some jargon incomprehensible to the travellers.

The unhappy major was told to strip himself, and lie flat on the ground on his stomach. He was wearing a diamond ring, and the brigands disputed whether they should cut off his finger or merely remove the ring. He forestalled the issue, by handing them the jewel himself. He was then soundly beaten with cudgels. After this, the brigands broke open the mail-boxes and abstracted the contents, rifled the luggage, and relieved the notable of his gold sleeve-links, but, after careful examination, declined to take his watch, because it bore his monogram.

The major's clothes were returned to him, after the pockets had been turned out ; but his gun was taken by the bandits as a souvenir of their meeting. The coachman eventually fetched other horses from the nearest posting station, and the coach proceeded to Silanus, where the unfortunate major, more dead than alive, took to his bed, and was unable to rise for quite a fortnight.

The story of the boastful officer's prompt punishment was received with keen delight throughout the island, and he was made the butt of so many jokes, that he became ridiculous, and was removed from his post by the authorities.

Occasionally the brigands work in large parties. Bands of mounted men scour the country, stopping peaceful folk on the high way, and compelling them to give information as to the wealthier inhabitants and landed proprietors. At such times, the entire country is on the alert, and parties of as many as fifty men will be told off to watch day and night at any village where a raid is anticipated.

Such a state of things may appear incredible to the dweller in more fortunate countries, where life and property are as secure as civilisation can make them ; but the reader has only to refer to the files of the Sardinian papers to find ample confirmation of all that is written above. Moreover, ancient historians, in speaking of the Sardinians, apply to them the epithets *pelliti* and *latrunculi* ; and Strabo tells us that the plains were constantly exposed to the raids of the mountaineers, who lived like savages in the clefts of the rocks.

No doubt, one of the causes which has revived the instincts of rapine, inherited by the Barbaracini from their ancestors, is their extreme poverty.  The Sardinians groan under taxation, and it is stated that fully one-third of the island has become State property, owing to the proprietors abandoning their estates, the produce of which is not sufficient even to pay the taxes.  A sheriff's officer, who found nothing else to seize at a house in the village of Tetti, tore out the earrings of a poor woman.

Heaven knows how the people manage to subsist in some of the poorer villages in the Barbagia and Nuoro, where the only fare of the peasants is barley-bread, garnished with a little *Gadoni* cheese, and in hard times often only bread, made from acorns, or even potter's clay, with, occasionally, boiled beans.  They grow plenty of potatoes, but sell these at Cagliari, in order to purchase necessaries. Is it, therefore, matter for surprise that *grassazione* should be so frequent during the hard, dark days of winter, when the men of Barbagia and the Nuoro are dying of cold in their miserable huts?

As to the people of Fonni, they are brigands by nature, having in their blood all the violence and savagery of their race.  It is they who generally organise the midnight raids, and recruit men from the poor folk of the neighbourhood.

Fonni is the highest village in Sardinia, and the winters there are extremely severe.  The hamlet is surrounded by forests, and the Taloro torrent, which rises in the Gennargentu, passes through the wild gorge, above which the village is built, and, after a rapid course, falls into the stagnant waters of the Tirso, which are the chief cause of the unhealthiness of Oristano.

The inhabitants of this Sardinian Siberia rear cattle and make cheese.  They are a wild, semi-barbarous race, of a type which presents considerable affinity to that of the Moors.  But, rough as are the people, and savage as are the surroundings, the village possesses a church dating from the thirteenth century, and a fine cloister.  Several other torrents besides the Taloro pass near the village, and provide the motive power for some picturesque, primitive mills.

For my excursion to the Gennargentu, I secured, after considerable difficulty, two Sardinian guides who could be trusted, and one fine morning found me bestriding my pony, and riding up the narrow village street, where my head nearly brushed the bottom of the overhanging balconies. The villagers stood on either side to see me set off, the men ranging themselves along the wall and solemnly saluting as I passed, the industrious women just looking up from their interminable weaving and wishing me a smiling good day. After passing the last houses, the road followed the dry bed of a torrent, and when this came to an end, the path became a mere groove in the rock, apparently hewn out by the constant passing of horses and mules. The bluish schist, of which the roadway was formed, was very slippery, and in places even dangerous. Up and up we went, in the mellow shadow of the chestnut trees, through the autumnal foliage of which the sunlight fell across the ground in a golden trellis-work. The leaves linger on the trees in Sardinia long after they have assumed the tints of decay, and fall from the lowermost branches first, so that the denudation proceeds regularly, and the foliage always remains graceful, with none of the raggedness seen in more northerly climes.

Ascending above the forest-line and leaving the trees behind us, we crossed a vast, lonely expanse of common, where the only vegetation consisted of furze and whin, and the only sign of animal life was one solitary vulture, a mere black speck, circling against the intense blue of the mountain sky. Beyond the common-land came a waste-place of rock and stone.

My guides were silent, and paced along with the true mountaineers' step, without hurry, yet without weariness, regularly, mechanically, and apparently unconsciously. Over against us rose a bare crest, looking as if it had been peeled. Underfoot was a pathless tract of boulders and rough grass.

Behind the crest towards which we were ascending, Bruncu Spina, the highest peak of the Gennargentu, rose with a gradual but majestic slope, its snow-covered ridge standing out coldly against the sky. It looked quite close ; but when we reached the shoulder of the hill, we saw between us and the mountain a deep, savage valley covered with forest. An icy wind blew in our faces, and our feet stumbled among loose stones and lumps of frozen snow. The guides showed me the *Fontana congiada*, frozen spring, where the people of Aritzo and Belvi obtain the ice which they supply to all parts of the island in summer.

After a short rest, we began the descent of the valley separating us from the mountain, and soon entered the forest, where we rode for several hours without meeting even a single shepherd. We reached the foot of the Gennargentu towards evening, and camped for the night under the beech trees, sleeping on a bed of leaves, with our feet outstretched towards a fire and goatskin coverlets on our shoulders.

The intense cold prevented any inclination for laziness, and before dawn we were up and afoot, climbing towards the summit. The sun rose as we ascended, a pale disc, barely showing through the mists, which were floating round us and gathering over the ravines. The crest of the mountain was entirely hidden, and the higher we went, the more icy grew the wind.

After an hour's heavy walking, the guides asked if I wished to go any further, remarking that the mist was growing denser, and that, what with the fog and the depth of the snow, we should only be incurring needless risks if we persevered in the ascent. I reluctantly yielded to their counsels, and, turning my back on the mountain, redescended to the valley.

As we approached the forest, the sun gleamed out for a moment through the clouds, and my guides pointed out a herd of *mouflons* speeding along in the distance. The herd was a large one, but the animals moved with incredible swiftness, and soon disappeared in a gorge. Stags, wild boar, and *mouflons* abound on the Gennargentu, but in our two days' march we only had this one glimpse of the animals, and then they were far beyond the range of our guns.

Towards evening we found ourselves back at the crest, from which we had seen the snowy mountain on the previous day. The sky had cleared and the sun was setting. Even from here, the view was superb, comprising fully one-half of Sardinia, extending on the west from the marshes of Oristano to the mountains of Iglesias, and the vast mining district of Montevecchio and Monteponi, with the sharp peaks above Masua and its argentiferous lead mines. Nearer at hand, stretched the immense tableland of the Giara, famous for its wild horses, which are caught with lassoes as on the South American pampas.

The mists over the lowlands, which looked so beautiful from this height, with their tints of violet and rose, were really charged with miasmatic poison. When the wind is westerly, they are often carried up by the breeze from the marshes to the mountain districts, and cause sudden outbreaks of malaria in places otherwise most healthily situated.

As the sun-rays became more oblique, the schistous rocks sparkled like rich metallic ore, and the yellows and browns of the chestnut forests turned to rich gold. We descended rapidly into the lengthening shadows of trees and rocks, regained the steep, slippery pathway, and entered Aritzo as the first star shone out on the forefront of the saffron-coloured evening sky.

November was nearly out, and winter was at our doors; yet the weather continued like spring. The sun shone brilliantly in a sky of incomparable purity, and the days were warm. But the mornings and evenings were decidedly fresh, and we never dined without a *brasero* under the table, while a great fire of branches crackled in the bedroom. I began to understand why the Sardinians wore such thick clothing. They not only have to protect themselves against the heat of the sun, but also against the sudden chill felt in the shade, and the keen breath of the wind. The two mountain chains along the Sardinian coasts run north and south, and the island is often swept by an excessively cold wind under a blazing sun. In clothing themselves as they do, therefore, the natives ward off the sudden chills to which they are constantly exposed, and which, more than anything else, engender the *intemperia*, as malarial fevers are called.

I had received a timely warning at Cagliari, not to venture to shake hands with the Sardinian women or to attempt to joke with them. The Sardinians are extremely jealous; and an innocent familiarity may often be taken by them as an insult, and be followed by a thrust from a dagger without any preliminary warning.

The Sardinian women, beautiful and remarkably chaste as they are, never appear at meetings of men, and it is not the custom to introduce them to strangers

At Cagliari and other large towns they do not go out to do their shopping like the women of other countries, the task of buying provisions being generally entrusted to servants or men. At the markets there are always crowds of little boys with baskets on their heads, who, for a few halfpence, do the ladies' commissions and carry the provisions home. These boys are called *picciocus de crobi* (little ones with the baskets).

One evening, I heard sounds of quarrelling in the lower room of the inn, and, going downstairs and looking through the half-opened door, saw a characteristic picture. Through the thick smoke of half a score of pipes, I perceived a number of men standing round the table. They had been playing the Spanish game of *morra*, which is very popular in Sardinia, and some dispute had arisen. The savage-looking players, clad in fleeces, with frowning brows and glittering eyes, were growling at each other like wild beasts, thumping their clenched fists on the table and making threatening movements, which bid fair soon to lead to actual fighting.

Suddenly the stalwart innkeeper appeared.

" Hold your noise ! " he cried in a voice of thunder. Then, turning to me, he added, " Do you see the knife-blades glittering ? If I didn't stop them, blood would flow. I've more than once seen a man's hand nailed to the table with a dagger."

His words or his presence imposed order, and the players quietly resumed their game ; nor was the night again disturbed, save by the strange sound of the Sardinian rhythm, with which some of the men soothed their ruffled spirits.

I never grew tired of hearing these weird folk-songs, whether sung by professional singers on Sunday afternoons in the village, or hummed by the peasant women, as they gathered chestnuts and beechmast in the golden silence of the woods.

The words of many of these sad ditties were composed by a native bard, a young poet of Aritzo, who was smitten by an unrequited love, and was murdered at the hour of vespers in one of the streets of the village,—a victim to the jealousy aroused by his hopeless passion.

The memory of this hapless mountain bard is held in great reverence and affection by the women, who lighten their toil and rock their children to sleep to the sound of his verses.

Warping the Woof.

One Sunday afternoon, the young Frenchman from Belvi station came to visit me, and we went for a walk together. Passing down the chief street of the village, we came to the little cascade where the women were accustomed to draw water. The light filtered through the yellow leaves of the overhanging trees on a bevy of girls in bright red bodices, washing linen in a natural basin of foaming water, white as snow.

We then followed a path through the chestnut woods. The setting sun made the forest look as if it were on fire, and the dead leaves on the hillsides resembled plates of gold.  As we turned back, we caught occasional glimpses of the village, the white and red houses of which, surmounted by a coronal of blue smoke, seemed as if lighted by a furnace.  Near at hand, birds were twittering in the branches ; and far below, in the valley, the shadow of night was slowly rising upwards like a moving veil of gauze.

As we paced slowly along by a rushing stream, we heard the sound of bells.  We were not far from the village, and hurried on to see the procession which had already left the church.

At a turn of the road, I saw it winding among the tortuous streets, in the darkness of which the white-clad penitents, seen against the grey walls, had the appearance of phantoms.  The waving banners, the tall, shining, brass crucifix, the priest in his vestments, the women all dressed in scarlet, the widows all in black, the tinkling bells, the sound of the blended voices singing a canticle, gave a strange, vague charm to the procession, in this village encircled by forests, on the slope of a great mountain, at the last hour of declining day.  But gradually the shadow of the hills extinguished the brilliancy ; twilight and then night enfolded the scene, and the only sound was the soothing, indescribable harmony of mountain silence.

Ancient Cart with Spokeless Wheels.

## ✓ CHAPTER VI.

Desulo.—Sardinian Poetry.—*Furia-furia.*—Complicated Cookery.—The Fair of San Mauro.—Wooing by Proxy.—"Waking" the Dead.—The Birth of a Firstborn.—The Flumendosa.—The Wild East Coast.—The King of Tavolara.—Fever.—Farewell, Sardinia.

FROM Aritzo, the railway ascends the valley as far as Sorgono, the terminus, passing the station for Tonara, a picturesque village like Aritzo, in a similar position on the slopes of the Gennargentu, but nearer the summit.

The road affords a far pleasanter way of travelling than the railway, however, and was the route by which I elected to go from Aritzo to Desulo.

The upper portion of the valley is said to be the very district first occupied by the Barbaracini in the days of the Vandal king.

On the road, we pass some travellers from Busachi on the Tirso, travelling in antique cars with spokeless wheels, like those used by the Romans. The vehicles are laden with homespun stuffs, which are being taken to the south for sale.

Then come some women of Atzara, a village on the hills opposite Desulo. Their dress is a genuine relic of past centuries, for, like all the natives of these mountain hamlets, they take pride in adhering to the picturesque costumes of ancient days. Sardinia has about two hundred villages, and each one of these has its own distinctive dress, but in no district is the variety so marked as in the Barbagia.

The women of Dorgali, a township on the east coast, are dressed like Albanians, with narrow, stiff petticoats, and bodices with long sleeves, tight from shoulder to elbow, but puffed on the forearm, with slashes to show the white chemise underneath, and buttoning round the wrist. Their head-dress is of thick, bright-coloured cloth, which enframes the face and falls in folds over the shoulders.

In the Nuoro, as at Osilo, the women are distinguished by a head-dress which would give them the appearance of nuns, were it not for the great richness of their costume.

The strangest attire of all is that worn by the women of Tortoli, which is characterised by a remarkably low-cut bodice, with a chain passing under the chin to hold in place the veil covering the head.

Beautiful and even magnificent as the Sardinian dresses are, they are unlike the dresses of more civilised regions, in being made strictly on natural principles. The bodice is evenly laced at the back, giving support to the spine from the waist to the level of the shoulders, but the edge curves downward from the shoulder blades, so as to come round the front below the breasts, which are thus supported but not compressed, and are covered by a slight chemise, which hides them without concealing their form.

From this cause, the women of Sardinia have been celebrated from of old for their busts, and such a thing as a mother being unable to nurse her child is hardly known in the island.

But to return to the road to Desulo and the nut trees of the valley of Iscra. After two hours' riding, we reach a gorge, at the bottom of which a torrent hurtles down, in the shadow of century-old oaks and chestnuts, above which we see the white church of the township, displaying as many cupolas as a mosque. Thick forests descend in dark cascades down the steep slopes, on which two-thirds of the village are built. Paths wind upwards in the folds of the mountain, skirting precipices and climbing rocks. Mountaineers follow these perilous ways, holding their horses by the bridle. The men have an

Women of Atzara.

24

austere appearance suited to the asperity of the landscape, and the
head-dresses of some of the women resemble knights' helmets. As
we ascend, flocks and herds led by shepherds pass us on the way
downward, raising clouds of dust as they go. We hear the bleating of
sheep, the tinkling of bells, the barking of dogs, and the shouts of the
shepherds. Winter is nigh at hand, and the flocks are descending to
the Campidano, to return to the mountains with the first swallows
in spring.

We soon enter the winding streets of Desulo, and my young
companion, the Frenchman from Belvi, guides me to a house, where
our arrival is expected. The head of the family receives us with
great cordiality, and tells us that we must consider ourselves in
our own house. Such was his polite form of words, at least, and
I must admit it was no empty phrase ; for his hospitality was most
generous.

The houses of Desulo are higher than those of Aritzo, but the
village is a similar congeries of narrow alleys with overhanging
balconies. Almost everywhere, wooden shingles replace the roof-
tiles, which are frequently cracked by the frost, the village being
situated some 2,000 feet above the sea.

The mornings at Desulo are delightful,—fresh, bright, and in-
vigorating. Looking from the window, one sees a whole panorama
of mountain, forest, valley, and diaphanous distances, veiled in mist,
through which the sunlight strikes on a point of colour, such as a
scarlet bodice, the peltry of a *mastrucca*, or the horns of the oxen
drawing a country cart.

Hooded women hurry along in the shadow of the walls to early
mass, and yonder on the uplands the woods are bathed in wave upon
wave of golden light and purple shadow, which spread down to the
valleys, till the whole country stands revealed in the joyous brightness of the new day.

Like all primitive mountain folk, the Sardinians, especially those
of the Barbagia, are fond of expressing themselves in poetry. Even
the arrival of two strangers like myself and the Frenchman was
made the theme for an improvisation, not of great merit perhaps,

but interesting as evidence of the poetic faculty of the people. This facility for utilising even the most homely occurrences as a fit subject for versification is only found nowadays in out-of-the-way corners like Sardinia or the Isle of Skye. In the latter, I knew a certain herdsman with a great local reputation as a bard, who composed quite a long and remarkable song about the arrival of a new bull.

Sitting of an evening by the warm hearth of my host at Desulo, while the women spun their wool and the humming of the wheel made a cosy accompaniment to the recitations, I heard many ancient verses, some of which were marked by great poetical feeling. Such was the following sonnet by the famous Sardinian poet Madao :—

| | |
|---|---|
| *De sa rosa impares humana bellesa* | Go learn of the rose, O beauty of youth, |
| *Tantu presumida, superba et altera ;* | So lofty, so presumptuous, and so proud ; |
| *In ipsa ti mira, in ipsa considera* | An image of thee her petals enshroud ; |
| *De bellas retractu, figura e primisa.* | Go, see thyself in a mirror of truth. |
| *O cantu innamorat cun sa gentilesa,* | What charm in her form, what love in her face ; |
| *Su tempus chi durat, una rosa vera !* | The while she's spared by Time's uncertain ruth, |
| *Ipsa sola regnat in sa primavera,* | Sole queen of the springtide, princess of youth, |
| *Inter sos flores, una pompa et grandesa.* | Amid her flowers she reigns by beauty's grace. |
| *Pero o disingannu pro dogn' hermosura !* | Alas ! too soon, she gives all beauty pause, |
| *Sa bella renia mudamenti narat,* | And mutely tells that all must pass away, |
| *Chi, o bellesa umana, sed de pagu dura ;* | That neither she nor maidens fair may stay. |
| *Sa caduca sua purpura e cultura* | Bereft of love and life by nature's laws, |
| *Su breve regnare florida imparat* | Her fading tints and falling petals say |
| *Ch'has in d'una die pompa et sepultura.* | That beauty rules and dies in one brief day. |

The sentiment is quite that of George Herbert ; trite, maybe, but

The Church of San Mauro.

charmingly expressed in the original tongue. And here, perhaps, the observation may most aptly be made, that of all the dialects of Latin origin, Sardinian most nearly resembles the language spoken by the Romans ; not in the grammar, which differs greatly, but in the words themselves, of which over five hundred are absolutely identical. So many phrases are common to both languages, that some poets have written entire poems, which can be read either as Latin or as Sardinian. Curiously enough some Greek expressions have also been left by the Byzantines or the ancient Greek colonists, and there are a few words presenting no affinity to any existing European language, probably a relic of the tongue spoken by the aboriginal inhabitants.

The oldest Sardinian poems were inspired by Biblical subjects, and treat of the Passion of Christ or the legends of the saints. They were mostly the work of priests and monks. The common people still sing old hymns to Saint Antiocus and Saint George, and a versified prayer for rain, which is used once a year at processions in the height of the dry season.

Love is naturally the favourite theme of the profane poetry, which generally takes the form of the laments of jealousy or unrequited affection.

One evening at Desulo, I was regaled with the national dish, to wit, sucking pig, without which no banquet or public or private festivity is considered complete. It is roasted in a peculiar manner, called *furia-furia*, which demands great skill on the part of the operator.

The animal is fixed on a prong and held quite close to the fire by an old woman, who turns it rapidly, so that all the sides are equally cooked. The process is very rapid, and the result is delicious.

The shepherds have the reputation of being the best roasters in the *furia-furia* manner. They also cook the pig by placing it in a hole in the ground, wrapped in branches and leaves, under a layer of earth which is stamped down, and a fire then kindled on the top.

It is said that this method was invented by pig-stealers, and that the owner has often been known to come and warm himself at the very fire beneath which his stolen animal was being surreptitiously roasted.

On great occasions the cookery is more complicated. A bullock is disembowelled, and stuffed with a sheep also eviscerated; and the sheep in turn is made the receptacle of a sucking pig. The operation of roasting this hybrid joint lasts the whole day, and often longer.

From Desulo it is an easy walk to Sorgono, the terminus of the railway, whence a path through the oak woods leads to San Mauro, a church surrounded by a few huts and two or three houses, on the slope of a wooded hill.

It is at San Mauro that the most important of the three great fairs of Sardinia is held annually in May. During the elevation at mass on the first day of the fair, a wheel hung with little bells is set in motion, and is the signal for a prodigious clamour of crackers, squibs, and guns, while at the same time a sort of parade of all the oxen and horses takes place before the porch. The oxen have their horns decorated with oranges, ribbons, little mirrors, and garlands of flowers, while round their necks are hung rosaries, scapulars, and charms. The horses bear saddles of bright-coloured velvet embroidered in arabesque, and their manes and tails are plaited.

Immediately after mass there is a procession, led by the best horseman in the district, who unfurls the banner of San Mauro. He compels his horse to go backwards, and from time to time to kneel down. The decorated oxen follow the procession, which makes the round of the church, the men being bareheaded, with their Phrygian caps on their shoulders.

The introduction of oxen into processions is a custom common to several villages. At Quartu they lead the way, and sometimes there are as many as two hundred yoke, with their skins rendered lustrous for the occasion, all wearing magnificent housings, gaily decked out with tinsel, tiny mirrors, coloured paper, and woollen cloths.

Processions in Sardinia serve the purpose of district agricultural

A Booth at the Fair of San Mauro.

competitions, and proprietors emulate each other in showing the finest
and most carefully tended beasts.

At some of these festivities it is customary to choose a *patronesa*,
or, in Sardinian dialect, *sa guardiana*—generally a young girl, like
the "May Queen" in Old
English sports. She has
the privilege of decorating
the statue of the saint to
be carried in the pro-
cession. Before the feast-
day she goes round to all
the houses of the village,
carrying a statuette of the
saint, in order to collect
offerings. She offers the
statuette to be kissed, and
holds out a bag for the
offering. She is accom-
panied by a man carrying
a sack for the contributions
of the poor, which are
always gifts in kind, generally consisting of corn.
The office of *patronesa*
cannot be held by the
same girl two years in
succession.

The church of San
Mauro and the surrounding
houses are deserted all the
year round, except in May,

A Seller of Homespun.

when not only Sardinians flock thither from all parts of the island,
but Sicilians come to the fair to buy horses, especially the wild breed
from the plateau of the Giarra.

The booths then present a unique opportunity for studying the

different types of peasantry—women from Busachi with their home-spun, men of Gavoi and Santo Lussurgio, renowned as forgers of bits and spurs, people of Desulesi with wooden utensils (*talleri*), peasants from Milis with great carts piled with oranges, and merchants from Oristano and Solarussa, vendors of *varnaccia*, a local white wine much esteemed in Sardinia.

Many come as pilgrims in fulfilment of vows made during illness or other times of misfortune, bringing all kinds of *ex-voto* offerings, in the form of waxen arms and legs, or tresses of hair. Many of the children again are dressed in monastic habits, being dedicated to this or that order in tender years, and wearing the Capuchin, Dominican, or Franciscan dress until they are eight or ten years old. Children thus attired may be met even in the streets of Cagliari.

Among other strange customs, those connected with marriage deserve mention. Not the young man himself, but the young man's father, makes the proposal for a girl's hand. Choosing a fine day, he presents himself at the house of the maiden's parents, and thus addresses the father :—

"I am growing old, and to charm and console my old age, I seek a dove of immaculate whiteness, which is hidden, I fancy, in the house which I have just entered."

The father makes a feint of not understanding the allusion, and replies that there is no dove in his house, that she must be at some neighbour's, or perhaps in the depth of the wood. After a long argu-ment, the girl's parent goes into another room and returns with the oldest of the women, saying, "Is this the dove you want?"

Finally, after the suitor has been introduced to all the women, the father brings out the girl whom he has known all along to be the one meant. It is the maiden's part to resist to the uttermost, but at last she does appear, and the young man's father calls out, "Yes! that is the white dove I was looking for!"

Dove is the prettiest but not the invariable figure of speech used at these wooings by proxy. Often the girl is designated as a filly, a lamb, or even a goat.

After the choice has been made, the girl withdraws, and the

two fathers discuss matters and fix a day for the exchange of presents.

On that day the father, dressed in his best, goes with great ceremony to the house of the bride-elect, followed by his friends, called for that occasion, *paralimpos*. The procession halts before the house, and the father knocks at the door; but no answer comes until, after persistent rapping, a voice calls out, "What do you want?" whereupon the *paralimpos* make answer in chorus, "Honour and virtue."

The door is then opened, the host making excuses that he did not hear the first knocks, and the company enters. The *paralimpos* spread out the young man's father's presents, and the girl's parents display their own gifts. The evening concludes with a banquet, which is not attended, however, by the young couple. A week before the celebration of the marriage, a procession is organised to fetch the furniture to the new home, headed by the prettiest girl in the village, carrying on an embroidered cushion the pitcher, venerated in all Sardinian households, with which the bride will draw water for the first time on her wedding day. The rear of the procession is always brought up by a donkey, carrying the hand-mill for grinding corn. The animal is richly housed, and wears gay trappings of scarlet and gold, with bells round his neck, and often a crown of myrtle on his head.

It is the custom for the bridegroom to carry into the house the first mattress for the nuptial couch. His friends carrying other mattresses bar the way, and then ensues a battle royal, generally more amusing for the spectators than the chief actor, who usually ends by being buried beneath a mass of bedding.

On the wedding day, the parish priest and the *paralimpos* go to fetch the bride from her parents' house. As soon as she sees them coming, she falls in tears at her mother's feet and implores her blessing.

The mother consoles the girl, lays her hands on her head, and confides her to the priest. The bridegroom, with the priest of his own parish, meanwhile goes to the church to await the bride. After the religious ceremony, the civil contract is signed before the syndic, and the wedding party then adjourns to a banquet, at which the newly married eat out of the same plate, with the same spoon.

The bride, mounted on a white horse, is then escorted to her new home, on the threshold of which she is met by her mother-in-law, who greets her with outstretched arms, and offers her an Etruscan vase, in which she throws grains of corn.

In the evening there is another banquet, followed by a dance.

All this celebration entails much expense ; hence, it comes about that, among the poor, the young couple live together from the time of their betrothal, and only get married when they are able to afford it.

At Cagliari, as in Minorca, courtship is frequently conducted from a balcony, and the young man is only received by the girl's family after the date for the marriage has been fixed.

Death in Sardinia, as in Corsica, is made the occasion in certain villages for dramatic scenes.

At Samugheo, a noted village near the castle of Medusa, the custom of " waking " the dead is still observed. An *attitadora*, or keener, is hired for the occasion, and mourns all night by the side of the body, surrounded by the family. Occasionally she tears her hair and scratches her face till the blood flows, and then resumes her dirge, certain verses of which are accompanied by the family in chorus.

Relatives never follow a funeral to the cemetery. Even at Cagliari this pious office is fulfilled by friends, who, on their return, announce the accomplishment of the burial to the family by the words " *Faiddi coraggio !* " (" Have courage ! ").

The birth of a firstborn is also accompanied by quaint customs. Day and night for a week there is nothing but feasting and rejoicing in the house, often in the very room of the young mother. As soon as one party of visitors goes, it is replaced by another, and the unfortunate father, in entertaining his guests, has scarcely time to snatch a wink of sleep.

In some villages of the Campidano, it is considered the proper thing for the husband to go to bed instead of his wife, and, in her name, to receive the presents and congratulations of friends and relations. Occasionally both father and mother receive their guests in

Sunday Morning at Desulo.

the birth chamber, and, as at their wedding, eat out of the same plate with the one spoon.

To return to Desulo, the most charming walk in the neighbourhood is that to the alpine village of Tonara, past the waterfall called the *Fontana di Monsignore*, and some picturesque mills, halfhidden, like hermitages, in the recesses of the rocks.

From Tonara, I visited Gadoni, famed for its goat cheese, and its embroidered linen spun by the women of the village, who also make woollen and cotton coverlets; the former called *fressadas* or *burras*, the latter called *fanugas*, and spun in strange patterns of animals and flowers.

Not far off is the river Flumendosa, noted equally for trout and for eels. It is spanned by a singular bridge made of tree trunks resting on three natural piers of rock, the tops of which approach each other so as to form segments of arches, through which fall three cascades.

It is said that a thief who had just "annexed" a cow, and was peacefully engaged in cutting it up on this spot, was surprised by the carabinieri in hot pursuit, and,

Man of the East Coast.

throwing a quarter of the animal over his shoulder, cleared the river in three leaps of from twelve to fifteen feet, jumping from rock to

25

rock, there being at that time neither trunks nor planks across the stream.

The mountains on their eastern side descend in abrupt escarpments, while towards the west the slope is long and gradual. The country at their feet is clothed in virgin forest, and the valleys running up between the high precipices are the wildest in Sardinia. Foaming waterfalls hang like white beards from the lips of the crevasses, and carrion crows circle over the lofty summits. Wildly beautiful as it is, the entire region is cursed by fever, which yearly decimates the scanty population of the scattered villages.

There is only one natural harbour along the east coast, the Gulf of Orosei, on which is situated the small seaport of the same name, the *Cedrinus* of the ancients, where the Cagliari steamers call once a week. The Golfo di Terranova in the north, which looks on the map as if it would be a good harbour, is sown with reefs, and the Golfo di Tortoli in the south, is far too small. There are several islands in the Gulf of Terranova, one of which, Tavolara, was at the beginning of the century a kind of independent kingdom. A shepherd of the Isola della Maddalena, named Giuseppe, having fallen out with the law officers, who would not let him live quietly in a state of bigamy, took possession of the uninhabited island and settled one of his wives there, doubtless in the hope of founding a dynasty. The other he established on the desert islet of Santa Maria, north of the Isola della Maddalena, where he used often to visit her. This shepherd was called in derision, the king of Tavolara ; but he became very rich, and his son and successor on the throne continued the family. It was a model monarchy, the throne being unshakable, since it consisted of rock, and the subjects never guilty of rebellion, since they were goats.

A journey along the east coast is, however, not to be undertaken lightly. The kidnapping of Mr. Charles Wood by brigands, who demanded a ransom of £1,200, was an event too recent to be any encouragement to explore this desolate region, where the people are few and far between and quite uncertain in the manner of their welcome.

The fear of brigands alone would not have deterred me from

making the venture, but I felt that I was in for an attack of
fever. A weariness of wandering grew upon me, my head felt
as if bound by a circle of iron,
and I had pains in all my
limbs. To be utterly alone in
such a condition seems to increase
one's ailments, and I returned to
Desulo.

My entertainer was delighted
to see that I had kept my promise
of not leaving the Barbagia without visiting him once more, and
said that I had just come in time
to take part in a domestic festivity to celebrate the arrival of
some relatives from Sar-
rule. Nevertheless, he was
anxious at my pallor and
generally worn-out aspect,
and after urging me to
accept his hospitality for
a few days, as the weather
was bitter and I looked
as if I needed rest, finally
advised me to lose no time
in returning to Cagliari.

The next day found
me in bed at the *Ristor-
ante de la Escala di ferru,*
in the capital, and the
doctor told me I was
suffering from a sharp
bout of malarial fever.

Woman of Sarrule.

Strong remedies averted any danger, but for over a week I could do
nothing but lie in bed and listlessly watch the boats rocking in the gulf

I was reluctantly compelled to forego a projected visit to the mining district, and also a hunting party organised in my honour by M. Georges Chapelle, who was unremitting in his attentions during my illness.

The Sardinians, who, like all islanders, are deeply attached to their country, greatly deprecate any one speaking of the unhealthiness of the island. They themselves naturally suffer less from fever than strangers, who dare not even breathe the air of certain districts in summer, lest they fall ill and die. In the middle of June, the landed proprietors of the Campidano fly from the country, and take refuge in the towns, while the care with which even peasants wrap themselves up show how they dread the *intemperia*.

Many of the Sardinian proverbs refer to the fever for instance :—

| | |
|---|---|
| *Sa frebbe terziana non est toccu de campana.* | The tertian fever does not make the passing bell ring. |
| *Sa frebbe attunzale o est longa o est mortale.* | The autumn fever is either long or mortal.' |
| *Sa frebbe senza sidis, malu signale.* | Fever without thirst is a bad sign. |
| *Sa frebbe atterat finza su leone.* | Fever prostrates even the lion. |

As soon as I was out of danger, my doctor told me to leave Sardinia immediately. "Go away," said he, "go away. At this time of the year the island is poisoned ; but in April and May you can come back, and go wherever your fancy leads you."

I had no resource but to do as he bade me, and early one morning found myself in the train speeding back to the north. I had one brief glimpse of the rock, on which stands the dismantled castle of Ugolino ; crossed the Campidano ; saw from afar the mountains of Iglesias, " the flower of the world " ; perceived the lagoons of Oristano glimmering in the sun ; and watched the vapours rising to the sky and obscuring the hills like a pale winding-sheet.

For a brief moment, I saw a player of the *launedda* leaning against the trunk of a tree, and heard the flute-like notes, like the warbling of a lark. But at the same moment a deep, rough, groaning sound spoilt the melody. Did it come from the marshes of the

Campidano Maggiore, which we were passing and which sometimes make sounds like the lowing of bulls? I do not know. The train carried me on.

But the joyous notes of the flute, broken by a melancholy cry, appeared to me typical of the whole of this Tyrrhenian Isle, at once beautiful and accursed. But for long after I quitted its shores, I still felt as if I had been travelling through time as well as space, and had returned from a mediæval pilgrimage through fabulous lands, where wild men and robber-bands alternated with mild-visaged chatelaines and chaste madonnas.

The civilisation of Sardinia is merely a gloss of officialism. Under the veneer of the modern state is still hidden the old oak of mediævalism. The Church has more influence than the law, and old custom is even more potent than the Church.

Looking back upon my journey, it seemed to me as

Young Man of Sarrule.

if I had been turning the pages of a palimpsest, where the old

heathen record is still visible beneath the miniatures and illuminated script, penned by some visionary monk in the vari-coloured hues of a stained-glass window.

Quaint and gorgeous costumes, strange manners, remote mountain solitudes, and unknown villages, all seemed to me like the memory of a day that is no more.

A Player of the Launedda.